News and the Net

News and the Net

Barrie Gunter

LEA
2003

LAWRENCE ERLBAUM ASSOCIATES, PUBLISHERS
Mahwah, New Jersey   London

Lawrence Erlbaum Associates, Inc., Publishers
10 Industrial Avenue
Mahwah, NJ   07430

Cover design by Kathryn Houghtaling Lacey

Library of Congress Cataloging-in-Publication Data

Gunter, Barrie.
News and the net / Barrie Gunter
        p. cm.
   Includes bibliographical references and indexes.
ISBN 0-8058-4499-6 (alk. paper)
ISBN 0-8058-4500-3 (pbk.paper)
1. Electronic newspapers. I. Title.
PN4833 .G86 2003
070.1'72—dc21   2002031902

Books published by Lawrence Erlbaum Associates are printed
on acid-free paper, and their bindings are chosen for strength
and durability.

Printed in the United States of America
10   9   8   7   6   5   4   3   2   1

Contents

Preface

This book examines the growth of news provision on the Internet and its implications for news presentation, journalism practice, news consumers and the business of running news organizations. Much of the focus is placed on the migration of newspapers onto the Internet, but references are made to the establishment of news Web sites by other news organizations, including broadcasters and news agencies.

The book begins examining the growth of online technology as a source of information and entertainment for media consumers. It considers how this development can be framed within models of communication, and comments on the apparent shortage of new models to explain the use, role, effectiveness, and impact of online communications. It then considers the early history of electronic news delivery, involving technologies that predate the Internet. These systems included online news provision in the form of news agency feeds designed specifically for professional news reporters, and then the emergence of corporate online information systems and news online for the general public in the form of text services provided via television broadcasting. With the establishment of Internet technology and, through this, the World Wide Web, a new channel opened up for the provision of online news that ordinary citizens could access via desk-top computers. Recognizing the future potential of the online market, newspapers began to publish electronic editions of their hard-copy publications.

In their rush to establish an online "presence," however, many newspapers gave little thought to the wider implications of electronic publishing. In a world in which the Internet rapidly achieved wide penetration, the corporate potential of this new medium was quickly recognized. Within a few years, thousands of companies launched business Web sites and consumers realized the potential to conduct financial, retail, and business transactions online. This technological revolution brought with it new expectations on the part of customers about the service they expected from online suppliers. The Internet was trumpeted for its increased efficiency, speed of turnaround and response, and financial economies. Many online businesses floundered within the first 2 years after their launch because they failed to cater fully to these customer expectations. News organizations were as guilty of online business immaturity as many other types of online business.

The bandwagon effect that led to so much online business growth influenced many newspapers in their decisions to move online. However, running an online business requires a "re-think" of corporate culture and business strategy. Many initial news Web sites were accused of offering little more than "shovelware," that is, hard copy shoveled onto the Net. But Web consumers want and expect much more than this. Certainly, it may be useful to consumers of a domestic newspaper to be able to gain access to it via the Web when they are thousands of miles away overseas and unable to find a hard-copy edition. More usually, though, Web users expect certain enhancements to be in place when venturing online for their news. The Web offers the potential for virtually unlimited information access. Current news can be linked to other related information in archives or on other Web sites. Hyperlinks can quickly get the consumer from one site to another with the click of a mouse. News on the Web can also be updated more readily and economically than is the case with hard-copy newspapers—where updates require a fresh (and relatively expensive) print run. Most significantly, the Internet offers interactive capability, whereby consumers can select precisely what they want to read or view, and through which readers or viewers can (or should be able to) communicate directly with each other and with the journalists producing the news. Consumers expect all these things and they expect them at no charge. Hence, newspapers that migrate onto the Net must consider how their electronic editions will financially support themselves.

The Internet offers many presentational opportunities. The Web can present information in multimedia formats. The notion that print news must remain in text form only, perhaps supplemented with the occasional still photograph, become outmoded within the world of the Web. On the Internet, information can be presented in video and audio as well as in text and graphic formats. Indeed, the establishment of news Web sites by broadcast organizations has meant that newspapers on the Net must seriously consider format enhancements. The Internet has created a single level playing field on which news organizations from different offline markets (e.g., print and broadcasting) now compete for a share of the same consumer market.

The presentational implications of news on the Net mean that journalists must be prepared to change the way they work. The increased use of computer-mediated technology in the newsroom has meant that journalists can no longer rely purely on traditional reporting skills. News sources are available online. The entire production process is a desk-top activity and journalists must be able not only to write but also to compose a complete presentation package on screen. The lack of skills and resources has frequently meant that many early online editions of newspapers failed to utilize the full range of Internet technologies. Journalists have voiced concern about the implications for their profession of this new online world. News librarians have also experienced anxiety that they may be cut out of the loop by online systems that provide journalists with direct access to information services that were formerly provided by them.

Publishing in an online environment presents other issues that the journalism profession and news as a business must consider very carefully. The legal status of the "publisher" of information can be called into question on the Internet with important implications for liability in the case of problematic content. The enhanced interplay between suppliers and consumers in cyberspace, whereby readers can contribute content to electronic newspapers in a more accessible and immediate fashion, may leave established news publishers vulnerable to legal action should that content cause offense to other parties. Online publishing opens up opportunities for local and regional news publishers to reach international markets. In so doing, however, their content may be subject to legal action under jurisdictions other than the one in which the publisher resides. Hence, accompanying its wider opportunities, the Internet invokes the need for broader awareness of legal issues that may impact upon news publishers and their operations.

Finally, for the public, online news provision holds great promise. Information can be obtained online either from intermediaries, such as journalists, or directly from sources in the form of corporate Web sites, online press releases, and so on. The problem resides in the huge volume of content that is released each day onto the Net and the ease with which this content can be searched such that consumers reach those items of most interest to them. Hence, there remains a need for skilled practitioners who can search, digest, and summarize information for others who are too busy or lack the skills to do so for themselves.

The underlying principle of the Internet is that it provides a channel that enables anyone to publish their views on any issue. Although this may be seen as a good thing from the perspective of democracy and freedom of information, there is a downside. Users do not always know how credible or trustworthy are different information providers on the Net. The major news organizations have reputations founded on many years of news provision, and citizens learn to know which news providers they can trust to supply accurate and unbiased accounts of events. Even in a world in which communications technologies open up greater choices for consumers, ordinary people will still need access to reliable news "brands." The challenge therefore remains for major news providers in the offline world to migrate their services onto the Net and continue to provide citizens with trusted accounts of world affairs, but adapting to the new online environment and meeting the enhanced delivery expectations of Web users.

—Barrie Gunter
April, 2002

Chapter 1

The Expanding Online World

The 20th century witnessed the emergence of more new forms of communication than any other period in history. As successive new media have come into being, ordinary people have enjoyed an expanded quantity, range, and choice of entertainment and information content. Further, they have been given greater personal control over the reception of this content and, of late, have moved from being mere passive recipients to content creators and information senders courtesy of sophisticated communications technologies.

The expansion of mass media has not simply meant more competition for the owners of these media, and the producers and distributors of media content, it has changed the nature of media audiences. Audiences have become more fragmented. Hence, established mass media can no longer depend on a virtually guaranteed market of consumers of their products. Moreover, "mass" communication has become integrated with "interpersonal" communication, meaning that media consumers now expect to be able to select what they want to consume when it suits them by placing individual orders at their own convenience.

Such developments have had important implications for the provision and consumption of news. News provision is one of the most important functions of the mass media. Indeed, the first truly mass media were the newspapers of the 19th century. The subsequent establishment of first radio and then television as mass media was founded upon their news services. As such, mass publics became accustomed to the reception of news in prepackaged formats—whether in print or as sound or video transmissions. The development of communications technologies in the late 20th century, however, opened up new possibilities for news delivery. Perhaps the most significant development is the transition to digital transmission systems that facilitate the convergence of broadcasting, publishing, telecommunications, and computing technologies. New digital appliances, such as the "flat screen" mark the evolution of the traditional television set into an interactive, multimedia entertainment and information center (Fidler, 1994).

Such technological convergence leads to business convergence, such that newspapers, magazines, television, and radio will no longer operate as separate services—where the separation is most clearly marked for consumers in a technological sense. These services are received via a single type of technology and users are able to switch seamlessly between them. Instead of choosing whether to tune in to news from a particular television channel or radio station or to read a particular newspaper, news consumers are able to decide the specific news stories they want to receive information about from a multitude of information sources and can also decide whether they want it only in text or as a mixture of text and video (Negroponte, 1995). Individuals are able to print off their own "newspaper," edit their own newsreel, or download an electronic news sheet onto a portable flat screen device (Fidler, 1994).

THE GROWTH OF ONLINE COMMUNICATIONS

Online communications can be traced back to the 1970s, but flourished only during the 1990s. With the growth of the Internet and commercial online services, the increased capacity of the public telecommunications network and the increased speed of communications modems and personal computers, online communications have become an effective, worldwide communications medium.

Consumer online services provide personal computer users with an electronic commercial link to a growing network of other computer users. By subscribing to an online service, such as Prodigy™, American Online™, or Compuserve™, users of personal computers equipped with a modem, appropriate communications software, and a connection to a Touch-Tone telephone can dial into a broad array of electronic services. These Internet service suppliers are providing ever easier access to the Internet, the global web of computer networks, through graphical user interfaces. The potential market for online services has grown significantly. In the early 1980s in the United States, for example, only 2 to 3 million homes were equipped with personal computers, whereas by 1994, the number had risen to 35 million machines. Nearly ⅔ of these homes (62%) had a modem (Pavlik, 1996).

The potential market for online news is growing all the time. In the United States, for instance, estimates at the close of the 20th century projected the Internet market at 144 million adult users by the turn of the millennium (Nielsen Media Research, 1996; Office of Research, 1999). By September 2000, worldwide Internet users aged 12+ were put at 360 million (NUA, 2000). There were over 1 billion Web pages on 5 million unique servers, though it is estimated that 70% of traffic goes to less than 5,000 sites (Savage, 2000).

The appeal of the Internet as a possible news medium stems not just from the volume of potential consumers to which it provides access, but also in terms of the composition of that market. Internet use is popular among younger people, in contrast to news consumption via traditional and older established media, especially newspapers. Women represent another group of Internet users on the increase. Jupiter Communications reported that more than 46 million women were online in 1999. *NetSmart*™ predicted that women would make up more than half of Internet users by 2002 (see Pavlik, 2001).

Internet diffusion internationally has been widespread and rapid. Across the top ten economies in the world, by 1998, average Internet use was 43% of the population (Juliussen & Petska-Juliussen, 1999). Although these figures are encouraging to news producers who have migrated onto the Web or who are thinking about doing so, it is important to put them in perspective. Even if there are 360 million Internet users around the globe, that still leaves 5.64 billion people (94%) of the world's population) without access (Pavlik, 2001).

The prevalence of the Internet is not just a result of its open and dynamic nature; its rapid spread has been facilitated by its increased user friendliness to noncomputer literate people. The advent of the World Wide Web (WWW) and the freely distributed smart point-and-click browsers, such as Netscape™ and Explorer™, have made surfing the Net as a source of knowledge and entertainment more attractive. Despite concerns about issues such as privacy, copyright, cultural identity, and pornography, the Internet continues its expansion, rendering it a medium that is impossible to ignore. As a result, publishing industries have begun to explore new, Internet-related markets, services and products in response to the recent advances in information and communication technologies (Scupola, 1999).

Today, news and information from any part of the world can be read with just a click of a button. A new breed of media businesses has emerged in association with the Internet that have become the information world's obsession (Nicholas, Williams, Cole, & Martin, 2000). Even the newspaper industry, never one traditionally quick to embrace technological change, has looked seriously at new ways of adapting its business to this new technology (J. Katz, 1994).

News media uses of the WWW and Internet have grown rapidly since the middle of the 1990s. Some commentators have referred to the Internet as the future for news (Katz, 1999). Although the dominance of the Internet over other, longer established forms of communication may still be some way off in the context of news dissemination, there is growing evidence that new online technologies are having an impact on journalism practice and the business strategies of news organizations (Alshehri, 2000; Chyi & Sylvie, 1998; Singer, 1998, 1999). A rapidly growing number of printed newspapers established Web sites and electronic publications during the final years of the 20th century and that growth has continued apace during the new millennium. Many of these sites have been established simply to obtain a Web presence, with minimal resources devoted to them; in other cases, their publishers have regarded the transition from print to electronic distribution as a key component of the future business strategy (Noack, 1999).

THE LATEST COMMUNICATIONS ERA

The widespread penetration of the Internet and the establishment of the WWW and digital forms of communications facilitated through a merger of computers and telecommunications networks has been envisaged as the sixth major communications revolution (Fang, 1997). The "information superhighway" that has been constructed out of the convergence of text- and image-based systems of electronic communication represents a key milestone in the development of communications—an important aspect of history in the making.

Fang (1997) divided the history of communication initially into five revolutions. The first revolution began with the invention of writing in Greece around the 8th century B.C. The second revolution was the invention of the printing press by Gutenberg in Europe in the second half of the 15th century. The third revolution began (in western Europe and the eastern United States in the middle of the 19th century) with the convergence of advances in paper production and printing press technology, enabling, for the first time, the mass production and circulation of communications, in the form of newspapers and magazines. During the same period, an entertainment revolution emerged as the fourth phase toward the end of the 19th century, with the emergence of the affordable camera and motion photography. The fifth revolution was the creation of what Fang calls the "Communication Toolshed Home" that evolved during the middle of the 20th century, transforming the home into the central location for receiving information and entertainment, thanks to the telephone, broadcasting, sound and video recording technology, improvements in print technologies, and cheap, universal mail services. A sixth revolution, as noted, embraces the merger of formerly distinctive technologies, such as telecommunications, broadcasting, and computing to create a digitized, multimedia, interactive communications interchange in which the division between senders and receivers becomes blurred.

CAN TRADITIONAL COMMUNICATION THEORY HELP?

With the establishment of mass communications, in the form of print media, sound broadcasting, and audiovisual broadcasting, film and video recording, scholars turned their attention to explaining the social, psychological, and political significance of these technologies and the messages they conveyed. Accordingly, "media research has evolved over time, in part reflecting paradigm shifts and the evolution of analytical models in the wider social sciences" (Gunter, 2000, p. 9). Media historians have noted a number of distinct milestones in the development of mass communications theory (De Fleur & Ball-Rokeach, 1989). Theories of mass communication focused variously on media production, the way the media represented various aspects of society, the structure and organization of the media, and media effects (McQuail, 1987). Much theoretical development took place during the era of Fang's (1997) fifth communications revolution.

Initial mass communications theory development focused on the role of the mass media as propaganda machinery especially, though not exclusively, during wartime. Early filmmakers and the printing presses were co-opted as arms of the dominant political ethos within countries at times of internal or international conflict during the early part of the 20th century (Gunter, 2000). Later on in the century, radio and television came to be used in similar roles as their penetration of societies grew. An early assumption was that mass communications could exert direct effects on the populace at whom they were aimed. The impact of such media messages was powerful enough to shape public opinion and influence patterns of behavior—especially behavior linked to the political process, such as voting. During the time of World War I, there was a general belief that mass communications could act as a magic bullet. Propaganda messages were fired at mass audiences and readerships and exerted a direct influence on the public's thought processes (see De Fleur & Ball-Rokeach, 1989; Lasswell, 1927). This all-powerful concept of media effects, however, was to be found wanting when put to more serious test in later years as research methodologies evolved.

Further tests of the media as a key aspect of political propaganda machinery during World War II led to a more moderate view of the impact of mass communications (Hovland, Lumsdaine, & Sheffield, 1949; Lazarsfeld, Berelson, & Gaudet, 1944; Star & Hughes, 1950). A revised notion of media effects dropped the idea that they acted directly on individuals to change them, and instead hypothesized that the media operated on their audiences and readers in a less direct fashion. The impact of mass communications was modified by the social context in which media and audiences interfaced, by the functions the media served for their users, and by other influential interpersonal forces. Indeed, in many ways, the media came to be regarded less as forces for change, and more as reinforcers of the status quo (Klapper, 1960).

One important model that emerged in the 1950s conceived of media influences operating in more than one stage. A two-step flow idea emerged to explain the effects of mass media in the political context, whereby the media were believed to act initially on opinion leaders within the community, who then in turn influenced the political thinking of the remainder of their community (Katz & Lazarsfeld, 1959).

The apparently weakened position of mass communication as a source of social and political influence was not universally accepted. A number of prominent writers observed that there were occasions on which the media could be seen to exert direct and quite powerful effects on the public. On some of these occasions, however, such influences were quite subtle (Blumler, 1964; Halloran, 1965; Lang & Lang, 1959). The "minimal" effects model therefore came under serious theoretical and, in due course, empirical challenge during the 1960s and 1970s. One commentator observed that fashions in media effects models and the tendency to veer from maximal to minimal effects orientations reflected to some extent the stability of society at different times (Carey, 1978).

During the economic depression years of the 1930s that led to international tensions and war, there was a need to understand the role of the increasingly popular mass media in this process. During the period of stability of the 1950s and 1960s, there was less reason to view the media as a source of social upheaval. Changing economic conditions and civil and political discord that characterized the late 1960s and 1970s once again drew attention to the media as arbiters of unrest.

The effects of the media were distinguished, however, by the level at which these effects occurred. Thus, although powerful effects of mass communications were conceived to be possible, they did not occur indiscriminately at any psychological level. The idea that the media could shape people's behavior was supported by an accumulating body of evidence concerned in particular with media effects on antisocial conduct. There remained a dominant school of thought, nevertheless, that media influences on public opinion and behavior needed to be understood in the context of mediating factors. Direct effects of media operated at a more superficial level such as by setting the public agenda or telling people which issues were the most important ones for them to think about (McCombs & Shaw, 1972).

As communications theory continued to evolve in the 1970s and 1980s, there was growing recognition that relationships between mass communications systems and the public are circular. The media can act on their audiences and audiences can act on the media they choose to consume. It is no longer informative or helpful to our understanding of the role and impact of mass communications in society to think about media effects as operating in one direction—whether such effects are deemed to be powerful or minimal.

Regardless of whether media effects are envisaged to occur in the form of agenda setting, the cultivation of social beliefs, learning of new information and knowledge, or attitude change or behavior modification, they are, for the most part, likely to be moderated by users' reasons for media consumption, the cognitive information processing systems brought to bear on interpreting media content, and social contextual factors that represent other forces of influence on public knowledge, opinion, and conduct (Gunter, 2000).

With the development of communications technologies, the public are experiencing new kinds of relationships with information and entertainment media. The Internet revolution has changed the face of media provision and patterns of media consumption. The key aspect of change is increased interactivity between the senders and receivers of messages and the redefinition of media consumers as senders as well as receivers. This means that traditional theories of mass communication, grounded as they have been in the fifth communications revolution, characterized by a communications environment in which there is clear distinction between senders and receivers, may be inappropriate to explain the significance and possible impact of the new electronic communications systems operating through merged broadcasting, telecommunications, and computing technologies. Instead, there is a need for an evolution in conceptual modeling in which theory grounded in a one-directional flow of information context embraces thinking that can accommodate bidirectional message flows.

This kind of thinking was reflected in a model put forward by Kincaid (1979). This Convergence Model defined *communication* as a process in which participants create and share information with one another in order to reach a mutual understanding. Information shared by two or more participants in the communication process may lead to collective action, mutual agreements, and mutual understanding and the communication process has no beginning and no end. The convergence model represents human communication as a dynamic, cyclical process taking place over time.

Unlike traditional mass media that represent a one-to-many communication model, the Internet represents both many-to-one and many-to-many models (Hoffman & Novak, 1995; Morris & Ogan, 1996). Many consumers can initiate communication to the same Web site at the same time. This many-to-one scenario is unique to the Web because many points of origination and destination co-exist in cyberspace. With such features as cyberchat and the listserve mailing list that simultaneously connect people with common interests, the Web becomes a means for many-to-many communications. There is no single source of message origination or single destination on the Web. All information is digitized, which renders it readily transformable into a variety of presentation formats. With this flexibility, information can be customized to the demand of the consumer. According to some writers, new computer technology will increase the power of the consumer and "blow apart all the monopolies, hierarchies, pyramids and power grids of established society" (Gilder, 1990, p. 31).

THE NEED FOR THEORETICAL DEVELOPMENT

The new interactive communications media requires new theoretical conceptualizations. Interactivity between communicators, such as those using the Internet, can occur at a number of levels. In varying instances, communications can be from one to one, from one to many, from many to one, or from many to many. In some situations, therefore, Internet communications can be conceptualized as forms of mass communication; in other instances, however, they represent a form of interpersonal communication (Kaye & Medoff, 1999).

The need for fresh impetus and direction in communications research has already been noted by eminent scholars who have made a point of following theory developments across the decades. A pessimistic view has surfaced that, of late, there has been a lack of creativity in theory development. In his examination of this issue, DeFleur (1998) argued that research in mass communication in general has stalled. He asked, "Where have all the milestones gone?" Defleur's main argument was based on his belief that there is a decline of significant research (milestones) on the process and effects of mass communication. DeFleur noted that most of today's theories on the process and effects of mass communication appeared between about 1930 and the early 1980s. "Since that time, few studies have made significant theoretical contribution" (DeFleur, 1998, p. 85). He asserted that "since that 'golden' period of well-funded, large-scale efforts conducted with 'important objectives' and based on 'standards of methodology,' there has not been a similar level of production of such seminal studies" (p. 86).

Even the most noteworthy studies of recent times have focused on restricted topics or have represented efforts to explore issues raised by the earlier milestones. When asked by a publisher to produce an update on his earlier review of milestones in mass communications, DeFleur (1998) claimed that he "could not identify even one [new milestone] that fit the same criteria as the earlier investigations" (p. 86). The reasons he outlined for this state of affairs included a change in social sciences' research agenda, a lack of a programmatic approach by media scholars, a shift to quantitative and critical modes of analysis, and changes in the work conditions of the academy (university systems).

Likewise, Wilbur Schramm, one of the founding fathers of communication theory, wondered rhetorically whether "we have produced only ingredients of communication theory" (cited in Mancini, 1994, p. 108). Mancini commented that Schramm's statement implicitly singled out how much his fellow researchers felt a lack of legitimacy. According to Mancini, scholars in this field had been unable to produce an exhaustive, complete theory of communications.

Shoemaker (1994) attributed the problem of mass communication research to the fact that most of the theoretical work is derived from other sciences. Media researchers must find ways to build more theory themselves rather than relying on theories borrowed from other disciplines. The field lacks a systematic theory building effort and even existing research interest groups often explicitly deal with neither theory nor methodology. Shoemaker (1994) discussed this "crisis of theory" and suggested that "we must be more theoretical in our research and more scholarly in our curricula" (p. 389). Shoemaker analyzed the "communication crisis triangle": theory, curricula, and power in demonstrating resentment of some media scholars about the status of their field.

Theoretical models to explain the use of interactive technologies and their impact on users have been slow to emerge. Part of the reason for this is the fact that widespread public utilization of the Internet has a short history.

The principal models adapted so far have been *diffusion theory* and the *uses and gratifications perspective* (Leung & Wei, 2000). Some studies have viewed use of the Internet and Web within the context of diffusion of innovation theory. According to diffusion theory, the adoption of technological innovations is a function of one's innovativeness, or willingness to try new products. Rogers and Shoemaker (1971) defined innovativeness as "the degree to which an individual is relatively earlier in adopting an innovation than other members of his social system" (p. 27). Although this has been but one of many competing definitions of innovativeness, scholars have yet to account fully for the psychological dynamics driving technology adoption. Indeed, it may be more appropriate to talk in terms of a diffusion framework than a diffusion theory.

In broad terms, diffusion research addresses the characteristics of innovations and those who adopt them. Rogers and Shoemaker (1971) initially distinguished between continuous innovations—those representing a variation of existing channels—and others that are more discontinuous (i.e., more difficult to adopt, perhaps involving the purchase of a separate piece of hardware). Building on that framework, Krugman (1985) proposed a dynamically discontinuous category to reflect innovations (e.g., VCRs) that require a specific purchase and a dedicated set of user skills. Studies of computer adoption (e.g., Lin, 1998) suggest that computers are perhaps the most discontinuous of media technologies, given the relatively high financial and skill barriers associated with their adoption. Because the same study uncovered a link between computer adoption and intention to use online services, the Internet can also be characterized as a dynamically discontinuous innovation.

Studies conducted within this perspective have discussed the spread of the new technology in news organizations and in the general public (Garrison, 2000; Maier, 1999; Niebauer et al., 1999). Although diffusion research has value in understanding the flow of information or a new innovation through a system such as newsgathering, it does have limitations. Like information flow theory, diffusion theory is source, not end-user, dominated (Ha & James, 1998).

Other theoretical perspectives have proven to be problematic in their application to use of interactive media. Uses and gratifications research, although focusing on the receiver or user of a medium and his or her purposes for using it, offers an approach or model at best and is not very theoretical (Severin & Tankard, 1997). The research literature does not reveal a deep foundation of uses and gratifications research aimed at understanding new technologies and active audiences. However, the literature on uses and gratifications of new technologies such as cellular telephones, computers, networked computers, and other interactive media is evolving (Leung & Wei, 2000).

THE INTERNET AS "MASS" MEDIUM

The concept of *mass* is both empirical and conceptual. In statistical terms, the Internet and associated WWW can be regarded as a mass communications system by virtue of the sheer volume of users around the world. By the mid-1990s, the Internet had achieved over 16 million Web site hosts, attracting many millions more users (Huizer, 1997). This growth from just four networked computers of the Advanced Research Project Agency Net (ARPANET) at the University of California had occurred in a little over a decade. Future growth was predicted to dwarf these proportions (Hilgemere, 1996); although making projections where the Internet is concerned is a risky business, with early forecasts often proving to be inaccurate (Batty & Barr, 1994).

In conceptual terms, whether the Internet can be classified as a mass medium depends on the nature of use as well as the volume of traffic flowing through it. The original concept of the *mass audience* for instance, embraced the idea of a collectivity of people defined by the fact that they shared a particular media-related experience. Conceptually, the phenomenon of mass in this context was differentiated from other social collectives such as the *group*, the *crowd* or the *public* (Blumer, 1939; McQuail, 1997).

In a group, all its members (usually) know one another and interact with each other with a certain pattern of regularity. They may also share certain values. A crowd is a gathering of individuals on a temporary basis and rarely re-forms with the same composition from one occasion to the next. Any shared identity it has is driven less by a common value system than by an ambient mood that persists for a limited period, but may be powerful enough to drive the gathering to perform a collective action. Once this action has achieved its purpose or run out of steam, the crowd dissipates. The public is an abstract concept that embraces the notion of a body of people, much larger than a group, who embrace the same values and may engage in debate about issues in a democratic environment. It reflects the notion of a societywide collective that has primarily political goals and the creation of a sociopolitical system within which the majority would prefer to exist.

The *mass* represents a distinctive concept that grew out of conditions created by the modern, industrial, urban society, characterized in particular by a shift from small, close-knit, rural communities to larger urbanized communities with more anonymous and transient populations. According to McQuail (1997), these populations comprised large aggregates of detached individuals, often not known to each other, "... but with their attention converging on some object of interest that is outside their immediate personal environment or control" (p. 7). Unlike a group, the mass lacks a stable structure or single coherent value system. With the emergence of information and entertainment media, that thanks to technological developments in production and transportation, could be made available or distributed on a large scale, the notion of mass became attached to and to a great extent defined by the consumption of common media outputs. Hence, readers of the same newspapers in the 19th century represented the first truly mass audiences. Specific newspapers might be read across a nation; therefore, they in turn became the first mass media. To the extent that online newspapers can also attract large numbers of users, the Internet (or more especially the WWW that can be accessed through it) might also be conceived to be a mass medium. However, the fact that Internet technology can also be used to provide two-way, one-on-one, interpersonal communication, or interactive communication involving small numbers of individuals, it also represents a group or interpersonal communications medium (Kiesler, 1997).

In continuing the debate about theoretical approaches to the study of new media, Jankowski and Hanssen (1996) noted that "one of the frequent points of discussion among communication scholars is whether existing theoretical models and notions are adequate to the task of understanding and explaining new communication technology" (pp. 7–8). They argued that mass communication models and theories—in general—fail to consider the distinct features of many new communication technologies because they are conceptually tied to the dominant characteristics of mass media. Even recent theoretical developments have tended to be "captive" to the inherent limitations in empirical data based on traditional mass media use studies.

To move forward in this theoretical debate, it is important to identify the stage of development that has been reached with the emerging media technologies (Fidler, 1997). Part of the problem is that there must also be some idea of how information technology innovations are likely to be affected by other technological and social developments. To achieve this, according to Fidler (1997), "we must first enlarge our perspective and discard most of our commonly held assumptions, particularly about the speed of change" (p. 9).

The Internet and related digital technologies are advancing so fast that it is difficult for anyone to predict future developments. Research needs to deal not just with technologies, but also with technological systems consisting of physical artefacts (e.g., electric power grids, railroad lines, computers, and networks), institutions (manufacturers, distributors, regulatory agencies, universities), people (designers, managers, consumers), and culture (Pang, 1998).

It has become trivial to state that the Internet and its applications have had a profound effect on modern society, especially in the last few years. Although, some describe new media as a big puzzle (Sikes, 1997), the Internet has without a doubt emerged as an effective form of communication that offers access to and exchange of information, linking communities in ways never before imagined. Furthermore, it arguably offers opportunities to contribute to the fulfillment of four basic needs: power, freedom, belonging, and pleasure (Glasser, 1986). Hence, the academic world as well as the business sector found itself facing a new challenge in defining and examining this hybrid communications system. The term *hybrid* is used here because the information superhighway represents a confluence of merged technologies that have previously been categorized and used as separate communications and information-processing systems. This concept of *convergence* envisages that formerly disparate communications systems should be treated as a single subject. Hence, separate industries such as the broadcast and motion picture industry, the computer industry, and the print and publishing industry can be regarded as overlapping and integrated (Fidler, 1997).

This model represents a complex technological marriage, but still does not add significantly to the theoretical problems surrounding the need to understand the implications of this media technologies merger for users. The phenomenal growth of the Internet and related technologies has to some extent perplexed researchers and business. Traditionally, media theorists have dealt mainly with one-way communications systems in which members of the public are passive receivers of information.

The interactive nature of the Internet requires a different form of conceptual model to explain its use and its impact. Its ability to bring together elements of the printed page, graphic, photographic, cinematography, including video, film, and animation into a dynamic and interactive environment that requires specialized hardware and software to function has put media researchers in a real dilemma. The complexity of the Net stems from the volume and variety of content that it makes available, and the way in which that content can be accessed. The Internet can provide content in a multimedia format and its software allows consumers more control over reception than is available with traditional mass communications. The Internet in one sense, resembles a huge shopping mall that users can peruse at their own pace. They seek out the items they wish to consume and do so at their own convenience rather than that of the producers. The Internet is more than a technology, however. It is a potential cultural force that can be used by consumers not just to obtain information, but also to send it (Strangelove, 1994).

In some ways, the growth and increasing use of the internet in recent years is believed to be the trigger of a true revolution that is the driving force behind the definitive transformation of a postindustrial society into an information society. Whereas it took many years after the invention of their founding technologies for the conventional mass media to emerge as a significant social force, it has taken only a few years, since 1991 (when the U.S. government opened the Internet to private enterprise), for the Internet to reach between 100-150 million users (1998 figures) worldwide. This raises an important question about the need for more internet-communication studies to meet this tremendous technology change.

To many observers, the diverse elements that shape this new structure are changing in their totality the basic notions of many social, economic, political, and communication models dominant until now. Media scholars have only recently begun to look at the Internet as a form of mass communication and to start to evolve conceptual and theoretical approaches for studying the Net and its audience.

One of the most significant contributions to the search for appropriate theoretical modeling within the context of studying the Internet has been produced by Morris and Ogan (1996). In a paper titled, "The Internet as Mass Medium," they examined a number of approaches to the study of communication on the Internet, considered constraints on Internet research, and emphasised the importance of regarding the Internet as mass medium. They also examined possible ways of applying theories of computer media communications (CMC) to the Internet.

According to Morris and Ogan (1996), with millions of people communicating on the Internet, its potential as mass medium should not be ignored. They also warned that if mass communications researchers continue to largely disregard the research potential of the Internet, their theories about communication will become less useful. They argued that more flexibility was needed among those researchers who have traditionally organized themselves around a specific communications medium as technology changes and media converge.

The use of traditional theoretical models has constrained research on new interactive media, and the most basic assumptions behind researchers' theories of mass media effects have kept them from being able to see the Internet as a new mass medium requiring a new theoretical perspective. They illustrated this point with reference to DeFleur and Ball-Rokeach's (1989) attitude toward computers in the fifth edition of their book *Theories of Mass Communication*, as typical. DeFleur and Ball-Rokeach compared computers to telephones, dismissing the idea of computer communication as mass communication. These authors assumed that to "have a new system of mass communication, the average person would have to have both the hardware and the skills to be able to use computers in daily life" (p. 335). Nevertheless Morris and Ogan's (1996) contention that De Fleur and Ball-Rokeach (1989) totally rejected the idea of the Internet as a mass medium is not a true reflection of their ideas in that they predicted in the same book that "computers will become the cornerstone of future modes of mass communications" (DeFleur & Ball-Rokeach, 1989, p. 331).

Morris and Ogan (1996) drew attention to the Internet as a multifaceted mass medium; that is, one that contains different configurations of communications. Its varied forms show the connections between interpersonal and mass communication that has been an object of study since the two-step flow associated the two. The Internet plays with the source–message–receiver features of the traditional mass communication model, "sometimes putting them into traditional patterns, sometimes putting them into entirely new configuration" (Morris & Ogan,

1996, p. 42). This may explain why Morris and Ogan urged scholars to rethink their terminology. One key distinction between the Internet and traditional mass media is the interchangeability of producers and receivers of content. One of the Internet's most widely touted advantages is that an audience may also be a message producer. This represents a departure from the traditional distinction between producers and receivers in the mass media context.

Likewise, Strangelove (1994) observed an entirely new form of human communication—mass participation in what he called bidirectional, uncensored mass communication, created quite by accident because of the open and distributed technology of the Internet. Mass communication is a relatively new phenomenon anyway that has always involved controlled broadcasts to passive audiences who never had any significant input or control over the content of communications. With the Internet, these characteristics of mass communication have been radically changed. For Strangelove, the Internet is a new form of mass communication with massive numbers of people broadcasting information to massive numbers of receivers. The Internet has empowered its users, turning them into producers as well as receivers of content.

The empowerment of the public via the Internet has been witnessed in the new kind of web site known as "the blog." *Blogger* is a simple Web technology based on a Web site called Blogger.com. The software enables the user to set up their own Web site and post to the web any content they choose. According to one report, in January, 2002, 41,000 new blogs were created, while Blogger itself boasted more than 150,000 users (Sullivan, 2002). These sites involved ordinary individuals giving their views on national, local, or personal events. Sullivan (2002) established his own blog in October, 2000. Within 6 months, he pulled in 5,000 individual visits a day. His site developed into a 24-hour broadcast. In the aftermath of September 11, 2001, the site contained reflections on those events. By November, 2001, it was receiving 500,000 visits a month.

DEFINING THE COMMUNICATIVE NATURE OF THE INTERNET

The key debate about the Internet at this time centers on whether to classify this relatively new communications technology as a mass medium. There is little to doubt that the Internet has become a widespread form of communicating, with the numbers of people linked to the Net already in the hundreds of millions worldwide, and growing all the time. The way in which communication happens on the Internet, however, is not the same as with traditional mass media such as newspapers, radio, and television. Although the Internet has the capacity to transmit messages from one person to many receivers, this is not the way it is invariably used by people. The Internet is a hybrid communications technology, the use of which can switch between mass communication and one-on-one or interpersonal communication. In developing theories to explain the way the Internet is used and the impact it can have upon consumers of its content, researchers must therefore be mindful of the distinct nature of the medium and the switching nature of its usage.

Although the Net has the basic four elements of communication, which include a sender, a receiver, a message, and a medium, the sender, in this context, is different from the usual sense of that term in that it could be a computer using an automated user ID and may not need someone to operate it. Thus, the traditional concept of the *sender* is no longer tenable.

Part of the dilemma concerning this new (mass) communication medium is how to define the "person" on the receiving end of a message in a global network that comprises people and machines. Is the receiver a *customer* doing some online shopping or a member of an unknown audience visiting a Web site with information about holidays, university courses, the corporate activities of a large global conglomerate, or the latest movie releases? Is the receiver downloading a popular computer-based game or the reader of an electronic newspaper? In these different cases, the relationship between sender and receiver varies. In some of these instances, the Internet performs much like a traditional mass medium.

A significant point of difference lies in the interactive nature of the communication process. Furthermore, the receiver can only make a link to this communications medium provided he or she has access to the necessary equipment. If individuals decide to create their own web sites, which can be visited by others, they then become message senders as well as receivers. Where the individual can not only link into Internet sites, but also inject their own content directly into them, and then receive further feedback from that site, a degree of interactivity emerges that is analogous to holding a conversation with another person.

As Brand (1988) pointed out in *The Media Lab*, instead of "broadcast," the situation is changing to one of "broadcatch." Here the consumer actively seeks or "catches" information being disseminated by or available from a variety of sources on the Internet. So it is clear that among the consequences of the new communication technology and its quickening pace that "it is no longer quite so easy to say what is *mass* communication and what is not" (Severin & Tankard, 1992, p. 8). Severin and Tankard (1992) argued that the boundary between different forms of mass communication is no longer so clear and that "communication theories must be developed or revised to keep up with the change" (p. 12). Similarly, December (1996) discussed the wide range of facilities supplied by the Internet and asked researchers to rethink the practicality of using the current notions of media to define communication on the Internet.

Nevertheless, in studying media processes and new technology, one must draw a distinction between classic mass media such as radio, television, and newspapers, which carry information in one direction, and what Poster (1995) called a "second age of mass media" with online services that operate in two directions. Users of an online newspaper, for example, expect commitment and responses from the producers. Online newspapers also allow articles to be available for months or years with large collections of data that would never appear in the print product (Alshehri, 1997).

From the mass media literature, one fundamental defining characteristic for a mass medium is the "one (few)-to-many" communication access model. But now the Internet has emerged as a "new interactive medium," which follows a "many-to-many" communication model (Hoffman & Novak, 1996). Jurdi (1995) argued that an electronic medium is "a medium that offers 'random access'; it has no physical beginning, middle, or end" (p. 393). Jurdi (1995) looks to this new communication form as a combination of multiple media that opens up such exciting possibilities for radically new ways of communication. Online news is read on screens instead of pages. At the same time, it contains most of the same articles as today's paper and can be updated at any minute. That flexibility explains the race to adapt old media to new media such as the Net and why "traditional journalism organisations—newspaper, television, and radio organisations—are moving rapidly to establish a presence on the Internet" (Friedland & Webb, 1996, p. 55).

Randle (1996) stated that it is "an especially exciting time for communication scholars to be studying mass media" (p. 16). But Jones (1994) noted earlier that most major research universities have guidelines for researchers, based on the "Nuremberg Code and/or the Belmont Principles." He observed: "… research in cyberspace was clearly not on the minds of those drafting these guidelines" (p. 31). Morris and Ogan (1996) noted that until recently, mass communications researchers have overlooked the Internet and the entire field of computer-mediated communication, staying instead with the traditional forms of broadcast and print media that fit much more conveniently into models for appropriate research topics.

Arant (1996) observed "the information superhighway is dangled before educators as a fount of unending educational benefits" (p. 1). Immediate access to the work of colleagues and a "virtual" library of millions of volumes and thousands of papers affords them the ability to incorporate a body of knowledge heretofore unthinkable (Arant, 1996).

Electronic publishing is one area of contemporary business that seems to offer rich opportunities for the fruitful application of academic theory (Pang, 1998). There is a tendency, however, to overstate the differences between electronic and printed media. The rhetoric of disruption, of total difference, of an imminent conflict between old media and new leads to an oversimplified view of both electronic and print media. This kind of debate blinds us to the many important and subtle continuities between them, and obscures some very promising avenues of future study. Some writers have observed, for example, that it is possible to apply theories and methodologies derived from interpersonal communications to the way people engage with new information and communications technologies, such as personal computers and other interactive media (Reeves & Nass, 1996). Others have wrestled with the challenge of determining whether theories developed in the study of "old" media can be applied to "new" media (December, 1996).

Clearly, the Internet is challenging the concept mass communication process long held by established communications theories. Research into new communication technology applications faces three major problems. First, the accelerating pace of change in new technologies means that academic research models are constantly struggling to keep up. Second, communication scholars have, for the most part, been reluctant to gamble with their reputations by joining in an unpredictable research arena. Third, the Internet is a new phenomenon advanced mainly by young (professional) researchers who may be lacking the necessary theoretical and philosophical knowledge and experience.

Nevertheless, it is becoming increasingly accepted that the Internet is a legitimate area for research and that as this new communications technology becomes even more widely established, it is vital that we understand more about its operation. Attention needs to be given to appropriate paradigms and models to investigate and understand the communication processes within this new media arena, and to study their impact on individuals, society, and business performance.

There is a need to establish some sort of common conceptual framework and general principles to know exactly what communication type(s) we are referring to when talking about the Internet. This means that there is a need to identify, at the very least, the broad answers to questions such as: What communication theory could be used to examine the use of the Internet by both user (consumer, reader) and provider (publisher, producer) of the content? What is (are) the economic model(s) that could be evaluated and examined when producing or investigating certain online news content? What are the relations of early media to new media? We are witnessing the emergence of a communications platform that is rapidly permeating daily life. This medium is dynamic, disorganized, and yet widely accepted by the masses. In terms of researching this new technology, it is unwise to cling only to a "who says what" doctrine. This doctrine may need to be re-phrased and turned around into an analysis of "who receives what."

There is clearly much more work that needs to be done, theoretically and conceptually, to define the nature of the Internet as a communications environment. Although often referred to as a new "medium," the Internet actually embraces a number of distinct channels of communications—textual, audio, and video—and operates at a number of communications levels, including interpersonal, group, and mass. It is therefore more akin to a collection of media rather than comprising a new medium in its own right. In the next chapter, attention is focused on the electronic delivery of news, an activity for which the Internet has become a conduit.

Chapter 2

Electronic Delivery of News

The phrase, "electronic delivery of news and information" refers to a broad concept of presenting news and information in an electronic form. This includes publishing on CD-ROMs as well as making information available through online services such as the case of the WWW. One definition of an electronic publication considers it to be "a publication which requires the user to employ an electronic device at some stage for its reception and/or its reading" (Vickers & Martyn, 1994, p. 4). Thus, with electronic publishing, information is distributed and/or stored electronically so that any one can access it via some form of electronic delivery system. Electronic publishing has also been envisaged as electronic commerce in "digital goods" and services that are intended for consumption by the human senses (Clarke, 1999).

According to Salem (1996), no one gave any attention to the "new" term, *electronic publishing*, when it first appeared in the mid-1970s. By the early 1980s, however, it started to attain a more serious prominence as a topic of discussion and inquiry. This change of emphasis occurred as some press organizations started to look to it as a vital tool for their operations and activities as part of a drive to establish upgraded computer software to facilitate their daily work.

In terms of the publishing tools available currently, electronic publishing can be divided into four main categories: (1) desktop publishing applications that provide tools for document creation; (2) portable document software that enables document conversion to a format that can be distributed to various platforms such as Portable Document Format (PDF); (3) hypertext publishing that allows structure free-form information collection from multiple sources for the creation of master documents; and finally (4) mark-up languages such as Hypertext Mark-up Language (HTML) and Simple Mail Transfer Protocol (SMTP) that provide a set standard to describe the structure and content of an electronic document (Grenier, 1998; Shay 1995).

Another fourfold classification system was presented by Lancaster (1995), who outlined four basic and co-existent steps in the evolution of electronic publishing: (1) Using computers to generate conventional print-on-paper publications allowing printing on demand or producing customized publications personalized to individual needs; (2) Distributing text electronically, which is the exact equivalent of the paper version; this includes full-text articles available through commercial vendors such as DIALOG; (3) Distribution in electronic form of print publications providing value-added features such as search capabilities and data manipulation; (4) Generating publications that take advantage of such electronic capabilities as hypertext, hypermedia, sound, and motion.

In sum, the information delivery world is undergoing profound changes as a result of the widespread usage of personal computers and the rapid growth of the Internet. A consequence of these rapid technological developments is that the electronic delivery of news to significant and expanding readership markets has not only become feasible, but has also become sufficiently accessible that a demand for this form of news publishing has emerged with some force. Although the publishing industry has a long history of adapting new technology, the new electronic media may represent the most significant new direction for newsmakers to date (Ackerman, 1993; Bender, 1993; Christopher, 1994; Koch, 1996).

EARLY HISTORY

The first serious attempt to use electronic means to deliver news (to a screen) was in the early 1970s and involved videotext technology. The idea of videotext is to deliver printed information electronically via hard wire (a telephone line or TV cable) either to a TV set or to a personal computer. Britain's Prestel™ service, which was launched in the early 1970s, was one of the first videotext systems in the world (Beckett, 1994; Carlson, 1996). Launched in 1979, it offered news bulletins, home banking, flight bookings, and other information via special TV-like monitors. High costs and other difficulties meant that by 1986, only 65,000 people had subscribed to the service and by 1993, usage had dropped to 30,000 (Beckett, 1994).

Ceefax™ also arrived during the 1970s and has continued to flourish up to the present day. It was developed by the BBC out of research into subtitling programs for the deaf and hard of hearing. The fall in the price of computers, development of ROM techniques, and advances in data transmission techniques all helped the project. It soon became clear that it had potential beyond its original intended application. Test pages were operational by 1973 and trial broadcasts begun in 1974 leading to a national launch in 1976. Oracle™, the version of teletext put out by the United Kingdom's commercial television broadcast service (ITV), was developed in tandem, with television set manufacturers also being consulted at each step. The potential to transmit live news in text form became apparent during the test phase.

Adoption of teletext services was slow to begin with, with only 3% of the United Kingdom's households having access up to December, 1981. Growth became more prominent in the 1980s, with take-up at 17% by 1987 (Greenberg & Lin, 1987). By the end of the 1990s, teletext broadcasts in the United Kingdom reached mass audiences, with 6 in 10 households (60%) possessing at least one teletext television set. The service was used daily by 9.4 million people and weekly by 19.2 million (see P. Williams & Nicholas, 1999).

A similar service called Minitel™ was launched by the French in the mid-1970s. Minitel terminals contained the contents of the local telephone directories and were given free to telephone subscribers. The Minitel service continued to attract a market for many years. At the end of 1986, more than 2.2 million "Minitels" had been installed, showing a fourfold increase in just 2 years (Pailliart, 1989). By the early 1990s, ⅓ of the French population above 15 years old used Minitel. The success of the French version was really exceptional for services of this kind. One reason for its success was that Minitel provided a significant amount of locally relevant content and services. Having said that, other statistics put the significance of Minitel as a news service into perspective. Although firmly established in many households, only a small percentage of users made a significant proportion of calls on the system. Furthermore, from the mid-1980s, games and personal messaging surpassed news and information as the major uses of Minitel (Charon, 1987; Pailliart, 1989). Another reason for its success was that reception terminals were given away free by the socialist French government (Beckett, 1994).

Videotext systems were introduced in a number of other parts of the world. A Japanese videotext service, Captain™, was introduced in 1979. The same year witnessed the launch of the Canadian videotext service—Telidon™ (Dusseldorp, 1998; European Commission, 1995, 1997; Jones, 1991; Ryan, 1995). In the United States, there were a number of experiments conducted at about the same time (Carlson, 1996). American workers tried to develop the first system (Startext) to deliver news and information to computers in 1981. Then came Key Calm, an experiment of the *Chicago Sun Times* between 1982 and 1986. This was an idea similar to videotext, designed to deliver information services to television sets via a dedicated terminal that the user had to buy. The whole project closed in 1986 after losing an estimated $30 million. Knight Ridder Newspapers, who own a number of large newspapers in the United States, came up with another ambitious experiment called Viewtron, using cable and telephone linked to television sets to deliver the service.

This ambitious project failed to survive after losing $60 million, which forced the company to close it in 1986 (Carlson, 1996).

Although most videotext ventures failed, the modified idea of *teletext*, that delivers textual content via a broadcast signal instead of videotext hard wires, has fared much better. Teletext services became firmly established across Europe, and especially in the United Kingdom, during the 1980s (see Greenberg & Lin, 1988). All the major broadcasters in the United Kingdom—terrestrial and satellite alike—continue to provide teletext services offering news and information on a wide range of subjects. In a sense, teletext is part news service and part entertainment magazine.

The failure of videotext was due mainly to the slow response to consumer inquiries, low-resolution texts, and the noninteractive nature of the system (McAdams, 1995b). According to Mueller and Kamerer (1995), of all the videotext experiments, only computer applications have provided an electronic method of delivery that bears a sufficient resemblance to printed newspapers to significantly augment or, perhaps eventually, to replace them.

EMERGENCE OF NEWS ONLINE

Initial electronic text news services were clearly tied to the prevailing electronic media of the day—most especially television broadcasting. The emergence of home computers and the evolution of telecommunications technology beyond traditional voice transmission services opened up fresh avenues for the exploration of news delivery.

It is significant that the newspaper industry was involved in most of these experiments, especially in the United States. Newspapers were driven to explore new methods of content delivery in response to declining circulation figures and increasing costs of production in the early 1980s (Strauss & Schoder, 1994). Early online news publishing ventures represented remarkable efforts at the time. Despite being at the cutting edge of the available technology, there was little market demand. A radical shift in market potential had occurred by the 1990s, opening up the possibility of launching financially viable electronic publishing services.

Possibly encouraged by Mintel's success, IBM and Sears developed a news and communication network called Prodigy. The launch of this in 1987 coincided with the advent of affordable home personal computers (PCs) and expanding interconnectivity between computers, especially at academic and research institutions. Computer networks thus opened up effective new communications channels for electronic news delivery.

Further online databases and information archives were developed from the 1970s to which subscribers could gain access via a computer with a modem. In 1973, Mead Data Central of Columbus, Ohio developed Lexis™, the first online full text database. Lexis featured case law, judicial rulings, and other information for the legal profession. Five years later, Mead Data Central debuted Nexis, the first online database containing national news publications, including the *New York Times*, the *Washington Post*, *U.S. News and World Report*, and Associated Press (AP) News Service information. Dialog™, a major commercial database network distributor, opened in 1972, and by 1979 had made available its National Newspaper Index, a bibliographic database later converted into a full text service. Compuserve, a major online consumer service, also began selling access to its network to computer hobbyists as well as professional groups in 1979.

Before the expansion of the Internet in the United States, companies that were providing more general online services that paved the way for the mass market potential of the internet, such as America Online (AOL), and CompuServe, offered electronic editions of national newspapers on an experimental basis. For instance, AOL provided online versions of *Time*, *Omni*, *Compute*, *Wired*, *The Chicago Tribune*, and the *San Jose Mercury News* (Liebman, 1993). By the mid-1990s, CompuServe offered online versions of *Florida Today*, the *Detroit Free Press*, and Gannett Suburban Newspapers in White Plains, New York, to 1.6 million subscribers. *Time* magazine went online in the autumn of 1993. After 3 weeks, *Time Online* was accessed 126,563 times. *Time* logged its 1 millionth online visit on Thursday, January 24, 1994. Total weekly usage reached 100,000 within 6 months of operation (Long, 1994).

Some of the most significant steps in the development of online newspapers came from the Mercury Center, in San Jose, California. The local paper, *The San Jose Mercury News*, went online in 1993 and became established as a cutting edge electronic news publisher. The paper pioneered value added services such as a news archive dating back to 1985, expanded local information, and an electronic bulletin board for readers to communicate with each other and with staff. In another innovation, the paper incorporated a personalized news service in which readers could enter keywords, weighted by the user in terms of degree of relevance, and receive articles dispatched via e-mail (Bates, 1999).

An online collaboration between the *Atlanta Journal—Constitution* and prodigy Services Company, Cox Newspapers, Inc., offered its readers a new electronic service called *Access Atlanta*™. The service provided a variety of information ranging from news stories and photographs to classified advertisements and current sports scores. *Access Atlanta* had signed up 11,500 subscribers in 10 weeks (Thalhimer, 1994).

Even the New York Times Company and the Washington Post Company launched online news products. On June 9, 1994, *The New York Times* launched an interactive news service on America Online called simply *@times* (Thalhimer, 1994). *@times* included a variety of offerings, ranging from news stories, reviews, and information on cultural, arts and leisure activities in New York City to an electronic bulletin board. The service was offered free to anyone subscribing to America Online.

The *Washington Post* produced an online service called *Washington Post Online* in 1994. It maintained as much as possible in online form the look of the *Washington Post*, featuring the same typeface in its banner, with the term, *EXTRA* added to the *Washington Post*. The left side of the on-screen menu listed major sections, such as news, arts, lifestyle, features, and displayed lead stories in the main part of the screen. Advertisements and computer functions were in the lower part of the frame (Arlen, 1994).

In England, the Web newspaper pioneer was *The Electronic Telegraph*, the online version of *The Daily Telegraph*, with its first Internet edition appearing in November, 1994. *The Times* had launched *ST—Online*™ in September of that year, which included an interactive discussion forum, but this was a modest text-only service not incorporating the then very new Web technology, although it did provide a gateway to the Internet. The full Web editions of *The Times* and *Sunday Times* were launched on January 1, 1996, and were the first United Kingdom papers to include the full text of the hard copy versions. *The Electronic Telegraph* had adopted an early policy of editing or reshaping stories for the online reader. Eventually, the Web copy evolved to include much unique copy not carried by the hard-copy edition.

The potential for accessing news online was not missed by newspapers publishers in the United Kingdom. Beginning with *The Guardian* in 1985, World Reporter (now FT Profile) mounted a campaign that was to see the near full text of all broadsheets, most tabloids, and a number of regional newspapers on the service by 1993.

By 1995, newspaper publishers were caused to observe that the Internet, once established among the general population, would become a force to be reckoned with. Newspapers would either need to take advantage of this new medium, or be left behind by it. Phillips (1998) noted that the

> online news and information business is exploding at a pace never seen before in the development of a new media industry. Current estimates are that the Internet will reach critical mass for general acceptance in around 5 years. It is already accepted enough to begin draining serious audience attention from our traditional media. (p. 1)

INTERNET NEWS SERVICES

Internet technology, in the way it accesses and presents information, is changing the rules of publishing and news distribution in many ways. The challenge posed by the Internet for the publishing industry is unprecedented. In some ways, Internet applications could provide a fresh impetus to the industry. News publishers are faced with an aging readership, declining revenues, sinking circulation figures, and a fragmented sense of mission (Orr, 1997). Hard copy newspapers risk losing a large segment of their readership that exhibits a particular preference for electronic information and entertainment sources, namely the younger generation who form the majority of Internet users. Internet traffic to online newspapers can be as significant as the readership of hard copy versions. In March, 2001, the online version of the *Sydney Morning Herald* in Australia had 240,000 visitors a day, roughly in line with the paper's physical circulation (Bitta, 2001). According to Nicholas, Frossling, Martin, and Buesing (1997):

> What is even more worrying in the long run is that the young, for whom newspapers never played a big role in the first place—not being considered a sufficiently "hip" medium (and regarded as something associated with their parents generation)—have deserted the press. (pp. 29–30)

Similarly, with a different approach, The *Financial Times* (1995) noted that newspaper readers, who are enviably affluent, educated, and middle-class, are getting old and are not being replaced in sufficient numbers. The *Financial Times* asked newspapers to not just stand back and watch the Internet, but to be part of it (*Financial Times*, 1995).

At the same time as having to consider the best ways of attracting younger readers, publishers are still wrestling with many broader questions about online publishing, such as how this new medium can be most effectively utilized (Powers, 1997). What is the ideal format for an online news site? What should it contain? What are the best way(s) to present online news to attract readers, regardless of their age, and eventually advertisers who wish to gain access to specific markets? What are the best pricing mechanisms? Lapham (1995) stated that the only certainty now is that there is no one right way to do things. Each newspaper must discover its "niche" and provide insightful and original content in a format its readers want. Much remains to be learned about the potential of the Internet, and what it can do for publishers and their customers. So far, though, little is known about publishers' visions and readers' expectations toward this new communication phenomenon.

In terms of user satisfaction and retention, no Internet-based news service can claim that it has yet achieved a satisfactory degree of customer loyalty or advertiser confidence to be sure of long-term market buoyancy. The market for electronic publishing is made no easier to handle by the fact that new software systems for handling online content are being developed all the time. Problems are created by the introduction of new devices to the market virtually "every other day" and means that only a few people can make sense of what is happening (Elderkin, 1996).

By the mid-1990s, although some revenue had begun to flow for many of the online information services, with commercial enterprises such as America Online turning a profit, few news content providers in the United States were in the black. Most of these companies viewed online services as a low-cost opportunity to experiment with electronic products. One service that did make a profit early on was the *Electronic*

Trib from the *Albuquerque Tribune.* The *Electronic Trib* was available via Prodigy and offered readers access not only to the content of the day's paper but also to additional material that did not make it into the hard copy paper, live chat sessions with reporters, and transactional services such as online classifieds. It had a small staff, low overhead, and its advertizing revenue exceeded its production costs (Pavlik, 1996).

A study of the multimedia marketplace in 10 European countries revealed that a big part of the problem faced by the electronic publishing industry is the lack of a clearly defined business model (McDermott & Fay, 1997). The study stated that this fact acts as a damper on the industry's growth as companies operating in the industry are unsure of their place in the value chain and the best way to profit from their activities. The study emphasised the importance of a well-defined business model that would help companies to understand how the industry operates and where its clients fit into the electronic publishing value chain. In addressing participants and potential entrants into the area of electronic publishing, the study also asserted that the Internet is quickly becoming the most significant electronic publishing medium, and that by the year 2002 it will be bigger than all other publishing media.

For users, numerous Web sites and free software packages are currently available providing online news and information in different formats. For instance, Netscape, the Web's first browser site, has a service that allows users to create a customized page on the Web, which displays personalized information whenever the user accesses it. Yahoo™, the Web's most accessed search engine, has Reuter's headlines and offers customized free news services for Yahoo subscribers. InfoSeek™, Excite™, and other search engines provide similar services. Some of these services are offered in a package with software that forms an essential part of the content delivery mechanism making real-time delivery possible.

One of the major imperfections of some of these packages is that they consume a large amount of computer screen and memory. The subscriber may therefore miss important news items because of the software's demands upon computer capacity. In addition, news and information can be found also in newsgroups, news discussion sites, and instant chat rooms.

Although these groups tend to discuss and spread special news about a certain field or industry, they remain a vital news source to Internet users. In addition, there are Web sites maintained by radio and television stations, which form another important set of news sources that attract more and more users based on the reputations of their providers. Good examples of this kind of Internet-based news service are the Web sites provided by the news services of the British Broadcasting Corporation (BBC) in Britain, and the American television networks, NBC and CBS.

To some, this growth of Internet news services is giving the user more personal control over his or her daily menu of news and information. The trend has been referred to as *news personalization* (or customization). According to one writer, Michael Cunningham, research/project co-ordinator of *The Guardian* and *The Observer*, this development

> is shifting power to the people, and threatens the dominance of traditional mass media forms. The "digital consumer" will be able to pull out the information and entertainment they want, when they want it, in a format they want—whether images, audio, text or graphics, or a mixture of four. (cited in Kwan, 1996)

Boutin (1997) asserted that there are some serious hurdles to be cleared before the new "Webcasting" model will eclipse established news sources. Web content providers, sponsors, and investors all hope "push technology" will provide the medium to carry their messages to audiences broad enough to finally turn these new media into mass media. However, it is important to understand and clarify the differences between each news service in order to assess the validity of this conclusion about the future of online news services. These services can be divided into two main categories; *push technology* (news tickers, e-mail news delivery) and news Web sites (*pull technology*). The following sections examine each online news and information service in more detail (Rademann, 1997).

PUSH TECHNOLOGY

Despite the many names push technology has been given, there is not much argument about its definition or its function. This service is also known as Webcasting, personalized news, netcasting, personal broadcast applications, channel technology, and Internet news broadcasting. All these names refer to one type of online news application. With this service, instead of readers looking for news themselves, it comes to them at times convenient for them and with the content of their choice, thus obviating the need to go looking for it on the Web.

Users can get all preselected types of news and information "pushed" to their desktops via e-mail updates, screen savers, tickers and, with the new 4.0 or 5.0 browsers, users can sign up to have specific news delivered direct to their computer screens. Individuals no longer have to surf for news and information; instead, news will find them (Lasica, 1997). This "third wave of net news" refers to the concept of *delivering* [pushing] content to Internet consumers rather than expecting them to seek out a Web site as in the "pull" model. The first wave was when newspapers launched primitive sites with cumbersome search tools hosted by commercial online services like CompuServe, Prodigy, or America Online. The second wave started in the early 1995, when the public and mainstream media discovered the WWW and started to put up their own Web sites. The impetus behind the third wave (push technology) has been conceived as confluence of three factors: technology, money and a receptive public (Lasica, 1997a, 1997b, 1997c).

In one analogy, the pushing model versus the pulling model of news delivery has been envisaged as being similar to the difference between getting home delivery of the newspaper and going down to the corner newsstand to get the paper (Toner, cited in Lindoo, 1998). Although there are news push services experiments to mobile phones and pagers, the main applications under the umbrella of push technology can be divided broadly into news tickers and e-mail news delivery.

News tickers is an online form of news delivery mechanism whereby the subscriber to this service needs first to register to download special software that will enable him or her to select from a "channels" menu, the topics of most interest. News in those areas is forwarded automatically to the user's computer.

There are number of companies offering this kind of service. The best-known example is PointCast™[1] which has five software editions, three of which are in English (United States, United Kingdom, and Canadian editions), one in German, and the other in Japanese that enable user to download and use the service for free.

News summaries by e-mail.   Subscribers to these services can receive a daily message of news briefing in standard (plain text) e-mail message or in HTML format that enables those who want more in-depth information to follow links to more extensive reports and news archives. News providers send news via e-mail to subscribers who have chosen their news preferences while signing up for the service (Sands, 1999).

An example of such services is InfoBea (InfoBea.com) which claims to have 3.5 million subscriptions to their e-mail news services. Subscribers can personalize the services by choosing only the information they want to receive via text or graphically rich HTML e-mail provided by its 100 staff members.

NEWS WEBSITES (PULL TECHNOLOGY)

With pull technology, the consumer is required to go to the news source rather than wait to be sought out by that source. Even with these news sources, however, a degree of personalization of services can occur. With *customizable news Web sites*, a service is offered to users to set up tailormade news profiles that contain keywords and similar queries identifying the fields of interests of individual subscribers. Several Web sites offer such news customizations for free. CNN Interactive is one example of this type of service. It has one of the most popular free news Web sites on the Net (cnn.com). CNN's decision to offer news for free was taken in the light of the amount of free information circulating on

---

[1]In May, 1999, Launchpad Technologies acquired PointCast and now is called EntryPoint™ offering the same service.

the Internet anyway, according to Clare O'Brien, account executive of Turner Interactive Broadcast (Liu, 1996). CNN's slogan, "the world's news leader," has meant that besides its successful television news station and the news Web sites on the Net, CNN has been forced to lead the way in offering customized news services via e-mail, pagers screens, mobile phones (CNN Mobile launched in February, 1999), and via small obtrusive frame (ticker) at the bottom of Internet Explorer 5 browser. Traditional newspapers are trying to join this race by experimenting with news customization services on their own on the Internet. For instance *The Times* (London) and *The Wall Street Journal Interactive* allow their readers to set up such services on their online editions.

A similar free service to these is a Web-based news site called Create Your Own Newspaper (CRAYON; cryon.net) that describes itself as a tool for managing news sources on the Internet and the WWW. CRAYON uses a simple analogy that lets the user create customized news page with daily information from a collection of links to mainstream news sites such as the Associated Press, Time, and PC Week.

BUSINESS NEWS SERVICES

A group of online services that outweighed news services in the mid-1990s provided financial information. Leading players in this market included *Reuters, Dow Jones Telerate,* and *Bloomberg Business News. Bloomberg,* for example, was founded in 1990 by Michael Bloomberg, a Wall Street investment banker with a PhD in physics. The company provided real-time information services for financial traders. It followed news about financial events. Within 3½ years, *Bloomberg Business News* had grown to 225 journalists and 40 editors serving thousands of clients worldwide. It operated 24 hours a day, 365 days a year. As well as financial traders, the *Bloomberg Business News* was used by other news organizations in the print and broadcast sectors. It produced a multimedia news product that offered an electronic news service with text, graphical, audio, and video information. Clients were required to lease a Bloomberg terminal, which enabled the supplier to update its software without having to worry about the compatibility of the software to the hardware used by clients. Clients paid a monthly lease fee. In another interesting development at the time, many of Bloomberg's journalists were teleworkers, working from home.

NONCOMMERCIAL INFORMATION SUPPLIERS ON THE NET

Much online activity is the result of noncommercial interests and organizations, including not-for-profit groups as well as governmental agencies. These organizations and their new media products often serve audiences unable to pay for commercial services or unattractive to advertisers, such as the urban poor, children, the homeless, the aged, and persons with disabilities.

Among the most well-known and widely available noncommercial services are the freenets, public access computer systems designed for the free exchange of information among members of both local and global communities. The first freenet was created in 1986 at Case Western Reserve University Medical School in Cleveland, Ohio (Shade, 1994). Originally, a small bulletin board service for doctors, the Case freenet quickly grew in response to public demand and came to serve more than 22,000 registered users, processing some 5,000 logins per day by the mid-1990s. The freenet featured more than 300 information and communication services, ranging from e-mail to medical information to project Hermes™, which contained the full text of U.S. Supreme Court decisions. The network also offered users free access to the online version of *USA Today* and Academy One, a K–12 electronic schoolhouse (Grundner, 1991). Since then, freenets have been established in dozens of communities around the United States and internationally.

ELECTRONIC NEWSPAPERS

The decline of print newspapers and the accompanying rise of Web-based news services have been the subject of much discussion among academics and news professionals who have explored the potential impact of these new technologies on the public and publishing industry. Newspaper publishers have been encouraged by market pressures to adopt the new medium and to conduct experiments in online news provision despite the uncertainty about how profitable such ventures are likely to be in the future.

The long-established business model for print newspapers, in which revenues are generated mainly from subscribers, newsstands and advertisers is no longer applicable in the new online marketplace. Although there may be a market (readers and advertisers) for Internet news, the big question is whether this market will pay off and how. According to a survey conducted by a leading American market researcher in 1997 (NPD Group), 60% of consumers who use the WWW frequently read newspapers and/or magazines online. The survey also showed that newspapers are the most popular type of publication on the Internet, with nearly 40% of those polled saying that they frequently read a newspaper online (NPD Group, 1997). Of the factors that makes e-news a good (alternative) news delivery channel is its ability to employ technology to deliver the same content as traditional newspapers to a larger readership with less cost and in real-time distribution. Elderkin (1996) forecast, "as will be seen, the newspaper industry is no more dead now than the buggy and carriage industry was when the world shifted to cars and trucks" (p. 4).

Today, e-newspapers are a reality and one that is growing rapidly and can be read all over the world. The recent rate of growth and penetration of electronic newspapers signifies that they are a phenomenon that is here to stay. Literally hundreds of newspapers have entered the online publishing arena. This trend already marks a major shift of news delivery from conventional formats.

In terms of access practices, electronic newspapers can be separated into three categories: (1) completely free access to the information, (2) free access with prior registration and (3) access for a charge (Angevine, Salido, Yarri, & Zapfel, 1996). An overwhelming majority of electronic newspapers, however, offer unrestricted free access. This concession reflects the high degree of uncertainty among conventional newspaper publishers about the robustness of the market for subscription electronic newspapers and their lack of experience in this new commercial market.

Although it is true that, in theory, anyone can set up a Web site and calls it an electronic newspaper (Akinfe, 1997), producing a news site that is likely to attract readers in large numbers and over time requires more than simply putting up a standard Web site with the name of a newspaper on the top.

GROWTH OF ELECTRONIC NEWSPAPERS

Newspapers' Web sites are growing at a rapid pace, but the rate of change in the online world is accelerating even faster. There were just 20 internet newspapers in 1993. By 1996, more than 1,300 online news sources were recorded, including established news publishers and newer computer bulletin boards and news groups (Lasica, 1997c). More than 150 newspapers had begun advertising online services through the Newspaper Association of America's Web page (Editor & Publisher, 1998). There were 5,400 online news sources worldwide by April, 2000 according to NewsLink's online database (ajr.org). The global growth of Internet use has pushed a similar growth of online newspapers worldwide, which indicates that Internet publishing is an international phenomenon.

Despite this phenomenal rate of development, the growth of electronic publishing has experienced a few casualties along the way. A Newslink census, conducted in July and early August, 1997, found that more than 100 newspapers had pulled the plug on unprofitable Web sites (Meyer, 1998). Meyer warned that, in spite of the trend toward online publishing, which began among larger U.S. dailies, and then extended to smaller U.S. newspapers and to newspapers abroad, hard questions remain about long-term viability in a market in which less than $\frac{1}{3}$ of all online newspapers expect to be profitable.

Likewise, Chyi and Sylvie (1998) discussed the hard questions that accompany the growth of e-newspapers, most of which focus on profitability, as publishers wonder whether sufficient advertising revenue exists to support the new medium and whether online newspapers can adequately distinguish themselves from other online services. Although these points are important, the political and technological orientations are toward a digital future in which only digital goods will survive. In the case of newspapers, Elderkin (1996) noted that within 20 years, the newspaper business will be in the middle of the greatest change in its history. Thus, it is just a matter of time before newspapers are transformed because of two basic reasons: (1) they cannot continue to make revenues on paper, and (2) they can make a killing when they go digital. In an attempt to turn this media evolution into an opportunity, Randy Bennett, Newspapers Association of America's (NAA) New Media director, advised publishers to establish an electronic presence early, and to start an electronic relationship with readers and advertisers as soon as possible (Bennett, 1996).

Putting aside the economic issues associated with setting up a publishing venture online, electronic newspapers are enjoying an increased presence in many parts of the world. In the United Kingdom, for instance, by March, 1999, there were 247 online newspapers (national and local) and other regular news resources. In Germany, there were 81 daily newspapers by May, 1997 (Neuberger et al., 1998). By 1999, Europe was the second most wired continent for newspapers in the world after North America, with 728 online newspaper sites; after the United Kingdom, Norway had 53 online newspapers; Asia (led by India) had 223 online newspapers; South America (led by Bolivia) had 161; and Africa (led by South Africa), had 53; Australia and other islands had 64 online newspapers. Thus, Internet newspapers have achieved a significant worldwide presence and penetration (Alshehri, 2000). Yet the main question is whether the new e-newspaper will replace the conventional hard copy one, and how the outcome will affect journalism.

The development of easy-to-use Internet facilities encouraged many Arab publishers to take the initiative and introduce online versions of their newspapers in the 1990s. Rapid growth in general Internet usage was witnessed in the Arab world during this time (Alshehri, 2000). The Internet was observed to have been of particular benefit to journalists and the press in the region (Alterman, 1998). Indeed, Arab newspapers have mirrored the press in the Western world in the emphasis they have placed on establishing a Web presence. At the turn of the millennium, almost every major national Arab newspaper had a Web site, although none of these publications was making a profit from their online ventures (Alshehri, 2000).

Some researchers and critics argued in the mid-1990s that e-newspapers would not replace traditional, hard-copy publications at least in the foreseeable future (Boulter, 1995; Kwan, 1996). Many publishers treated their electronic newspapers as additions, not replacements, to their print versions (Orr, 1997). Indeed, some commentators have observed that e-newspapers are supplemental services with little in common with print newspapers and that they could not replace print (Outing, cited in Erlindson, 1995).

The local technology presents further restrictions on the use of electronic newspapers and therefore on the growth of the e-newspaper market. It has already been noted that limited computing capacity coupled with the screen and memory demands of e-newspapers mean that the provision and formatting of electronic news is not as flexible or user friendly as it could be. E-newspapers are not readily transportable onto laptop computers either (Kwan, 1996). These limitations will delay the time when e-newspapers totally replace their hard-copy ancestors. In contrast, Nielsen (1998) observed that this is just about the end of legacy media (newspapers, magazines, books, television networks) and predicted that most current media formats will die and be replaced by an integrated Web medium in 5 to 10 years.

OTHER ONLINE NEWS SERVICES

Newspapers have not been the only medium to explore the opportunities afforded by the Internet to reach new market for news and information. The broadcasting industry has been a very active developer of Web sites. The significance of these broadcaster-run sites is that they often contain print formats that resemble the electronic versions of newspapers. As such, they may be regarded as direct competitors of electronic newspapers in the online environment.

By April 2000, the database maintained by *Editor & Publisher* online (mediainfo.com) offered links to 1,895 radio stations' Web sites and 1,305 sites maintained by television stations. These statistics showed a remarkable growth in the use of the Internet by broadcast media. The user markets for these sites were expected to grow as well. According to research released in January, 1999 by Edison Media Research/Arbitron, online radio listenership among Web users had grown from 18% to 30% over the previous year. The same research also found that 35% of (American) online users said they were watching less television because of their use of the Internet (Arbitron.com, 1999). Yet even though online television and radio Web sites may have audio and video files, for the most part they still exhibit a very print-oriented design. This pattern was illustrated by the Web sites of CNN and MSNBC (NBC news) that contained links to the main news topics and to news programs regularly appearing on these networks. When following these links to more detailed content about the stories, however, users were led to full-text transcripts with photo enhancements that looked very much like a traditional newspaper or news magazine (Berry, 1999).

Traditionally, television and radio surpassed newspapers as the quickest forms of transmitting information, whereas print was able to convey larger quantities of news. The shift to the Internet, however, has created a more level playing field in the form of a hybrid communications medium that can convey large amounts of information and update its content almost continuously. Further, it can accommodate multimedia formats with news presented as text, soundtrack, or still and video images. Some observers have concluded that the Internet poses a threat to the dominance of the established print and broadcast media (Lapham, 1995). Others, however, have regarded the Net as providing exciting opportunities for both (Ducey, 1996).

CONCLUSION

Electronic news delivery predates the academic and commercial exploitation of the Internet by 20 years. Hence, the concept of transmitting textual information via electronic means was not borne with the Internet. Early forms of electronic news text transmission can be traced to business communications systems and to the use of television signals to transmit text news to the public. Initial online databases and information archives were available only to subscribers who could access them via computer terminals with modems. Some of these early services were supplied by newspapers. Teletext and videotext systems enjoyed mixed success and became more quickly established in some countries than in others. Although providing a wide range of content and a service that offered regular news updates throughout the day, teletext provided consumers with only limited interactivity.

By the early 1990s, however, newspapers were starting to migrate onto the Internet. At first, only parts of the hard-copy editions were posted on the Web with limited interactive facilities. Over time, however, more and more content was added with the full hard-copy edition plus links to more detailed information on specific stories contained in the newspapers' own archives or facilitated via hyperlinks to other sources.

It was not only newspapers that established Internet news sites though. Broadcast news organizations, news agencies, and start-up Internet news services have provided competition. Despite these developments, newspaper publishers have recognized the need to establish a presence on the Net, even if they have not always done so in a very adventurous way. Since the mid-1990s, there has been a rapid growth in the presence of electronic newspapers on the Internet as well as in the numbers of people who use them. This growth has occurred more quickly in some countries than in others, most notably the United States, but at the turn of the millennium, this growth was a truly worldwide phenomenon.

Internet news is therefore firmly in place. What, though, are the implications of this phenomenon for news publishing as a business, for journalism as a profession, and for the public as news consumers? Do news Web sites provide a real alternative to traditional forms of news publishing for a sector that has struggled to retain its customers? Have newspapers created effective Web sites that take advantage of the facilities provided by Internet-related technology? Does the migration of news onto the WWW mean that journalists will need to accommodate to fundamentally different working conditions? Will journalists' roles change in the future as the Internet empowers news consumers to obtain their news from a wide range of different sources? Can the public cope with huge volumes of information the Internet will make available? More importantly, can the public trust much of this information? These and other questions are considered in the remainder of this book.

Chapter 3

Business Implications of Internet News

Although the printing press as a dominant medium for mass communication has been challenged many times in the past as newspapers have yielded various functions to radio and television services (Dusseldorp, 1998), the press has nevertheless remained a major source of information and news. Newspapers have even successfully managed, to some extent, to take advantage of the broadcast media to promote themselves to their target markets. Newspapers feed off television, for example, and among the tabloids, in particular, much of their copy is devoted to entertainment news concerned with television programs and personalities.

The Internet, however, poses a whole new set of challenges for newspapers (Irish, 1997; McAdams, 1995b; Medsger, 1996; Orr, 1997). The Internet's role in the production and distribution of news has had significant implications for the printed product. Although the revenue base for the printed newspaper might be endangered by loss of readership and advertising revenues, at the same time, new opportunities for news production and distribution present themselves via this new technology. To utilize this new communication technology effectively, newspaper publishers and their editors must devise a strategy for taking maximum advantage of an electronic, digital environment that offers new possibilities for packaging, presentation, and consumption of news utilizing multimedia formats. Thus, the newspaper product may need to be redefined. Newspaper publishing could be transformed from a separate and independent enterprise into one of the products of multimedia production houses. The scope and character of the printed product may also change following its transition onto the Web. This new medium is virtually unlimited in space and can be updated or modified instantaneously. Lapham (1995) stated that

As we approach the end of the 20th century, two powerful forces have emerged to change the mass communication model. The first is the use of computers as a means of processing, analyzing, and disseminating information. The second is the constantly accelerating capacity of that technology to enhance communication so it is almost unbounded by time and space. (p. 7)

This digital revolution, according to Katz (1994) has pushed publishers still closer to the wall, unleashing a vigorous flow of news, commentary, and commerce to millions of people. Thus, the Internet is reality and its services are widely used, accessible, and acceptable. This new environment will create its own traditions and values. The fresh thinking required must begin with its concept of the readership market, that will become more fragmented than ever before. Indeed, the only attributes one could confidently expect consumers of this electronic publishing environment to have in common are that they possess an Internet connection and as such have signed up to what one might call "the culture of freeness" associated with the Net.

This culture depends mainly on the openness of hundreds of Internet services together with tens of well-established news sites as well as hundreds of daily newspapers that can be read online for free. Unlike earlier competitors from broadcasting, the WWW has grown into an alternative news medium almost overnight. It poses a challenge to all news producers—whether working in the established print or broadcasting media (Lindoo, 1998). For publishers to maintain some sort of control over their production, they have to acquire new equipment and a range of new skills necessary to utilize it. It is no longer the case, as in traditional publishing, that newspaper operators will have all the production skills they need "in-house" (McDermott & Fay, 1997).

It is not only print publishers who have focused attention on the Web. Many broadcasters have ventured into the online world with Internet Presence Sites (IPS). Some have gone as far as developing separate information sites (e.g., CBS's Marketwatch) and portal services (e.g., NBC's Snap.com). As broadband technology continues to grow, real-time and downloadable video over the Internet will improve in quality and speed. This will result in technology firms transforming into online information and entertainment providers. America Online's development of AOL TV after its proposed merger with Time Warner, Microsoft's acquisition of Web TV, and ABC's Webcasting of certain network news segments clearly signal a trend toward the convergence of formerly distinct media (Breznick, 1999).

The Internet, with its unique capacity of interactivity and personalization, is inherently very different from traditional print and broadcast media. The interactivity element of the Internet is perhaps its most distinguishing feature and means that in migrating onto the new platform it provides, established print and broadcast media must reorient their messages and structures of presentation when they communicate with their consumers in order to take full advantage of this new medium (Cho, 1999).

THE MIGRATION OF BUSINESS ONTO THE WEB: GOOD PRACTICE OR FASHION STATEMENT?

Adoption of Web sites by organizations across most business sectors has become a prevalent activity. Whether Web sites are always established for sound business reasons is another matter. The study of Web site development and the experiences of other sectors in this domain are highly relevant to news publishers engaging in this activity.

Early signs indicated that there may be financial advantages to having a Web presence. Although, another factor could be that companies adopt a "follow-the-leader" strategy where the Web is concerned. If their leading rivals have established a Web presence, they feel they must do likewise. A 1997 content analysis of the home pages of the Fortune 500 companies in America revealed that companies that had higher market performances measured by revenues were more likely to use Web sites to reach their customers. According to the same research, the goals of the home pages were mainly to (a) have a Web presence, (b) to promote the company's image, (c) to enhance public relations, (d) to attract users to browse products and services, and (e) to collect user responses and other related data (Maddox, Darshn, & Dubek, 1997). Other commentators have suggested that Web sites can (a) generate awareness, (b) explain or demonstrate the product, (c) provide information about a company, (d) help in the evaluation of company performance, (e) yield customer feedback, and (f) help project a favourable corporate image (Berthon, Pitt, & Watson, 1997).

Two broad categories of factors have been linked to Web site adoption by organizations: (1) the characteristics of organizations and their environments and (2) the benefits and advantages of the innovation itself (Damanpour, 1988, 1991; Downs & Mohr, 1976; Tornatzky & Klein, 1982). Big organizations tend to adopt new technologies more readily than small organizations. Younger organizations are also more likely than older ones to adopt innovations (Dewar & Dutton, 1986; Kimberly & Evanisko, 1981). The perceived benefits of a Web site, as with the adoption of other new technological devices, may be affected by the results of trials whereby the adopter runs a pilot test of the innovation for a limited period. In addition, information from other, reliable sources can be influential (Abrahamson & Rosenkopf, 1993; Rogers, 1995). Concerns over ease of access and use, security, and the unproven commercial benefits of Web sites mean that actual benefits are still not well understood (Bellafante, 1995).

Despite these reservations and concerns, organizations continue to adopt Web sites. One reason identified for this is social pressures operating at the interorganizational level. This can be especially true in the case of new innovations. The greater the ambiguity surrounding a new technology, the more important social pressures may become (Contractor & Eisenberg, 1990). So, what are these social pressures? Institutional theory proposes that the actions of organizations are influenced by those organizations around them (Scott, 1995; Scott & Christensen, 1995; Scott & Meyer, 1994). Under conditions of high uncertainty, organizations simply mimic the behavior of their competitors or similar organizations—a bandwagon effect.

Although organizations adopt innovations that are perceived to bring business benefits such as enhanced performance internally and better relations with customers, adoption may often take place without due consideration of the costs involved. Complex new technologies may require special skills that the organization does not currently possess. Optimal utility of innovations may require radical changes to long-established organizational practices and ways of working. Failure to understand the implications of such changes may result in no real benefits being achieved by early adoption of new technologies. Many organizations have been found to lack formal planning systems for adoption of innovations (King & Grover, 1991). Less formal and explicit criteria may be more powerful factors. Bandwagon pressures can influence the adoption of inefficient innovations as well as the nonadoption of efficient ones (Abrahamson & Rosenkopf, 1993). Organizations may be driven by "fashion" rather than a systematic appraisal of need and functionality. The fact that other similar organizations have adopted an innovation may be all the reason needed for an organization to adopt it also (Tolbert & Zucker, 1983).

Extraorganizational networks can also guide organizational decisions in this context. Organizations that perceive themselves to have high visibility within a business sector or to be leaders in their field might be especially prone to the effects of social pressures to adopt innovations (Galaskicwicz & Wasserman, 1989).

Social pressures, operating at the interorganizational level, have been found to have an effect specifically on the adoption of Web sites by businesses. The belief by organizations that other similar organizations were establishing Web sites was a powerful institutional force encouraging Web site adoption (Flanagin, 2000). Social pressure factors did not operate in isolation. Some companies did consider the business benefits of Web sites in terms of increased information flow through the organization as well as between the organization and its customers. Even so, it was clear that Web site adoption was often a fashion statement as much as it was a sound business decision.

Many online news sites have operated at a loss. Some have generated a profit, but many have accepted losses in the short-term with the expectation of profits to come in the longer term. Some large news organizations, such as Thomsen Newspaper Corporation have enjoyed profits from their online operations from fairly early on. Other established news brands such as CNN have had periods of profitability with their online edition (e.g., cnn.com). This initial success was underpinned by a commitment to dedicated staff to service the online edition and investment that enabled some development of interactive components to complement the standard news content. The provision of original content and the use of interactivity represent features essential to the success of online news services. Early research noted that online newspapers and broadcasters had recognized the need to produce original content and not just to reproduce offline content online (Middleberg & Ross, 1997, 2000).

THE EMERGENCE OF ONLINE NEWS

Newspapers' Web sites are growing at a rapid pace, but the rate of change in the online world is accelerating even faster. There were just six Internet newspapers in the early 1990s (Riley, Keough, Christiansen, Meilich, & Pierson , 1998), 100 at the beginning of 1995 (Outing, 1996), with the number expanding rapidly to 5,400 worldwide by April, 2000, according to Newslink's online Database (ajr.org). Clearly, it is the global growth of Internet use that has pushed a similar growth in online newspapers around the world.

Meyer (1998) warned that in spite of the trend toward online publishing, which began among larger U.S. dailies, and has since extended its spread to smaller U.S. newspapers and to newspapers in other countries, hard questions remain about its long-term viability in a market in which less than ⅓ of all online newspapers expect to be profitable. Meyer (1998) quoted a "plaintive note" on the front page of a still active online edition of a small newspaper from Georgia (United States) that summed up the problems: "Unless advertisers begin supporting newspaper Web sites, publishers will have to start cutting their losses".

Likewise, Chyi and Sylvie (1998) discussed the hard questions that accompany the growth of e-newspapers, most of which focus on profitability, as publishers wonder whether sufficient advertising revenue exists to support the new medium and whether online newspapers can adequately distinguish themselves from other online services. Although these points are important, the political and technological orientations are toward a digital future in which only digital goods will survive. In the case of newspapers, Elderkin (1996) noted that within 20 years, the newspaper business will be in the middle of the greatest change in its history. Thus, it is just a matter of time before newspapers are transformed because of two basic reasons: (1) they cannot continue to make revenues on paper; and (2) they can make a killing when they go digital. In an attempt to turn this media evolution into an opportunity, Randy Bennett, Newspapers Association of America's new media director, advised publishers to establish an electronic presence early, and to start an electronic relationship with readers and advertisers as soon as possible (Bennett, 1996).

DEFINING THE MARKET

The electronic newspaper is a distinct medium despite often being affiliated with, or even operated by, its print counterpart. The market for electronic newspapers may, to some extent, overlap with that of print newspapers. However, just as television and radio function in somewhat overlapped but different markets, so do the electronic newspaper and the print newspaper. *Market* is not a simple concept here. Electronic newspapers function in a dual product market—the information market for media goods and the advertising market for access to audiences (Chyi & Sylvie, 1998). Although most media markets are geographically confined to a particular area or region, the Internet opens up what is potentially a worldwide market with no geographical boundaries.

Breaking into new markets can often present a difficult challenge for new media operations in the traditional offline world of news publishing. Entry into the newspaper or broadcast worlds comes with high set-up costs. In contrast, entering the electronic newspaper market does not take much capital. The cost of running an electronic newspaper, for an established newspaper, can also be modest, although this can vary with the type of Web site being maintained. Simple "shovelware" production, whereby the print edition is placed on the Web in static form can be done cheaply. The problem with this type of electronic publication is that it fails to take advantage of Internet-related technology to provide the additional facilities and services Web users have come to expect. Maintaining a more complex multimedia site, which goes beyond the hard copy, provides links to news archives and other sites, and offers interactive capabilities, however, is a much more expensive undertaking both to establish and then to maintain.

According to Chyi and Sylvie (1998), four "markets" can be identified for electronic newspapers based on geography and type of content. Local and long-distance information and advertising markets can be distinguished on this basis. Thus, in a local information market, an electronic newspaper will compete against other local media, including local television and radio stations and local newspapers. How effectively an electronic newspaper can compete against traditional media in the local information market will depend on the degree to which the online publication offers something different or more attractive.

A survey of 489 adults in Austin, Texas examined readers' preference of print newspapers and electronic newspapers, given the same news content at the same price. Of those with Web access, 76% said they would prefer a print newspaper, whereas the rest said they would prefer the electronic edition—a clear preference for hard copy (Chyi, 1998). Although offering content for free to users can boost an electronic newspaper's market (but does nothing for short-term profitability), it may also take readers away from its print edition. Hence, the significant thing for online newspapers is to differentiate themselves from traditional media so that they appear to offer something different.

In the long-distance information market, print editions may not be readily available. But there are other challenges. Once the news gets on the Web, it reaches a global market. The marginal cost for delivering news to more people is zero. If an area can generate revenue that exceeds cost, it is worthwhile for electronic newspapers to explore wider markets that carry them beyond the geographical boundaries defining their print editions. How successful an online newspaper will be at attracting readers in the global marketplace is hard to predict. Experience has already shown that readerships for such publications can vary widely. Major newspapers such as *The New York Times* and *The Wall Street Journal* can attract significant numbers of visitors to their online editions from all around the world. Smaller local newspapers may continue to attract only a regional readership, even when they go online.

In the international arena, online newspapers may include business people needing first-hand information from another country or travelers seeking news of native lands. While residing overseas, these users may not have access to their regular hard copy newspaper and therefore turn to its electronic version instead.

Turning to the local advertising market, electronic newspapers face competition from offline and other online media operators. Printed newspapers often derive more than ¾ of their revenue from advertising. Electronic newspapers have no strong model in this context because of advertisers' concern over the endurance of the online readership and the online advertisement's actual penetration. The current model requires electronic newspapers to deliver content free of charge to attract sufficient visitors to attract advertising. To attract advertising, electronic newspapers must show an advantage over other media and over other online services.

In the long-distance advertising market, electronic newspapers must carry advertisements that have global appeal. This means attracting big national and international advertisers to advertise their brands on the Internet. An alternative is to persuade local companies to think globally and to explore international expansion on the Internet. There remains the problem of how to effectively measure audiences for Web advertising. Different measurement systems exist and disagreements have emerged about the effects of Internet advertising.

It is clearly important for newspapers that migrate online to study the demographic profile of the Internet market. Early figures indicated that men were much bigger users of the Internet than women. Nonetheless, even during the mid-1990s—early days in terms of the wider commercial use of the Net in the public domain—female use of the Web rose rapidly. In the United States, women represented 5% of Internet users in 1994, but 31% by 1996 (Pitkow & Kehoe, 1996). Some surveys revealed an even higher female representation than this in the Internet market (Lawson, 1996; Rackiewicz, 1996).

Age is another known discriminating demographic in relation to new technology adoption. Internet use was observed from early on to be far more prevalent among young people than the elderly (Pitkow & Kehoe, 1996). The strongest growth in Internet use was thought to reside among adults in the 20s and 30s (National Opinion Poll, 1997). Over time, however, Internet use has spread across all age segments and as the younger, computer literate generations grow older, so too will the market for the Internet.

EMERGENCE OF ONLINE NEWSPAPERS

The last chapter presented statistics underlining the rapid spread of on-line newspapers during the 1990s. This development led to debate about whether hard-copy newspapers would be superseded by their electronic counterparts. Some researchers and critics have argued that e-newspapers will not replace traditional, hard-copy publications, at least in the foreseeable future (Boulter, 1995; Kwan, 1996). Many publishers treat their electronic newspapers as additions to, not replacements of, their print versions (Orr, 1997). Indeed, some commentators have observed that e-newspapers are supplemental services with little in common with print newspapers and that they could not replace print (Outing, cited in Erlindson, 1995).

The local technology may present further restrictions on the use of electronic newspapers and therefore upon the growth of the e-newspaper market. It has already been noted that limited computing capacity coupled with the screen and memory demands of e-newspapers mean that the provision and formatting of electronic news is not as flexible or user friendly as it could be. E-newspapers are not readily transportable onto laptop computers either (Kwan, 1996). These limitations will delay the time when e-newspapers totally replace their hard-copy ancestors. In contrast, Nielsen (1998) observed that this is just about the end of legacy media (newspapers, magazines, books, television networks) and predicted that most current media formats will die and be replaced by an integrated Web medium in 5 to 10 years.

INTERNET AND NEWS AS BUSINESS

News organizations have different objectives for establishing Web sites. Such sites can serve a public relations function, operating as a brand-building tool. In this context, information is provided for free to users, because charging for exposure to a promotional feature is inappropriate. News Web sites may cover their costs through the advertising revenue they generate, as do print publications. Often, however, establishing this revenue "stream" takes time and an early entry into the on-line publishing market can enable a news publisher to learn important lessons essential to the maintenance of a viable Internet business in the longer term. As the online news market becomes established, the attitude to charging for content is likely to change.

Online news sites may also experiment with charging customers and need to test different pricing systems alongside the types of content or services for which charges are levied. Once again, on entry to this new market, where the expectations of customers are different from those who read printed newspapers, there is a period of experimentation needed to find out user tolerance for different access tariffs. Online news publishing experiments may also be geared toward selling tailored subsets of their information to specific market subgroups while retaining control over the full database (e.g., Reuters).

In Britain, the *Daily Telegraph* was the first newspaper to go online in November, 1994. Although offering access for free, it subsequently introduced charges for access to parts of its Web site. Other online British newspapers, such as *The Times* and *The Guardian* have also introduced charges or plan to do so (Godley, 2001). Newspapers have been wary about charging for access to their online editions for fear that it will drive consumers away. Even those that have introduced charges have not done so for the entire online edition, but have reserved charges for specialized parts of their electronic publications. One possibly fruitful development is to charge for access to online archives or to content that is not available in the mainstream publication.

There is no single "best solution" for all news sites. Each must find out for themselves the type of configuration of services and charges that works to their advantage. Some early online ventures, such as Disney's free *ABCNews.com*, have suffered significant financial losses (Evans, 1998a, 1998b). According to some writers, news organizations with committed strategies to offer free-of-charge services may win out in the end. Free news sites with highly developed interactive services offering hyperlinks to news archives or other news sites represent the most likely online services to succeed, provided they are easy to use (Webber, 1998).

Specialized services aimed at business clients, however, may find that access fees are readily accepted by their clients provided the service supplies the information clients need in a format they can readily digest and act on. For example, *The Wall Street Journal* has discovered that users are prepared to pay for access to strongly branded content such as financial information from Dow Jones.

The Internet has given newspapers access to new markets. Buying a subscription to a newspaper in another country has generally been very expensive because of postage costs. Sales of foreign newspapers therefore tend to be low unless there is a local printer/distributor. It is possible, however, that people might be willing to pay a lower subscription for access to a foreign newspaper's Web site. Although a number of newspapers have appeared to be contemplating the priced-for-foreigners/free-to-locals model, in practice, most of them have taken the free-for-all approach. Some newspapers, however, experienced indecision over their pricing strategy and in the case of *The New York Times,* switched back and forth between being free or priced for foreigners several times (Webber, 1998).

WHAT DOES THE FUTURE HOLD?

The future scenario for the traditional newspaper market is not very bright. New electronic publishing is not the only reason for this gloomy prospect, and electronic publishing may even bring fresh hopes and breathe new life into the news industry. Despite the increase of the global population, for some years statistics have shown that the circulation figures for printed newspapers are declining (Garneau, 1994). In the U.K. market, for instance, the total circulation of national daily and Sunday newspapers in 1962 was 40 million per issues; by 1994, however, circulation of these issues had dropped 25% to 30 million. Advertising expenditure in newspapers has also declined; in 1986, the percentage of advertising expenditure directed toward national newspapers in the United Kingdom was 14.5%, however in 1994, this percentage had decreased to 13.1%. During the same period, the advertising expenditure of regional newspapers also decreased from 19% to 18.4% (Kwan, 1996). In the United States too, a significant decline in the public's newspaper reading was observed over a 25-year period to the mid-1990s (Mings, 1997). The Newspapers Association of America (NAA) validated this with statistics showing that newspaper circulation had been in a steady downward curve since 1988 (Newspaper Association of America, 1996)

Research using brainstorming and forecasting techniques has been implemented among news publishers, editors, and other professionals with expert knowledge to investigate the future of the newspaper industry. Some of these techniques, such as the Delphi Technique, for example, invite panels of experts to respond to open-ended questions or to offer their views on prompted topics anonymously. Through a series of stages, these responses are fed back to other participants who then provide further reactions. In one such study, experts were questioned about the changes they expected to see in newspapers as new technologies emerge (Massey, 1996). What skills would newspaper journalists of the future need? What would be the implications for running a newspaper business?

It was envisaged that journalists would need better computer skills through which they would become more actively involved in the design aspects of news presentation. Information technologies linked to the Internet would provide more sources of information for journalists and for readers. At the same time, there would be serious business implications. Staffing levels were expected to fall, small newspapers would struggle to afford the new technology and trained personnel needed to operate it effectively, and there might be questions about copyright ownership of content. It was also expected that the level of competition from other operators would grow. There would be a need for more effective use of market research to stay ahead of the competition.

A major problem is that online publications are largely unprofitable at present. High-profile online publications are still struggling to turn a profit. Even large subscriber bases such as that commanded by *The Wall Street Journal Interactive*, which has 150,000 subscribers, have failed to turn in a profit (Dusseldorp, 1998). The unwanted solution may come from large companies operating global monopolies that will eventually control the electronic publishing industry. The past 10 years have already witnessed an evolving tendency among the larger media, software, and telecommunications companies toward joint ventures, mergers, and acquisitions. These companies are attempting to acquire both the distribution channels and the rights to the content (McDermott & Fay, 1997).

So what does the future hold for journalism in this electronic age? For the moment, this is a difficult question to answer in any definitive way. To some, the Internet is merely a new channel of communication in parallel to the more traditional print forms (Giussani, 1997). Others argue that the Net opens up the possibility for everyone to be a publisher, but to make a profit out of it is the real challenge. Thus, an important element for an online news service to be a viable commercial alternative is to generate a profit (George, 1997).

According to Katz (1994), the publishing industry should not ignore its past in figuring out how to respond to burgeoning competition in the electronic environment. Some strategists have advised newspaper publishers to differentiate between what is a threat and what is an opportunity on the Internet. Newspapers need to exploit the Internet and consider the different ways it can facilitate better access to the news for their readers (Chisholm, 1998). What newspapers need to change is not the delivery technology, but rather the content of their editions. Even if electronic publishers become very skilled in their use of information technology software, this will represent a marginal solution to a fundamental problem, and a diversion of resources that could be put to much "wiser" use (Katz, 1994). This wiser use of the Internet for news purposes still embraces the need for skillful journalism.

In the absence of reliable and comprehensive market research data on the Internet, publishers are faced with having to deal with largely undefined markets and unknown readerships, in addition to the special challenges posed by a new technology that is constantly evolving. The potential of electronic news publishing to generate revenue is, however, already being defined by the precedents being set by established free news services. Electronic publishers must therefore reconfigure their thinking about revenue generation in the future. They must also conceive of their markets differently. News consumers in the future may utilize electronic news in a variety of different ways—some of which may model traditional news consumption habits, but others of which will represent new styles of news consumption facilitated by the new

delivery and reception technologies. Future generations of news consumers may prefer more sophisticated media to the daily ritual of the
morning newspaper (Lapham, 1995).

In order to compete and maybe even to survive, newspaper publishers must develop new strategies, adopt new ways to attract customers,
and take the initiative by rethinking their industry (Lapham, 1995).
Lapham explains by asserting that newspapers must start by analyzing
and paring down the essentials of journalism as a craft and a profession.
Once this has been done, the "real essence" of the industry will emerge
and a predictive model will begin to take shape. This point was illustrated further by Michel Hooker, the former president of the University
of Massachusetts, when he wrote *Come the Millennium, Interviews on the
Shape of Our Future*, a project of the American Society of Newspaper Editors. Hooker stated that the newspaper publishing industry is in the
midst of a pivotal time in its history (the reason: the WWW). He asserted
that

> The challenge for you will be perhaps your greatest ever. As a producer of
> newspapers, what you must do first is determine how you conceive your-
> self. Are you an organization that supplies newspapers or are you an orga-
> nization that supplies information? Remington and Underwood saw
> themselves as being in the typewriter business. IBM saw itself as being in
> the word-processing business. The rest is history. (Hooker, cited in
> Lapham, 1995, p. 7)

Forecasting the attitude of the American public toward electronic
news, George (1997) noted that culturally, Americans are too accustomed to the printed newspaper to rely on a computer as their primary
source of news. A similar reaction came from Tony Ridder, chairman
and CEO of Knight Ridder, who argued that the U.S. newspaper industry
is basically healthy, despite the advances of television news and the impact of the Internet. He pointed out that even with the Internet providing endless information, 80% of American adults still read either a daily
or Sunday newspaper (cited in Dusseldorp, 1998).

Printed newspapers may face an increasingly challenging future in
holding onto readers, especially younger readers. This, in turn, will have
an effect on the advertising revenues they are able to command. Going
online is undoubtedly an option more and more established news publishers will be encouraged to pursue as the Internet becomes established
as a major news source that the public becomes accustomed to using.
Making money out of online news services will not be easy however.
Early adopters have become accustomed to many free information services being made available through the Internet. Consumers already have
to pay for access to the services of Internet companies who provide search
facilities to explore the plethora of information that is now available on
the WWW. Nevertheless, with their reputations and trusted brand
names, long-established newspapers have a unique advantage over new

online news sites, with no historical reputation as credible news providers. Their already established brand image could therefore help hard-copy newspapers to build a successful online presence.

It was noted earlier that electronic journalism could open up exciting possibilities for news provision as the Internet is not restricted in terms of space and time in the way that the printed page and television and radio broadcasts are. Cyber news also gives news consumers more choice over news selection. It can provide greater variety and the dynamic facilities that enable users to explore news archives as well as to consume from the contemporary news menu (Lazarus, 1997).

The fact that many Net users are accustomed to receiving information services for free may appear to be a stumbling block that may hold back the transition of hard copy newspapers to the electronic publishing environment. Business strategies will need to be rethought. Net revenues may not derive primarily from the sale of information to consumers. Instead, information may be supplied free of charge to entice consumers who then become the commodity that electronic news publishers sell on to advertisers.

With advertisers, the issue is more complicated. The measurement of audiences for Internet advertising is still in its infancy. There are insufficient data available to establish how effective such advertising is, compared to advertising in other longer established media. In consequence, advertisers have been slow to free up revenue for online placements. Although Internet advertising in the United States alone grew to nearly $600 million in 1997, of the top 10 Web sites in terms of advertising revenue generated, only one newspaper site, for *USA Today*, made the list at the very bottom (Phillips, 1998). So far then, the sums of money flowing into online newspaper services have been modest. This aspect of online business is going to take some time to build. In the meantime, the communications infrastructure is developing very fast compared with the slow movement of electronic publishing software.

According to Jeff Boulter, the founder of the first customized online newspaper in 1995, CRAYON (Create Your Own Newspaper), there remains much to explore and learn about the online publishing business. Although traditional print newspapers are rushing to claim their space online, most offer online news services that comprise electronic copies of their hard copy publications. Few have taken advantage yet of the interactive capabilities of the medium. Only a select number, like HotWired™, the online service of *Wired* magazine, have begun to explore the more dynamic information delivery possibilities of the Net (Boulter, 1995).

In one series of interviews with journalists and media managers in the United States, mixed opinions emerged about the future of journalism (Degen & Sparks, 1997). Some suggested that, over time, newspapers will have multiple formats, whereas others foresaw that there will be a continuation of traditional newspaper forms. Although most of the interviewees agreed that technology will have an enormous impact, they believed that traditional newspapers will not disappear (Degen & Sparks, 1997).

Another study examined assessments made by newspapers in New England of the benefits, drawbacks, and future of electronic publishing (Alexander, 1997). A survey was conducted of the region's 602 daily and weekly newspapers from November, 1996 to February, 1997. Data were obtained from 210 responses comprising newspapers with a combined circulation of 3.87 million, 2.31 for dailies and 1.56 million for weeklies. The newspapers responded to open-ended questions on the pluses and minuses of cyber editions.

The survey found that most of the benefits cited were related not to producing better journalistic product, but to business considerations. In addition, many of the aspects of online publishing that have been lauded as revolutionary—including the ability to deliver the news instantly, without regard to space limitations—are the same elements cited as drawbacks by some online publishers. By early 1997, 70 New England newspaper operated online editions, of whom 64 responded to this survey. Another 24 newspapers planned to establish an electronic extension of their print product within 12 months, while a further 15 were considering it.

Although most respondents (80% of daily newspapers and 63% of weeklies) said computer delivered news would never replace the traditional newspaper, 13 papers (6.5%) surveyed said the Internet—or some as yet unimagined technology—would eventually replace the print medium; four more (2%) said the demise of the print medium was possible.

The key benefits identified for being online were:

- encouraging journalistic innovation by avoiding the space, deadline, and print limitations of the traditional newspaper;
- being part of a savvy business strategy to allow the newspaper to evolve and thrive into the next century;
- attracting—even developing—new readers;
- expanding services for readers and increasing the newspaper's ability to respond to their concerns;
- elevating the newspaper's image by using the new medium to demonstrate cutting-edge technology and build links in the community.

A number of reasons were given for staying offline. These included no demand from readers, no way to make a profit, not enough time, not enough staff, no expertise, too expensive an operation to run, advertisers not interested, no idea where to begin such a service, and fear that sales of the hard-copy newspaper would suffer.

AN OPTIMISTIC VIEW

Some writers have predicted that the commercial prospects of the Web newspaper are considerable. As research techniques improve within this electronic information environment, advertisers will be better able to target specific promotional messages at specific readership markets.

Eventually, electronic newspapers may turn out to be a far more effective advertising medium than current newspapers, television, or home shopping schemes (Angevine, Salido, Yarri, & Zapfel, 1996). Electronic publishing may bring about a need for new marketing models, because the consumer marketplace covered by the Internet will not be the same as the markets covered by traditional media. Market structure is usually determined by geographic limits, nature of commodity, number of competitors, and barriers to entry (Chyi & Sylvie, 1998). Although these factors may still be important in the context of the Internet, the way they are utilized in this new context may not be the same as the way they have been used in relation to print and broadcast media. Understanding the electronic publishing industry will require a fresh structural analysis of the market.

GETTING THE PRICE RIGHT

Pricing news information services was one of the great unknowns of electronic publishing. At the outset, there was no market on which to base estimates of the likely success of these news services. Estimates for digital services, such as movies on demand, were based on charges made for comparable analogue services such as videocassette rentals. In some instances, introductory prices have been set low relative to the cost of the service in order to facilitate initial demand, with prices subsequently increased. This strategy has backfired on occasion, producing consumer resentment. In the case of cable television in the United States, the consumer backlash to price increases was so great that it produced reregulation of cable television prices.

Pricing for online services has presented a special case to the new media industry. In the early 1980s, many videotext services were priced too high and produced few adopters. Many of the next generation of consumer online services in the 1990s were priced much lower, such as *Prodigy*™ or *Compuserve*™, which attracted much greater subscriber bases. Unfortunately, although low subscription prices generated large numbers of subscribers, they did not produce enough revenue. Accompanied by somewhat limited advertising support, the financial well-being of some of the commercial online services has been in some doubt.

In the nonconsumer, commercial online services, pricing was designated somewhat differently. Because users tended to be corporate organizations, services such as Dialog or Reed Elsevier, which marketed the Nexis/Lexis service, prices were much higher. In the mid-1990s, Dialog introduced a new approach to pricing based on the number of people in a corporation who were authorized to read documents down-loaded from the computerized database service, Dialog Information Systems (see "A new fee structure to share on-line data," *The New York Times*, 1994). Using a formula of "multipliers," it was cheaper for a Dialog client to allow many of its users to share computer access to a single electronic document than to make multiple copies and distribute them electronically to every user.

In an analysis of 48 online newspapers in the Arab world, Alshehri (2000) found that only two publications (*Al-sharq Al-awsat* and *al-Nahar*) levied subscription fees from readers. In each case, subscribers completed an online subscription form and gave their credit card details. *Al-Sharq Al-awsat* charged the equivalent of United States $15 per 3 months, while *al-Nahar* charged United States $35 for the same period. Cheaper rates were offered to subscribers signing up for 6 months or 1 year. *Al-Nahar* also offered an information-on-demand service through which subscribers paid additional fixed charges to obtain news of specialized themes such as local news ($35), economics ($20), or sports ($15).

ADVERTISING ON INTERNET NEWS SERVICES

The Internet has provided a new medium for advertisers to promote their merchandise or services. There is concern about the effectiveness of Web sites as advertising locations, a matter that so far remains inadequately tested. An issue has also been raised about the danger of a *blurring*, or news with advertising on the net. "News" may be sourced by advertisers with marketing objectives who select particular types of information as an advertising context in order to attract specified markets (Williams, 1998).

On the Internet, advertisers may attain greater influence over the nature of news content that is presented if they are the principal source of revenue for electronic news publishers. A news agenda controlled by advertisers may lack the balance, comprehensiveness, and diversity normally expected of media news services. Hence, although news publishers on the Internet must produce attractive sites that will appeal as much to advertisers as to readers, there are important implications of this business strategy for the quality of journalism conveyed via the Net.

Research in the Arab world revealed little advertising on Internet newspapers. Hard-copy newspapers and magazines, and broadcast television remain the dominant advertising media. Indeed, much of the banner advertising found on Arab electronic newspapers was composed of self-promotion by the publications themselves (Alshehri, 2000).

The revenue-earning potential of advertising for online publishers remains an uncertain issue. Advertising is a source of deep insecurity in online media as advertisers inclination to take risks varies with the status of the economy—and is rarely high anyway. An optimistic view that is gathering support is that as online advertising becomes more sophisticated, its revenue potential will grow. In this vein, *The Wall Street Journal* spent 28 million dollars redesigning its business news Web site. While other online publishers had scaled back, so this move was against the tide. Although the revamped site continued to experience difficulty attracting advertisers, the enhancement was regarded as a sound investment that will reap dividends in the future (Hayes, 2002).

In sum, there are many areas still unclear for both publishers and readers, including clear and understandable pricing methods, suitable electronic format, copyright issues, back-issues availability, guaranteed accessibility, and other issues. Despite the growing market of online news services, many studies reveal that users are not likely to pay for content, even news they consider valuable, if free content can be accessed elsewhere (McMillan, 2000). So it would be unwise to rely on subscriptions to generate revenues in the short-term plans. But publishers should examine carefully the needs of the other important customer for newspaper—the advertiser—who may find it easier to advertise directly on the Internet, to put his advertisements with other popular sites, like search engines, or to set up his or her own Website.

KEEPING APPRAISED OF CONSUMERS

Attracting advertisers to Internet publications is very much dependent on the establishment of a solid customer base. It is essential that electronic newspapers should monitor visitors to their publications to track the behavior of users and define the size and nature of their market. Measurement of the number of visitors to a Web site is one of the essential processes in understanding consumer navigation behavior in online environments. After decades of perfecting methods to establish the circulation and readership figures for their hard-copy newspapers, publishers now find themselves in a new world where advertisers want to know how many people might see their [online] advertising messages (Gyles, 1997).

Yet, measuring the number of visitors to an Internet site still presents a challenge to marketing researchers. There is no single, agreed-on method for defining the Web audience (Ledbetter, 2000). Current measurement tools are regarded either as misleading or too simplistic in the interpretations they allow (Nicholas, Huntingdon, Lievesley, & Withey, 1999) or, in some cases, somewhat inaccurate and incomplete as measurement instruments (Randall, 1997).

In research with Arab online newspaper publishers, Alshehri (2000) inquired whether they systematically measured the visitors to their sites. Out of the 27 Arab newspaper publishers who replied in this survey, just four (15%) indicated that they did not use any form of visitor measurement. One in three (33%) said they used a digital counter, and one in four (26%) indicated getting server visitor statistics that provide hourly and daily reports based on the number of "hits" and the statistics produced from the log files. These methods revealed surprisingly high hit rates for Arab electronic newspapers, though advertisers still remain cautious about the validity of measures produced by digital counters.

IMPACT OF ELECTRONIC VERSION ON PRINT NEWSPAPER

The production of an electronic version of a hard-copy newspaper represents a potential competitor. Does the introduction of an online edition adversely or beneficially affect the readership of the hard copy? Research among news publishers in the United States found that around one in three felt that the online edition had a positive impact on the hard copy (Mensing, 1998). In the Middle East, Arab newspaper publishers were even more likely to claim a positive impact of an online publication on the print edition (Alshehri, 2000).

Indeed, publishers of Arab electronic newspapers felt that although some negative impact will be felt on the print journalism side of their business, once the Internet becomes more firmly established as a news source in that region, there will continue to be a stable market for the traditional morning newspaper for many years. Certainly, the younger generation of news readers were expected to be among the first to switch to the new medium, but for older readers, their loyalty to the hard copy edition was unlikely to be broken by Internet news publishing (Alshehri, 2000).

DEFINING THE RIGHT KIND OF SERVICE

Newspapers as carriers of content have had to yield various functions in the past to radio and television services, and now there are other categories of information that might migrate—this time to the Net. The printed paper risks losing revenue generators such as classified and personal advertisements, and thus may face the eventuality that it will become less profitable. New competitors, that have emerged through the Internet market may erode revenue share of printed newspapers. The Internet also offers a range of new advertising-based services on search engines, directory services, free homepage services, and on e-commerce outlets. These new online services can attract advertising money in competition with established media.

Another problem faced by newspapers is raising market awareness of their presence on the Internet. A huge amount of content is now freely available on the WWW. Finding specific types of content is not always straightforward. In adapting to the Internet environment, printed newspapers must offer in their online editions much more than a reprise of the printed edition's copy. Internet users are growing accustomed to more specialized services that take advantage of net technology. Thus, news services on the Internet must offer interactive capabilities, a richer mine of information through archives, and more regularly updated information. Readers of Net news can be given opportunities to contact journalists directly via e-mail or to engage in chat rooms to share their opinions with the news producers and other news readers. The news itself must be well-organized and easily accessible. Although Net news readers may desire greater range and depth of news provision, the news must still be easy to access and digest. Getting the mix right will provide a serious challenge for news businesses in the future. This aspect of Net news provision may be crucial to longer term success.

A FUTURE ON THE NET

In under a decade, the Internet has emerged as the news medium of the future. Newspapers around the world, whether operating across national or regional markets, have established Web editions in ever increasing numbers. It has become an accepted part of any business plan that investment should be made in the establishment or maintenance and growth of an Internet edition. As with print versions, however, online newspapers are shaped by their financial resources. The limited applications of many online newspapers, in which the full technological potential of the Internet is no where near fully exploited, can be explained largely in terms of the degree of financial investment the newspapers have received.

Publishing on the Internet is different from traditional hard-copy publishing. The difference lies not simply in the fact that a different communications medium is being used, but more significantly, in relation to the way consumers engage with the Internet and market expectations concerning how content will be paid for. Different models of revenue stream generation need to be contemplated in the Internet context. Shareholders need to show patience in waiting for a return on their investment because readerships for online publications need time to become properly established. Furthermore, readers who would normally pay for a hard-copy newspaper do not always expect to pay for an online edition. This means that greater reliance is placed on revenue streams from advertising and sponsorship. Although subscription charges can be made, readers are not always prepared to tolerate these in the Internet environment, especially not when they already feel they are paying for an online newspapers in terms of fees to Internet service providers and telephone charges. However, online news businesses can be successfully configured so that revenues are obtained from advertisers and directly from readers. But readers must feel that they are receiving a service with added value that is therefore worth paying the extra money for. This "value added" dimension is usually to be found in more specialized information services (e.g., archive and reference sources) that enable readers to go beyond the usual hard-copy content.

The important consideration for any news publisher contemplating migration onto the Internet is to ensure that this innovation is being adopted for sound business reasons and not just as a fashion statement. Research into business Web sites has indicated that organizations often adopt the Web only because the rivals have done so. Systematic planning does not enter into their thought processes. All too frequently, organizations fail to find out whether a Web platform is suitable for their business, what internal changes they may have to implement to ensure that they operate like an e-business, and what new skills they may have to acquire to handle the new technology effectively. All these considerations apply to news publishers as much as to other business sectors in relation to migration onto the Web.

The value of Internet publications to advertisers may stem from its ability to target specific groups of consumers in a more precise fashion than other media. Online news services may take time to establish a critical mass of readers to attract advertisers. However, if they can demonstrate an ability to attract particular categories of readers and provide effective exposure at an economical cost to advertisers, a significant revenue stream could be obtained from this source. Further, with electronic auditing technology, it should be possible to provide advertisers with rapid, ongoing feedback about the performance of their commercial messages in this electronic sales environment.

Chapter 4

News Presentation on the Net

As the rate of technological change continues, the media perhaps more than any other industry has been affected by computerization. Further, perhaps no other professional practice promises to be as completely re-shaped as does journalism in response to the evolution of the Internet (Trench, 1997). The WWW provides new opportunities for journalists. It also opens up the business of news provision to nontraditional entrants who may pose a challenge to journalists' traditional role as public information providers (Gordon, 1995; Schudson, 1996).

According to at least one observer, the Internet is creating new form of journalism

> by reproducing existing content and program structures (online editions), developing new modes of journalistic presentation for the WWW and, significantly, regarding the Internet facilities of e-mail, news groups, and Web services as authentic sources of news gathering (sometimes even replacing news aging material). (Volkmer, 1997, p. 52)

Presentation is important in relation to economic viability of a news Web site. According to an online report published by Editor & Publisher Co., Inc. (1998), three components—balanced content, proper user measurement, and savvy marketing—are critical to the profitability of a media Web site. As for the specific online activities that contribute to Web site profitability, the same research found that a Web site is likely to be more profitable if it (a) develops original editorial content; (b) provides advertisers demographic measurement of users, click-through data, and page-view data; (c) offers online surveys from users for content development; (d) uses online traffic usage reports; (e) has voluntary registration; and (f) provides secure electronic transactions of products and services. It seems that a Web design that combines appropriate content with marketing and consumer information collection tools is critical in evaluating the effectiveness of a news Web site.

Although news has steadily migrated onto the Internet, journalism has not always been equally ready to incorporate the multimedia presentational capabilities offered by Internet-linked technologies. Whether sites have been created by print media or broadcast organizations, the story has been the same. A lack of experience and dearth of skills needed to utilize this new medium to its full potential have resulted in fairly crude applications being typical (Pavlik, 2001). Even if the term, *crude*, seems harsh in every case, news organizations can legitimately be accused of simply shoveling their traditional content and formats onto the Net. The reasons for this lack of true innovativeness can be found in the shortage of staff with advanced multimedia skills, the failure of organizations to regard news on the Net as anything more than an extension of their usual news provision, and, perhaps, an attitude of journalists who have yet fully to come to terms with the requirements of electronic journalism to conceive of news delivery in nontraditional ways.

As we will see, there is also an internal tension created by the emergence of these new technologies within news organizations centering on the role of two traditionally distinct professional groups—reporters and librarians. The access to news sources that the Internet can provide to reporters may circumvent the news source finding and providing role of news librarians.

NEWS SITE DEVELOPMENTS

As we saw in chapter 3, new electronic applications are transforming the way news publishers do business. Internet-related technology allows an information provider to store information in a variety of formats, including text, still images, moving images, and sound. The technology also allows the Web page designer to enable a user to send electronic mail or to use connections (hypertext links) to move seamlessly to material provided on Web sites elsewhere (Kiernan & Levy, 1999; Krol, 1993).

The 1990s witnessed a proliferation of online news services. By 1995, in the United States, more than 110 daily newspaper were available online (Bjorner, 1995), together with the texts of more than 5,000 magazines, newsletters, and newswires. Evans (1998a) reported that more than 450 U.S. daily newspapers had developed sites on the WWW or were offering "electronic newspapers" through commercial online services. Interactive media initiatives were a high priority for all international news operations (e.g., CNN, Reuters).

The same period also saw a dramatic growth of Internet newsgroups, mailing lists, and Web sites. Evans (1998a, 1998b) observed several thousand Internet newsgroups and mailing lists, many of which served as important sources of news for participants. In this context, participants would often post news stories they had found elsewhere online and wished to share with others on the list (Lewenstein, 1995).

Online investors have access to many news sources about financial matters via the Internet. These include Web news sites provided by established news organizations such as the BBC and CNN. Print media also provide online information sources. Corporate Web sites have also grown dramatically in the past few years, with many companies placing press releases on their Web sites. Temple (2000) identified six main categories of news sites online:

- bulletin board newsgroups,
- usenet newsgroups,
- Web site bulletin boards,
- e-mail lists,
- online newswires and broadcasters,
- online newspapers and magazines.

The first four of these categories represent ways in which opinion can be exchanged with other investors. This is important for online investor because of the upsurge in the use of execution-only stockbroking services. Using bulletin boards as a sounding board can act as a partial substitute for the role normally performed by the traditional private client advisory stockbroker. Box 4.1 presents further details about each type of online information service.

FEARS FOR THE FUTURE

Given the milieu of new technology and new competitors, how will traditional news organizations respond? Many newspapers, television, and radio stations and news agencies have responded by creating their own Web sites that offer news and information to users (Fulton, 1996; Gunther, 1995; Lasica, 1996; Shepard, 1997). Racing to keep up with technological changes, established publishers are experimenting with many new methods of news delivery and are anxiously trying to keep pace with newer players competing to get their share of this young market. There is a fear among newspaper companies that new electronic publishers will emerge and take away their franchise (Carlson, 1996).

Although newspapers have traditionally had to compete for readership markets, the new competition is of a different kind. Equipped with the latest technology, electronic news publishers are targeting new markets of younger consumers not customarily renowned for their interest in serious news or for their reading of serious newspapers. The younger generation, however, is interested in the Internet and may therefore be more inclined to consume news from a screen than from the page. The threat of electronic publications was encapsulated in the remarks of one observer who noted that within the space of 1 year, "We have seen a

Box 4.1. Online Information Services

Bulletin Board Newsgroups

They can offer a source of comment and opinion. They represent a central point to which discussion and opinion from various sources can be posted and where it can be seen by all participants in the group. Newsgroups can be moderated and unmoderated. In the latter case, there is no filter or editing system applied to the content that flows in. Therefore much irrelevant material of little value may be placed. Furthermore, abusive content may arrive uncensored.

Usenet Newsgroups

The newsgroups operate in a broad hierarchical system that enables specific fields of interest to be identified more quickly. Topics can be separately identified and located. Most of these sites are unmoderated, meaning that irrelevant content can be posed on them. There may be blatant examples of self-promotion, irrelevant, or abusive postings, and other unsavory content.

Web-Site Based Bulletin Boards

These are better organized sites than the Usenet sites. The sites tend to be accessed by active investors who want news and views on stocks, without other irrelevant material getting in the way.

E-Mail Lists

Different from newsgroups. They may have a more limited number of participants. They are refereed and tend to stick to the topic in hand. The character of these lists is more like a private discussion group than the boisterous and anarchic exuberance of the Usenet newsgroups. Many of these lists grew out of scholarly conferences on particular topics and are still run and refereed by academics.

Online News Feeds

These services provide hard news. There are a number of categories.

ClariNet

Clari.net is an electronic publisher offering a series of newsgroups to which are posted (on a read-only basis) news stories from the main wire services such as Reuters, UPI, and AP. Covers stock market reports and economic news.

Online News Services

A number of large news agencies and similar organizations provide services that can be accessed either directly or indirectly via the Web. These

(continued)

include Reuters, Bloomberg, CNN, and others. Initially, some of these services charged their subscribers, but they have mostly switched to advertising funded services or by wholesaling subscription revenue.

Online Newspapers and Magazines

Can provide useful source of information for investors, as well as providing coverage of market events. They can also provide information about companies of a more general nature.

Source. Temple, 2000.

storm surge of new competitors roll over the media landscape to compete for ever thinner slices of what had been our business" (Phillips, 1998, p. 1).

With electronic news publishing, new rules and standards will be set to inform the way news should be provided in a world where consumers have much more control over the process of consumption and different assumptions and expectations of news services. New "cyber-publishers" driven by technology advancements, are seemingly leading the way. The old culture of a newspaper that presents news once every 24 hours is no longer tenable. On the Internet, it is possible for content providers to offer immediate, timely scoops of news around the clock. Furthermore, Internet users are able to experience a much expanded range of choices of news delivery that enables them to customize their news diet to meet their personal tastes and interests. Moreover, the Internet is offering all these services 24 hours a day (for free in most cases).

Online newspapers have been observed to have a number of important advantages over their hard-copy ancestry. They are not constrained by space limitations in the same way as are printed newspapers. With hard-copy newspapers, the news copy has to be edited to fit the available page space. In the latter case, readers are restricted to the news that is immediate and presented on the page. With electronic newspapers, online stories can be linked to archival news-story databases, enabling readers to go beyond the current copy and explore the background of the story (Henderson & Fernback, 1998).

Online newspapers can offer other kinds of flexibility to readers when searching for the news they want to read about. Key words can be entered to find stories of interest, both from the current news menu and from archived news (Geier, 1995). These searches are not tied to the present, but could retrieve stories going back many years. The electronic news archives exist for this purpose (Mannes, 1995). Furthermore, Internet technology allows readers some control over the information (content) received from the Web site whereby users can customize the news to their preferred topics (Williams & Nicholas, 1999).

The emergence of the Internet has marked the advent of hypernews. Online news sources permit users to explore links to related texts, sounds, images, and archives. In this environment, it is likely that no two users will pursue the same path. Studies of hypermedia will require fundamentally new ways of thinking about media content. Through the use of intelligent technology, some providers of online news allow users to create their own online "newspaper," to specify the topics in which they are interested, and even to customize the look and functionality of the newspaper. Electronic news clipping services can scan the online news environment in search of stories that match the user's expressed interests. Intelligent software will soon be able to discern a user's news interests without direct user instruction and find and recommend news sources accordingly (Nielsen, 1995).

WHAT IS AN "ELECTRONIC" NEWSPAPER?

An *electronic newspaper* on the Internet is defined as a publication on the WWW. Such sites use Hypertext Mark-up Language and other computer-assisted graphic devices to present text and graphics containing news information on a computer screen. Graphics, in this context, include photographs as well as charts (Kehoe, Pitkow, & Moron, 1997; Li, 1998). Internet newspapers have grown dramatically and represent an increasingly significant news source. As with television before it, the unique contributions of the Internet to major news events at key moments have helped to put it on the map as a news source. With television, events such as the 1953 Royal Coronation in Britain, the 1960 American presidential debates, the assassination of President Kennedy in 1963, and the first man walking on the moon in 1969 served to established the potency of this medium as an instant news source. With the Internet, the posting of the results of the 1996 U.S. presidential elections on Web sites drew the attention of the public to the power of this new medium (McChesney, 1999).

The Internet is believed by many of its supporters to afford significant fresh opportunities for the presentation and delivery of news that will benefit its readers. Many newspapers in different parts of the world began delivering information electronically through commercial services before the recent Internet era, but their presence in the field was limited until they started to publish electronic versions on the WWW. So what are the advantages of publishing news on the Internet?

Internet technology can free up a significant amount of space to present news (Lapham, 1995). The WWW offers a number of other presentational opportunities. It can present excellent color graphics. It can provide readers with access to extensive news archives. In addition, the news can be readily and regularly updated. Indeed, going online affords newspapers a whole range of opportunities. The rapid advances in technology, however, have left professional business practices behind and have been underresearched so far. Thus, knowledge of how to publish news effectively on the Internet is poor (Morris & Ogan, 1996). This point is particularly important in light of criticisms that have been leveled against the Internet.

Many early online newspapers lacked user-friendliness. Accessing all the content could prove difficult, time-consuming, and, ultimately, expensive (Katz, 1994). Navigating around some Web sites can lead to a frustrating experience especially when users try to locate a specific article and expect instant feedback from the newspaper server. Moreover, it would be quite frustrating for a user of this service in the long run because a lot of the services and some of the links appear and then disappear. Indeed, some researchers have contended that access to newspaper content on the Internet was a privilege belonging only to the most technically advanced readers (Mueller & Kamerer, 1995).

MODELS OF ELECTRONIC PRESENTATION

The rapid growth of online news publishing has therefore spawned many questions about (a) effectiveness of presentation, (b) ease of content access, (c) the computer skills required of consumers, (d) the multimedia presentational skills required of journalists, and (e) the new approach to business needed by newspaper publishers. For researchers, it has posed questions about methodology and, perhaps more significantly, about conceptual models that can be devised effectively to investigate and improve understanding of all these issues. A few models have so far been proposed for the analysis of electronic news publishing. Li (1998) discussed three such models: (1) the interactivity model, (2) the new hybrid model, and (3) the media transaction model.

Interactivity Model

Interactivity is a critical concept in computer-mediated communication because it is seen as the key advantage of the medium (Morris & Ogan, 1996; Pavlik, 1996). In a corporate context, interactivity can facilitate engagement in business transactions between a company and its customers.

Under the interactivity model, Rogers (1986) noted that the most essential capacity of electronic media is that of interactivity. Interactivity has been assumed to be a natural attribute of interpersonal communication, but has become a concept applied to new media such as the Internet (Rafaeli, 1988). Rafaeli offered a model that distinguished three levels of interactivity: (1) two-way (noninteractive) communication, (2) reactive (or quasiinteractive) communication, and (3) fully interactive communication. Cho and Leckenby (1997) offered a different threefold classification of interactivity: (1) interaction between users and messages, (2) interaction between man and machine, and (3) interaction between senders and receivers.

Rheingold (1993) also discussed the role of people in Internet communication as an interactive group and argued that this new communication revolution was shifting power to the people. This power shift seriously threatened the dominance of traditional mass media forms, especially television, radio, magazines, and newspapers, which were built from the one-to-many communications model. It is not just interactivity that is significant with new communication technologies. It is also the interconnectedness of new technologies that underlies the "logic" of electronic media growth that is significant. One-way systems become two-way or even multiple-user networks (Neuman, 1995).

There has been a tendency among some researchers to use face-to-face communication as a benchmark of interactivity and to evaluate the interactivity of mediated communication, such as the Internet, by how closely it simulates face-to-face interaction (Walther & Burgoon, 1992). This conception ignores the characteristics of computer-mediated communication, which allow asynchronous communication. Participants may choose the time and duration of interaction (Ha & James, 1998).

Ha and James (1998) proposed that interactivity should be defined "in terms of the extent to which the communicator and the audience respond to, or are willing to facilitate each others" (p. 461) communication needs. This definition accommodates individual differences in communication needs. Sometimes users want only low levels of communication, having the freedom to navigate within a Web site and to select from among its content options without direct interactivity with the organization behind the site. On other occasions, the user will want to interact directly with someone beyond the Web site (e.g., interaction with journalists who write for an electronic newspaper).

Ha and James (1998) outlined five dimensions of interactivity capable of fulfilling communication needs including: (1) playfulness, (2) choice, (3) connectedness, (4) information collection, and (5) reciprocal communication. Communication in a Web environment must cater to the need of the user to be entertained. The design should promote an enjoyable experience for the user and engage his or her curiosity. A Web site must offer choice, not just in terms of variety of content, but also in terms of levels of interactivity across a variety of platforms. It must not discriminate against users who do not possess computer equipment at the top end of the technological spectrum, by designing sites that require more sophisticated reception equipment than most users possess.

A well-designed Web site should offer a feeling of connectedness by allowing users to move around the site effortlessly and to jump from one part of the site to another, or from the site to other sites and back again, with ease. A site should collect information about its users so that future interactions can become more personalized. In particular, it is important to know about visitors' previous usage history with the site. Finally, a site should provide reciprocal communication. The Web site is not just a repository of information from which visitors can draw. It should promote interactivity in the form of user feedback, with dialogues eventually being established between the organization and its customers.

Ha and James (1998) analyzed Web sites of American companies involved in manufacturing, services, and retail sectors. Few business sites were classified as playful or as encouraging users' curiosity. Few bothered to collect user information and a significant proportion made no effort to encourage any form of consumer reciprocal communication. Most sites provided navigational schemes to facilitate ease of movement around the site, but the level of connectedness tended to be limited. In sum, many business Web sites tended to be relatively crude services that failed to capitalize on the full range of facilities offered by this technology in the service of establishing better relations with customers.

Hybrid Model

Under the *hybrid model*, it is believed that the Internet could open up previously unthought of opportunities for news delivery. *Multi-media presentation formats* mean that news texts can be accompanied by photography, graphics, animation, and video. The Internet could represent the site of a merger of previously separate news formats and delivery channels (Gilder, 1994).

By using computer technology to produce and deliver a new product, newspapers have welded both the old (literacy–print) with the new (computers–digital delivery) and created a hybrid model. According to Li (1998), however, this model does not address the impact of Web page design or effects of different approaches on the communication process. The hybrid model only provides a general idea of how the function of a newspaper is enhanced by computer technology. It does not measure the impact of relative levels of interactivity, nor does it identify where the old component, the convention of newspaper publishing, and the new component, the technology, stand in the model, and how they work together and react to one another.

Media Transition Model

The third model discussed in this context was the *media transition model*. Boedewijk and van Kaam (1986) developed a model when discussing the flow of information in new communication systems. The described four basic communication patterns and showed how they were related to each other.

1. *Allocution*. Information is distributed from the center simultaneously to many peripheral receivers, which is typical of the "old media" of mass communication.

2. *Conversation*. Individuals interact directly with each other by-passing a center or intermediary and choosing their own partners as well as the time of communication.
3. *Consultation*. This refers to a range of different communication situations in which individuals look for information at a central story of information.
4. *Registration*. This is the consultation pattern in reverse in that a center "requests" and receives information from a participant at the periphery (usually without their awareness).

Boedwijk and van Kaam (1986) concluded that the trend is moving from allocutory to consultative to conversational. This implies a broad shift of balance of communicative power from sender to receiver. However, it is not clear yet to what degree this shift of control is taking in Internet newspapers.

DIFFERENCES BETWEEN PRINTED AND ELECTRONIC NEWSPAPERS

In the case of most online newspapers in their embryonic form the bulk of the news they present has been "shovelware"; that is, content that was created for the print product and has simply been shoveled onto the Web or "re-purposed" for online distribution. Martin (1998) observed, for instance, that stories were typically moved from the newspaper production computers to the online staff for the mark-up needed for Web delivery. Other content changes were rare and relatively minor, such as changing headlines to fit the different space requirements. Online staff, however, did occasionally develop special content sections not available in print.

Other research has indicated that certain changes do occur between hard-copy and electronic versions of newspapers. Singer (2001) explored whether online papers reflect the content mix selected by gatekeepers at their print counterparts or whether they are giving their online readers a different view of the world. Six Colorado newspapers with circulations varying from below 50,000 to over 250,000 readers were analyzed for a composite week in June, 1998. Most attention was focused on stories in the news, business, and sports sections.

Overall, 1,383 stories appeared in these sections in the online editions compared with 3,403 in the print editions. Thus, Web editors were clearly reducing print content for online distribution. Of the online stories, just 158 or 11.4% appeared only in the Web editions. This compared with, 2,173 stories (or 45% of all news, sports, and business stories) appeared only in print. The same versions of 1,149 stories ran in both the print and online editions of the papers. Another 62 stories appeared both in print and online, but in different versions. Singer (2001) also noted that despite the Web's multimedia capabilities, many online newspapers were less visually enticing than their print counterparts—especially in terms of information-conveying graphics. Technological limitations are a partial excuse—pictures take longer to display online and the resolution is worse than in print. However, there may be other reasons connected with resources devoted to online editions and the degree of expertise invested in their production.

There is a perception also that printed and electronic newspapers cover the same areas of interest and will gratify many of the same needs of their readers and advertisers. Even though there are differences between them, electronic and hard-copy newspapers still perform the basic function of informing their readers and selling advertising space. Because the Internet is getting bigger both in the size of its subscriber or user markets and in the volume of its content and applications, this is bound to have a spin-off benefit for embryonic e-newspapers. Electronic and hard-copy news provision places different financial requirements on producers and consumers (Elderkin, 1996). The traditional hard-copy newspaper requires expensive equipment on the production side and no equipment on the reader's side. Conversely, the e-newspaper requires less expensive equipment on the production side and sophisticated reception equipment on the consumer side, which requires more investment up front on the part of the consumer. In other words, owing to the dynamic nature of technology, which is the backbone of the e-newspaper production and distribution system, and because of the different formats in which they appear, several important differences can be identified between e-newspapers and printed newspapers.

Internet technology allows for enhanced and improved information provision not possible in a printed, or even a passive broadcast medium. The key differences can be found in relation to the following features:

- Amount of content.
- Format and design.
- Access and customization
- Immediacy.
- Hyperlinking.
- Interactivity.
- Cost.

Format and Design

In terms of reading, e-newspapers can be read on a small screen in a horizontal scrolling format, whereas traditional newspaper information is organized vertically on large pages. With the latter, it is easy to scan an entire page in seconds; that is difficult when reading on screen despite the fact that online newspapers usually have an index facilitating links to other pages and related stories. Electronic newspapers have the advantage of being able to employ multimedia files to support stories, while with traditional newspapers, the reader is restricted to the information on the page (Hutton, 1997).

Exploration of the multimedia function of the Internet in online news publishing has been limited so far. True multimedia productions require a degree of technical expertise that most newspapers do not possess. Moreover, any such development effectively represents a move into the terrain of broadcast news. Multimedia presentations comprise not only text and photographs, but also audio and audiovisual elements. Newspapers, lacking experience in these forms of news presentation, are ill-equipped to compete with the online video reports produced by established broadcasters such as the BBC or CNN. Nevertheless, as the Internet news market evolves and the masses go online, sophisticated multimedia formats may be expected. Whether traditional newspapers will provide such services or not, in the face of competition from broadcast news organizations and new online specialists, remains to be seen. In all likelihood, newspapers may need to seek business partnerships with organizations that possess multimedia know-how. Such developments have already begun to emerge in the United States. News Web sites have become established with inputs from newspapers and broadcasters (Williams & Nicholas, 1999).

Amount of Content

One of the key aspects of online publications is their ability to publish a larger amount of content that provide greater depth of news coverage unlimited by space or time restrictions as well as enabling readers to refer to back issues and instant online archives. In the traditional newspaper, the reporter is bound by the available page space and may experience cuts to stories to accommodate the space available. With a traditional, hard-copy newspaper, updating the content can only be achieved by bringing out fresh editions. With e-newspapers, updating text is much easier and can be done almost as a continuous process.

Newspapers have recognized the fresh news delivery possibilities opened up by the Internet. Online editions generally include "value added" elements to enhance the quantity and quality of news that is delivered, as compared with the traditional hard-copy paper. Via the Internet, newspapers can provide more comprehensive coverage of current news stories and provide further background information to readers through links to news archives. Some online news services provide special sections on contemporary topics that give readers a better opportunity to understand key issues. Hard-copy editions are unable to afford the luxury of space needed to supply this extra service. In Britain, for example, *The Electronic Telegraph* has provided a special section on issues surrounding the development of the European Union. BBC Online provides special reports and background information on topical stories to accompany current news coverage (Williams & Nicholas, 1999).

Archive services can prove to be a particularly valuable value added aspect of online news publishing. As yet, online publications have not utilized this potential as fully as the technology can allow, but there are some exceptions. Some news organizations have not only recognized the potential of electronic archives, but have invested in infrastructure to support these services. News International in London has established computing capacity enough to house the complete Internet editions of *The Times* and *Sunday Times* for at least 10 years (Lloyd, 1996). *The Times* allows searches for back copies of its paper from the day it first went on-line on January 1, 1996. It also developed an *InfoTimes* section where important articles and historical information are provided. Retrieval is by a directory system rather than by word searching.

In the United States, archive access is more prevalent. The *San Jose Mercury Post* has a digital news laboratory housing more than 1 million articles. This service offers stories from the *Mercury* dating back to 1985 and archives of 19 other newspapers comprising the headline and first lines of stories. Readers can then pay extra to receive the full text. *The Washington Post* also operates an archive service with material less than 14 days old available free of charge and older material, dating back to 1986, available for a modest fee.

The development of Web editions has meant that many newspapers have been able to establish reference services. A good example of this phenomenon is *The New York Times* education supplement, which contains a great deal of information of value to teachers. This includes feature on special topics as well as lesson plans. *The San Jose Mercury News* includes a JustGo.com section with listings of local events.

In the United Kingdom, *The Times InfoTimes* section provides a general reference service for readers on such subjects as stress management, personal finance, and computing for small firms, plus a number of sports facts and figures. It also contains study guides and links to universities.

Customization and Access

With a computer and Internet connection, online newspapers are accessible any time, anywhere, whereas a printed newspaper has certain times for circulation and the reader must go to specific places to get it. A printed newspaper, however, does not require the reader to purchase special devices before it can be read. A hard–copy newspaper can also be carried out by the individual, whereas its online counterpart can only be read where a computer is available and plugged into the Internet (Orr, 1997). Most readers are accustomed to reading news from a page rather than from a screen. Furthermore, computers bring their own idiosyncratic problems. The machine may go wrong or crash. It needs to be free from viruses that may require the user to reinstall the whole operating system (nearly 45,000 known virus and Trojan files move from one computer to another nowadays).

The Internet not only enhances access to news for the public; it also offers facilities for the customization of news. This means, potentially, that readers have more control over the news they receive. This can be achieved in a number of ways. Readers may be invited to request only certain sections of each day's output—sports, politics, show business news—which is delivered by e-mail. A more sophisticated system involves creating a detailed user profile from very specific category options and prioritizing them for personalized clippings services. Another method of customization is to create functions whereby the reader can enter personal details and receive information according to stated circumstances. For example, a personalized traffic or travel news service might provide information about road conditions and transportation options in different parts of the country tailored to individual needs.

Customized Internet news services are being offered by search engines and directories as well as by news organizations. *Yahoo!* includes a "My Yahoo!" selective dissemination service. Users register to receive "personalized news" on their Yahoo browser page. There are several options including news and current events, business and investing, technology, entertainment, arts and culture, sports, lifestyles, and so on.

One impressive customized news service has been established in the United States by *The Raleigh News and Observer*, which offers a service called Nando News Watcher. This sends continuous feeds of customized local, regional, and national/international news to a small window on the reader's screen, where it can be enlarged and viewed as desired.

Immediacy

A major advantage of e-newspapers lies in their high news update frequency, which can take place any time around the clock. Online newspapers are freed from the constraints of print production deadlines and distribution timetables. The editor or reporter of a certain section of the e-newspaper can provide timely updated content throughout the day by uploading updated stories to the e-newspaper site from their PC or laptop. Immediacy, however, is limited by the constraints on labor to update news and stories as they unfold (Strauss & Schoder, 1994)

Numerous examples have already emerged of Web editions providing news scoops ahead of their hard-copy sisters. The online edition of *The Glasgow Herald* reported the Dunblane tragedy on its Web site 12 hours before the first print story appeared. (A terrorist bomb exploded on a Pan-Am flight that crashed into the village of Locherby in Scotland killing all passengers and many others on the ground.) In the United States, *The Dallas Morning News* posted the story of Oklahoma bombing defendant Timothy McVeigh's confession to the crime on the Net before the story of his confession was published in hard copy (Hanson, 1997). In

Sweden, starting in 1996, the national newspaper, *Dagens Nyheter*, regularly provided front page news on its Web edition the night before the print release (Nicholas, Frossling, Martin, & Buesing, 1997).

United Kingdom national newspapers, however, were found to not yet take up the option of continual updating of stories to any great extent. *The Times* adopted a simple approach of retaining the same front page throughout the day but included a "news update" option on its top menu bar. Breaking news was posted here. Other major newspapers (e.g., *The Guardian, Electronic Telegraph, Independent, Mirror*) were found to engage in no news updating during the day (Williams & Nicholas, 1999).

Newspapers in the United States have given more priority to the immediacy of coverage and to regular news updates. Many newspapers state the time articles were posted and the front page may change more than once a day. *The Washington Post* developed a system whereby it provides a Web twin for its hard-copy front page while also allowing the main body of its Web edition to reflect breaking news.

There may be a downside to the emphasis on immediacy. The rush to get news onto the Internet as quickly as possible may leave little time for more thorough investigation of the facts. The temptation to report what public figures do or say without proper analysis may result in incomplete reporting (Hanson, 1998). The normal standards of accuracy may be relaxed in the scramble to be first to post the news on the Web (Hume, 1995). There is a further problem with employing a system of constant updating of news. It consumes resources at such a rate than it may reduce capacity for in-depth investigation of issues (Hanson, 1997).

Hyperlinking

Hyperlinks are part of the very essence of the WWW. The name, *Web* itself implies interconnectivity between the different sites it links up. Such links have not proven to be a prominent feature of online news services. Many newspapers have exhibited a reluctance to link any of their stories to external sites, whereas some have been more adventurous. In a news context, hyperlinks mean that connections are made between stories told online and other related stories. Hyperlinks enable users to click through to this other content. Such content may reside on the same Web site or on other Web sites (Fredin & David, 1998). These links enable news consumers to obtain greater detail about stories, to find out about their historical background or other contextual features, and to get a more comprehensive and varied set of perspectives on a story.

Newspapers and broadcast news organizations in the United States have probably been the most forward thinking and active in this respect (Pavlik, 2001). For example, *The Washington Post* linked its Kosovo reports to an Associated Press photojournalist's photographs and diary notes from Kosovo, the Office of the High Representative in Bosnia and

Herzegovina, NATO, BosniaLINK, the US Department of Defense Information Service, the UN High Commissioner for Refugees, and others. All of these links, however, were to the sites of bodies representing U.S. or international interests. In contrast, CNNi offered links to the Albanian Ministry of Foreign Affairs and, representing the Serbian point of view, the official site of the Government of Yugoslavia. However, *The Post* also offered links to documents, such as the full text of the Dayton Peace Agreement and UN Security Council Resolutions. News media organizations such as APBNews (www.APBNews.com) have produced online services dedicated to the provision of varied, contextual, multisourced information on specific news themes such as crime and criminal justice (Pavlik, 2001).

This extra information provision gives host sites prestige and a reputation for being good information sources, in addition to their prowess in reporting events themselves. In the United Kingdom, the regional press seems to have capitalized on this feature more so than the national press. *The Northern Echo* decided that the provision of such additional information services would be appreciated by existing readers and would attract new readers. A background section provides readers with more detailed information about long-running stories and daily stories. The extra content is taken from the paper's own archives and from appropriate Web sites. With the latter, the material may be copied and pasted on to a preprepared template, with an acknowledgment of the source. Alternatively, links are made to the source site from the background index page (Williams & Nicholas, 1999).

Web sites made up exclusively of active hyperlinks are currently termed *portal sites*. These are dedicated to providing a gateway to other sites on a particular subject. The regional press in the United Kingdom has been far more enthusiastic about providing this kind of service than the national press. In addition to *The Northern Echo*, Eastern Counties network, the parent company of newspapers in the east Anglia region of England, incorporates links to business, tourist, and other sites on its Web pages (Williams & Nicholas, 1999). In a wider context of news provision on the Web, major Internet search directories such as Yahoo! contain hyperlink lists of newspaper and other news sites, and The Electronic Newsstand provides links to literally hundreds of online magazines from a variety of countries and in many languages.

Interactivity

Internet technology permits a far wider range of communication flow than that afforded by any other medium. Anything from private one-to-one e-mails to publicly broadcast newsgroup messages with a potential audience of millions are possible with the facility to reply to individual or all correspondents. In addition to this, the communication is almost instant, emphasizing an element of interaction more dynamic than in written correspondence. This aspect of the Internet is one that has helped it gain appeal as a truly different and alternative phenomenon and has led users to demand a degree of interactivity from the Web that would not be possible elsewhere. Type of interactivity may include bulletin boards hosting readers' comments on various subjects, where messages can be replied to individually or to the broad spectrum; reader to journalist, where the authors of particular articles of interest make themselves available to answer e-mailed communications; and reader or journalist to public figure, in a similar public discussion.

Internet applications, like e-mail chat rooms, provide opportunities for readers and e-newspaper staff to interact in an exchange of opinions. According to McAdams (1995), readers "are eager to let their opinions be known—not just in public discussions, but in personal e-mail to specific individuals" (p. 8). Williams and Nicholas (1999) noted, however, that unlike other types of online news providers, newspapers have been slow in recognizing that a fundamental condition of effective Web communication is *interactivity*. These writers further noted that most of the news reporters he interviewed were horrified at the idea that readers would send them e-mail about a story they wrote and might even expect an answer.

Evidence concerning the take-up of interactive facilities has been conflicting. In the United Kingdom, both *The Times* and *Electronic Telegraph* were receiving up to 100 e-mails a day in 1996 (MacArthur, 1998). According to staff at News International, *The Times* and *Sunday Times* were receiving six times that average by the beginning of 1999 (Erbach, 1999; cited in Williams & Nicholas, 1999). *The Guardian* reportedly received as many readers' letters via e-mail as through other media (Nicholas, Williams, Cole, & Martin, 1998a).

In the United States, interactive services are well established with papers regularly organizing online debates between the public and politicians. In addition, bulletin boards had already emerged by the mid-1990s that facilitated public comment on major news events, especially disasters and tragedies (Nicholas & Frossling, 1996).

Despite a surface-level enthusiasm for interactivity, however, many journalists have been reluctant to publish their e-mail addresses for fear of being swamped with messages from readers (Nicholas et al., 1998a). Indeed, although interactivity may be regarded as a step forward within journalism, many journalists acknowledge failing to answer their own e-mails (Rusbridger, 1999). Another problem can arise from the interactive facility and its use by readers to place "inappropriate" messages that may be obsessional, threatening, malevolent, or offensive. It was this reason that led *The Guardian* newspaper in the United Kingdom to discontinue its memorial bulletin board in honour of Diana, Princess of Wales (Williams & Nicholas, 1999).

It has already been noted that in the online environment, newspapers face direct competition from other news suppliers, including broadcast organizations. Even these new entrants to the online market, however, do not always use the new technology to its full potential. Chan-Olmsted and Park (2000) examined television stations' application of Web features that could be expected to contribute to the overall effectiveness of their Web sites. They also explored whether certain market factors were associated with the availability of these features. A sample of 300 broadcast television stations' Web sites was analyzed.

Home pages were analyzed in terms of appearance, content, linkage, special features, structure, and use. Specifically, use (i.e., ease of use, ease of navigation, and ability to get an overview of structure) was found to be more important, followed by content (i.e., usefulness of information, currency of information, concise, unique, and nonrepetitive information). The degree of interactivity is important to a Web site's overall success because it is a feature that is closely linked to the site being considered a top site by popular Internet portals (Ghose & Dou, 1999).

Chan-Olmsted and Park (2000) found that news-related content played an important role on these Web sites and interactivity and personalization were not readily observed on these sites. Broadcast television stations seemed to be following a safer route of expansion into this new medium by reassembling and reproposing their distinctive existing products for online delivery.

Headline news content appeared to be an important part of a station's home page as more than ¾ of the sampled Web sites offered top stories of the day. These stories, however, were presented mostly in simple text format with only 16% of the stations incorporating news photos in these reports. The most popular online program-related content was program schedules (79% of stations), followed by general program information (58%), and specific program information on upcoming episodes (52%). Web-casting of television programs was practically nonexistent (1.3%; four stations). Among nonprogram-related content, job listing was the most popular (49%), followed by business/market information (42%), local life guide (40%), yellow pages (40%), event calendar (25%), and public service announcements (15%).

Most of the stations did not provide their Web users with a more interactive communication mechanism as fewer than 10% of sites offered discussion forums/bulletins or chat rooms and just over one in three (35%) of the stations had feedback forms on sites. Only one in five (20%) of the stations offered some form of interactive shopping opportunity on their Web sites. Hence, the true interactive elements on these Web sites were limited.

Cost

As noted earlier, the absence of a reliable business model to accommodate online newspapers has hindered publishers' plans for future investments. However, online newspapers generally cost less than the printed paper. There is no paper or ink and no need for large warehouses for paper storage and delivery trucks to make the daily journeys to distribute the paper to subscribers or newsstands. Thus, in many ways, e-newspapers are more economical than their printed counterparts.

CONTENT OF ELECTRONIC NEWSPAPERS

Under this heading, it is not only the content of online newspapers that is an important consideration, but also the format and ease of access to that content. Electronic newspapers will attract readers not only because they provide quality news services in terms of up-to-date content, but also because that content can be readily accessed and is presented in a format that renders the news easy to digest.

Inevitably, there are technology issues that lie at the center of these concerns. Newspaper publishers must ensure they have the skills base to produce attractive multimedia news formats and news content databases that consumers find easy to search. Even the highest quality news reporting will not be enough to maintain a readership if that content is difficult to retrieve. A number of studies have examined this subject.

Issues Surrounding the Study of Electronic News Content

Analyzing the content of Internet publications has proven to be a topic of debate among communications researchers who have questioned whether traditional forms of media output analysis are sufficient to cope with such a complex medium. Content analysis has been a staple of media research for many years. Indeed, since 1965, content analysis has been used as the primary methodology in roughly ⅓ of the articles published in mainstream media research journals (Cooper, Potter, & Dupagne, 1994; Potter, Cooper, & Dupagne, 1993). Content analysis has frequently been used to assess media news—covering such topics as crime (Barlow, Barlow, & Chiricos, 1994); foreign policy (Wells & King, 1994); military conflict (Fico, Ku, & Soffin, 1994); biotechnology (Priest & Talbot, 1994); and AIDS (Gozenbach & Stephenson, 1994). Content analysis has also played an important role in research programs that have explored the relationships between news content and public opinion and behavior (Noelle-Neumann, 1993; Protess & McCombs, 1992; Viswanath & Finnegan, 1995).

Some writers have argued that traditional content analysis may be unsuited to assessing the role of news in the era of interactive media. News content is traditionally produced in discrete units called *stories* that are packaged into larger units called *newscasts* or *newspapers*. News consumers could then selectively attend to these news "units." They could not, however, readily override the constraints of the isolated story as the basic news unit. They could not readily find or create links across stories or locate additional information related to the story to which they were attending (December, 1996).

Another important assumption of early content analysis research was that the news audience was a mass audience that shared a relatively common culture. Content analysts assumed that the symbolic environment was relatively homogeneous and that the social context of news production and consumption was relatively unimportant (Evans, 1998a). The methods of content analysis have changed little since the 1950s. Traditional content analysis is ill-equipped to document and explain news content in an interactive environment. Online news users may select from dozens of news sources, can explore links across news stories, and access text and video databases. In this context, it may make little sense to conceptualize news stories as the basic content unit. When each consumer can create his or her own path through online news resources, there may be as many news "stories" as there are consumers (Evans, 1998a).

Past research concerned with the analysis of human communication on computer and networked communication systems have used a variety of frameworks for defining units of analysis. Researchers have examined the relationships between the characteristics of media systems and the attributes of individuals using them (Hiltz & Turoff, 1978; Johansen, Valle, & Spangler, 1979). Other studies have focused on sociopsychological components of human interaction with computer-mediated communication systems (Kiesler, Siegel, & McGuire, 1984; Lea & Spears, 1991a, 1991b; Spears & Lea, 1992; Spears, Lea, & Lee, 1990).

Further research has explored factors related to the diffusion and adoption of interactive media technology and has developed a variety of different types of analytical units to investigate societal and individual changes that result from the use of new communication technology (e.g., Harnad, 1991; Havelock, 1986; McLuhan & Powers, 1989) and the selection of new media by individuals and organizations (Daft, Lengel, & Trevino, 1987; Trevino, Lengel, Bodensteiner, Gerloff, & Muir, 1990).

An alternative approach to studying online communication has been to concentrate on language and rhetoric. Research in this domain has uncovered many interesting features about the structure and content of computer-mediated communication (Baron, 1984; Ferrara, Brunner, & Whittemore, 1991; Finnegan, 1988; Gurak, 1994; Murray, 1991; Shank, 1993; Spitzer, 1986). It has also examined a number of different schemes for defining units of analysis in online communication.

One study examined electronic documents and electronic mail used in interpersonal and smal- group communications systems within a proprietary context. A number of cognitive and contextual strategies were identified for writing documents on personal computers and for using electronic mail (Murray, 1991). Another investigation focused on electronic mail lists on the Internet and other networks and attempted to devise a method for analyzing online "discussions" (Shank, 1993).

These two studies utilized different methodologies and, in consequence, cannot be directly compared. What is more important is that their limited focus also rendered them insufficient to produce a comprehensive analysis of more complex communications systems such as the WWW with its hypertext links between documents and message systems (December, 1996; December & Randall, 1995).

There is a growing recognition that any methodology designed to analyze the Internet must recognize that it is not a single medium, in the sense that newspapers, television, or radio might be regarded. It is a collection of media—textual, photographic, audio, and video—that utilizes computer and telecommunication technologies to transmit and process data and information. It is therefore characterized by a number of distinct sensory modalities and any analytical protocol must be capable of handling all of these.

December (1996) differentiated between concepts of *media space, media class, media object, media instance,* and *media experience.* Media space is defined by a set of computer servers that provide information in one or more modalities to users or "clients" who have links to that service provider. Media class "consists of content, servers, and clients that share a defined set of characteristics" (p. 27). A media class could theoretically be equivalent to a media space. However, for most Internet users it is more likely to represent a subclass of the media space to which they have access as bounded by the services supplied by a specific Internet content provider. Media object is a member of a media class. It usually comprises a specific content domain available through a service provider. A media instance is "a media object at a particular time" (p. 28). This concept embraces the notion that content on the Net is evolving and changing all the time. A media experience is a particular user's perception of a specific media instance. Although this may or may not serve the analysis of the Internet well, it provides a useful pointer toward the kind of multidimensional analytical model needed to evaluate a "multimedia" communications system.

Although Web researchers have acknowledged the usefulness of content analysis as a methodology to explore the character of Web sites, the distinctive and dynamic nature of the Internet as compared to other major communications media means that it is essential to exert care in the way this methodology is applied. Problems can arise at the stages of formulating research questions/hypotheses, sampling, data collection and coding, and training coders (MacMillan, 2000).

Content analysis of traditional media assumes some linearity of content, whereas with hypertext content on the Web, linearity of content may occur in a quite different form. Nevertheless, aspects of the Web remain similar to content in print and broadcast media. Determining sampling units can prove difficult for some populations, especially where offline lists of sites may become quickly out of date, whereas online sources are updated so quickly that a sample drawn at one point in time may not exist in the same form even a short time later. When using search engines to find a sample, it is important to enter appropriate key words and to have a clear understanding of how that search engine classifies sites.

The fast pace of change of the Web means that data must be collected quickly, otherwise content coders may end up analyzing different content. It may be advisable therefore to download Web sites to obtain a snapshot of their status at one point in time. Rapid changes in the nature of Web sites may also affect reliability testing across coders, if two coders analyze the same site at different times.

CHARACTERISTICS OF ELECTRONIC NEWS SITES

With the emergence of electronic newspapers on the Internet during the 1990s, media researchers began to turn their attention to the analysis of these publications. These studies adopted primarily quantitative approaches consistent with traditional media content analysis. As much attention was paid to format as to content, however. Researchers were interested not so much in the news agenda being set by online newspapers as in the extent to which they took advantage of the presentational opportunities afforded by Internet-related communications technologies. To what extent did online newspapers provide hypertext links between different news content domains? Did they provide access to extensive news archives? Were interactive facilities provided for readers to gain more direct access to journalists? Were multimedia presentation formats being used?

Despite the significance of questions about the extent to which online news providers take full advantage of the new technology, it is equally important not to ignore traditional news-related issues such as the balance and diversity of news provision. Given the highly competitive nature of the online news environment, has this had an impact on the quality and range of news provision?

QUALITY OF PROVISION

Newspapers in competitive market environments have been found to devote more space to news and subscribe more to wire services, as compared with newspapers in less competitive settings (Litman & Bridges, 1986). A functional commitment model was mooted that posited that managers at newspapers operating in highly competitive markets secured bigger budgets to be able to compete more effectively. As this greater investment by the media company takes effect, a product may emerge that is more attractive to news consumers (Lacy, 1992). Newspapers in competitive markets also tend to employ more reporters (Lacy, 1987).

It is possible then that these economic principles operate in the online environment. Traditional news organizations that launch Web sites may invest more to create distinctive sites in the highly competitive Web environment. This differentiation may occur in relation to the content provided and the number of formats used to present information (Kiernan & Levy, 1999). Empirical evidence has so far failed to demonstrate conclusively that the financial commitment model operates in the Web news environment.

An exploratory study of Web sites launched by local television stations in the United States found little evidence to support the theory that competition influences content provision (Kiernan & Levy, 1999). One reason for this could be that the competition that can be found among local television stations in the offline environment has not yet transferred across to the online environment. Their new Web news operations are not yet the location where the key ratings battles are waged. Another factor is that the traditional competitive values of journalism have not filtered through to the staff responsible for the Web side of the business—usually different from the staff responsible for operating the mainstream offline news services (Shepard, 1997).

Types of Hyperlinks

In addition to the quality of content provided, a major issue with Internet news provision is the degree to which online news businesses utilize Web technology to enhance their news operation. The principal way in which this can be done is through archives, links to other sites, and interactivity. There are various types of hyperlinks that a news service can add.

- Internal links to its own news stories (in whatever format: text, audio, video).
- Quasi-internal links to material produced by partners (e.g., profiles of companies or people).
- External links to the Web sites of organizations referred to in a story.
- External links to related organizations or data.
- External links to other non-news services.
- Links to complementary non-news services.

If a news site is not going to develop at least some of these forms of interactivity, then it is failing to take advantage of the benefits of online publishing for users. According to Webber (1998), "By setting up layers of information into which you can drill for more detail, sites are adding value for which either people may be prepared to pay or to which they will return (thus adding 'eyeballs' for advertisers)" (p. 234).

The most common links are internal ones to other relevant stories. External links are more problematic, despite their usefulness to customers. One problem is the cost of identifying and adding appropriate hyperlinks to external sites. A further issue is the fact that this service is effectively encouraging users to leave the host site for another. On the plus side is the development of a reputation for the site that it is a useful source of information and offers leads to further information, and this in itself may be sufficient to attract users back to it again. This last feature may be crucial to success of business news sites that not only provide information of value in their own right, but also serve as portals to other sources of valuable data and content.

Conceptualizing Interactivity

What does *interactivity* mean in the context of the Internet? In the online journalism context, it is taken to mean Internet-enabled communication between journalist and reader (Bates et al., 1997; Foo, Tham, & Hao, 1999; Kamerer & Bressers, 1998; Riley et al., 1998). Interactivity has also been defined in terms of new forms of storytelling that derive from the Internet's architecture. Thus hyperlinks that lead the reader from text information to video or audio information represent new forms of interactivity (Bates et al., 1997; Kamerer & Bressers, 1998).

Elsewhere, interactivity has been defined in terms of expanded opportunities for readers to search for information and also in relation to the interpersonal channels the Internet can provide for readers to exchange views with one another, as well as with journalists (Tremayne, 1997). The possibility of customized news, the frequency of content updating, and other aspects of Web site design have also been included with definitions of interactivity. However, these various features should probably not be treated as belonging to a common category (Massey, 2000).

Within the context of online journalism, a conceptual model of interactivity has been explored that derived from one developed earlier by Heeter (1989) for communications technologies in general (Massey & Levy, 1998). Although the original model comprised six dimensions, just four of these were regarded as directly relevant to the analysis of news on the Web. These dimensions were:

1. *Complexity of choice offered to users*. Interactivity is conceived of as the range, or complexity, of content topics and content-interaction devices that Web journalists offer their audiences. The assumption is that consumers will experience greater interactivity when more choice is provided.

2. *Responsiveness to the user*. Online journalism offers interpersonal interactivity when Web journalists engage individual audience members through the Internet's technology. This kind of communication would be asynchronous, or delayed, as is the case with e-mail.

3. *Facilitation of interpersonal communication*. Interactivity, for this dimension, could be thought of as synchronous, or in real time, conversation. Online journalists would facilitate this by allowing

their Web sites to be used as conduits through which two audience members could engage each other interpersonally.

4. *Ease of adding information to the system*. Another way to conceive of Web journalism's interactivity is by whether content consumers are permitted to add their own messages to the news site. In this way, they become content producers as well as consumers of it. The interaction would be asynchronous and from one member of an audience to the many members.

To these four, Massey and Levy (1998) added a fifth dimensions of *immediacy*: "the one characteristic of online news that most clearly distinguishes it from news delivered by traditional print media" (p. 141). Immediacy was defined by these authors as "the extent to which Web news sites provide consumers with the most immediately available information" (p. 141).

News Web Site Research

Much of the early research was conducted in the United States where Internet penetration was ahead of that elsewhere in the world. However, a few studies have also been conducted among electronic publications in other parts of the world. Evidence collected so far has indicated that users of Internet news services are not experiencing the new medium's full potential for interactivity. Internet news service providers the world over have exhibited significant variation in the extent to which they have developed interactive facilities (Elliott, 1999; Massey & Levy, 1998).

Most of the research literature has focused on journalism practice at the Web companions of newspapers and television stations (Bates et al., 1997; Foo et al., 1999; Gubman & Greer, 1997; Kamerer & Bressers, 1998; Kiernan & Levy, 1999; Niekamp, 1996; Tankard & Ban, 1998). These studies have been descriptive rather than theoretically grounded and have reported variations among online newspapers in their provision of interactivity. This evidence indicated that the degree of interactivity may be related to the size of an Internet newspaper's staff and the market penetration of the printed edition that published it (Chyi & Sylvie, 1999; Foo et al., 1999; Gubman & Greer, 1997; Tankard & Ban, 1998).

Most of the previously studied news sites supplied e-mail access to their newsrooms or individual journalists. So "responsiveness," or at least the potential for it, is a rather well-developed dimension of interactive online journalism. The sites were also found to offer a fairly broad range of content topics, which is an attribute of "choice complexity" interactivity. Yet the choice for consumers tended to be limited to text-based news, sports, weather reports, photographs, and advertisements.

The findings for the more technologically sophisticated forms of content interactivity generally are mixed. Multimedia content was rare. Online news archives and Web-site search engines were relatively prevalent, except at the broadcast-news sites analysed by Kiernan and Levy (1999) and Niekamp (1996).

Kamerer and Bressers (1998), Li (1998), and Tremayne (1997) reported finding a great deal of hyperlinking at the Web news sites they studied. Most journalists surveyed by Singer, Tharp, and Haruta (1999) said that hyperlinks typically are added to the content published to their newspapers' Web companions. Tankard and Ban ((1998), however, found a low incidence of linking among the online newspapers they sampled. Further, most of the newspapers sampled by Tankard and Ban (1998) and Gubman and Greer (1997) uploaded content with the immediacy of a traditional daily newspaper.

Gubman and Greer (1997) carried out a content analysis of 83 sites produced by U.S. newspapers to examine whether the criticism directed to the industry for failing to adapt to new technology is well-founded. They examined five areas of importance on which newspapers must concentrate when going digital: structure, content, news writing, reader interaction, and user services. The study's findings showed that the structure of news was fairly standard. A significant minority of the newspapers studied (44%) presented some news on the first page. Indeed, a majority (70%) provided headlines and short stories on the first screen. Nearly every publication (89%) provided local news and the majority of the sites updated their content daily.

Turning to writing style, there was evidence that few electronic newspapers showed signs of adapting their writing style to fit the new medium. Only 13 (16%) of the newspapers surveyed used any type of linked boxes or nontraditional storytelling, three of which broke up the news copy into blocks shorter than one screen, three used blocks equal to one screen, and seven used blocks of text longer than one screen. In terms of reader interaction, virtually all the sites (95%) provided some type of reader feedback, and more than half (55%) even provided either the reporter's or editor's e-mail addresses or gave addresses for specific departments such as news, opinion, or features. The study showed that nearly 58% of the surveyed papers appeared responsive to reader comments.

With regard to the fifth criterion of user services, less than ⅓ of the sample offered free news searchable archives. Advertising was accepted by all but nine of the surveyed papers with just over half (51%) allowing users to search classified ads without further charge. Although this research corroborated some of the earlier criticisms of online newspapers, there was further evidence that in some areas, electronic newspapers were making genuine efforts to provide a better service to their readers.

Kamerer and Bressers (1998) examined the content and the technical features of some American online newspapers using systematic random samples in a developmental study (74 in April, and 166 in November,

1999) over a period of 6-month's time. The study showed a growing technical sophistication of online newspapers in the 6-month period of the study. For instance, the study found that graphics use and the ability to e-mail the papers from the Web site increased dramatically in the period covered by the study. The provision of online archives also jumped from 34% in April to 52% in November. However the study revealed that electronic newspapers remained poor in their multimedia features. With regard to their content, the sampled newspapers increased their national news coverage more than their local news coverage, but also exhibited an increase of the editorial coverage. Most of these newspapers were freely accessible with an increase in classified ads (51% in April, and 76% in November).

Kamerer and Bressers (1998) also found that daily newspapers had the most sophisticated sites in comparison with speciality papers and non-daily ones. The overall result of the study showed that e-newspapers grew in the 6-month study time and became both more technically sophisticated and more comprehensive in their news coverage. Although the content of these e-newspapers was to an extent dependent on content prepared for the printed editions, the researchers observed a growth in the interactivity of online newspapers, which represented a significant departure from how things were normally done in the print world.

Peng, Tham, and Xiaming (1999) examined the current trends in Web-based newspapers in the United States by looking into various aspects of such operations as advertising, readership, content, and services. They used a stratified sample of 80 newspapers including 6 national, 28 metropolitan, and 46 local daily publications selected to represent various regions and states. The study revealed that reaching more readers, income generation, and promoting the print version were consecutively the top three reasons for using the Web by publishers. The study also examined the style of the newspapers online and four different types of format were found: text plus graphics in addition to directories; headlines plus text and directories; headlines plus directories; or directories only. National and metropolitan newspapers tended to follow the traditional hard-copy format (59%), whereas local dailies most often (41%) chose a directory format only. As the Internet offers the capacity to provide additional services over and above those available with hard copy publications, such as archives, two out of three of those publications studied provided access to such services.

In the Far East, Massey and Levy (1999) studied 44 daily, general circulation English-language newspapers in Asia that published companion Web editions. The sample covered 14 different Asian countries. The selection of this type of newspaper was justified by the authors because English was commonly *lingua franca* in Asia and typically used among nations' educated classes. In addition, the newspapers were among each nation's most influential. The unit of analysis was the entire newspaper Web site beginning at the "front page." For about ½ the sites examined, the front page was accessible only through a home page. The *home page* was defined as the newspaper's initial, or opening screen on the Web. The front page could then be accessed through the home page or could itself serve as the newspaper's initial Web screen.

Each site was coded for the presence or absence of various types of content and features that tap into the technology of the Net. The Heeter (1989) typology of interactivity was used to guide the analysis of news Web site content. Four of Heeter's dimensions were used, plus one other added by the authors themselves. *Complexity of Choice Available* was conceptualized as five content subdimensions: news, entertainment, multimedia, commercial, and background/news customization. *Responsiveness to the User* was split into "potential for responsiveness," or the provision of e-mail links to journalists and "actual responsiveness." To gauge the latter, a standardized e-mail message was sent to the newspapers by the study's coders, requesting minimal data about how their sites functioned. Online letters to the editor, electronic bulletin boards, and reader polls on news topics of the day were coded as examples of the *Ease of Adding Information* dimension. *Facilitation of Interpersonal Interaction* was conceptualized as moderated and unmoderated chat rooms. *Immediacy of Information* meant the presence on a Web site of a publication date or an "update ticker."

The 44 English-language, Asian Web newspapers scored well on "news," but offered little "entertainment." Commercial content (product/service, classified, and "help wanted" ads) was scarce. These newspapers did not give users many options for hypertext linking out of a daily news story to such background content as same-day or archived information, or for customised news delivery. Multimedia content was found at two sites only. Cartoons were the most frequent form of entertainment. Commercial content was mostly for products and services and found at around ⅗ of the sites. About one in ten newspapers allowed readers to "jump" by hypertext link from a daily story to some form of onsite background content or to a relevant external Web site. Neatly three in four newspapers provided user-searchable archives, but only three offered customization features.

These electronic newspapers generally scored low on responsiveness. They averaged no more than two to six types of e-mail links. For actual responsiveness, coders' messages generated an 18% response rate. Sixteen of these newspapers did not allow users to create or add content to their Web sites. More than ½ provided one of the three features comprising the *adding information* dimension. Interpersonal communication facilities were observed at fewer than one in five of these newspapers. Only one site used both information immediacy features that comprised the dimension of *interactivity*. Thirteen other newspapers reported only their Web editions' publication dates. Although offering good content choice, these newspapers offered little in the way of sophisticated use of Internet technology. Although some interactive dimensions existed, these were not widespread or well-developed. The news quality was good, but the technological advantages afforded by Web technology were nowhere near fully utilized to add new dimensions to traditional hard-copy news reporting.

Another market-based model has been offered in the context of explaining the degree of interactivity in electronic newspapers (Massey, 2000). This is based on McManus's (1995) market-based model of news production. This model states that a commercial news organization will allocate its resources according to the need to maximize profits for its owners. Profitable or potentially profitable journalistic activities will be funded and staffed, and those that are not likely to be profitable will experience a dearth of investment. A primary goal for the organization is to generate revenue by delivering advertising to consumers. It does this by packaging the advertising in a news-information product that consumers will "buy" with their attention, time, and money.

The larger its audience, the more value the product will have as an advertising-delivery vehicle. And as that value grows, its publisher potentially would gain more ad-dollar profits. But the market model has a *least-cost rule*: a commercial news organization intent on maximizing profits likely would seek to produce its advertising-delivery vehicle as inexpensively as possible.

Massey (2000) hypothesised that the greatest multidimensional interactivity would occur at Web news sites published by large traditional audience news organizations and that such interactivity would be at its most developed in those organizations with the biggest staffs devoted to their online editions. He studied 17 Web newspapers in Southeast Asia. Each one was published by an English-language, printed-page newspaper. They represented seven countries, varying in their economic strength (Brunei, Indonesia, Malaysia, Philippines, Singapore, Thailand, and Vietnam). He analyzed the entire online newspaper, beginning with the home page, or screen visitors first saw when accessing the Web site. Content and technological features were then coded according to Heeter's multidimensional conceptualization of interactivity including a further dimension of *immediacy* devised by Massey and Levy (1998).

The *complexity of content choice* dimension comprised either subdimensions: hard news, entertainment news, value-added entertainment, opinion-editorial, hyperlinking, news personalization, multimedia, and photographs. Each of these categories of content was recorded. Immediacy was coded as the presence of two features: a home page link to a "breaking news" section or page, and an "update ticker" or scroll box on the Web newspaper's opening screen. *Ease of adding information to the system* was operationally defined as the number of electronic bulletin boards/news groups, reader polls, and letters to the editor found at the newspaper site. Interactivity as defined by *facilitation of interpersonal communication* was measured by counting the number of real-time chat rooms that a Web newspaper supplied. *Responsiveness* was defined as the number of unique e-mail addresses that a Web newspaper provided to its newsroom or journalists. Other data were obtained about circulation figures for the printed copy, staffing figures for the online edition, and amount of Web display advertising (display ads and classified ads). The local Web market was defined as the proportion of a country's population that used the Internet.

The most persistent forms of interactivity were *responsiveness* and *choice complexity*. The choice complexity interactivity appeared largely as traditional "hard" news and entertainment articles, opinion–editorial content, and photographs. Technology enabled forms of content interaction generally were rare. None of the newspaper studied here published multimedia material. Four of the e-newspapers (three from Brunei and one from Thailand) posted some content that was hyperlinked to topically related onsite or offsite information. Even they did not make wide use of this feature.

News customization was a more frequently applied layer of content interactivity. Seven of the Web newspapers supplied either archives or search engines, and seven offered both. All of the Web newspapers provided for potential responsiveness by posting at least one unique e-mail address to their newsrooms. The average was for three e-mail links. Four of the Web newspapers leveraged on the Internet's technological capacity to offer more than once-a-day immediacy.

The hypothesis that multidimensional interactivity in e-newspapers would be greatest for the large-audience, traditional, printed newspapers was only partially supported. This pattern was true in the case of choice complexity. Web news sites associated with the bigger printed newspapers offered more hard news, entertainment stories, value-added features, and opinion–editorial content. News customization was also related significantly to circulation.

Staff size was also correlated with certain aspects of interactivity such as ease of adding information and potential for responsiveness. It was not widely predictive of choice complexity, except for the number of hard news articles and customization features that the newspaper offered. In sum, organizational resource variables did emerge to some extent as predictive of how advanced the interactivity features are of online newspapers; but they were far from perfectly predictive and many aspects of interactivity were unrelated to resource commitment.

According to Massey (2000), his findings

> provide some theoretic support for the market logic of "shovelware." A large-audience news organization would have the financial means to fill its traditional product with a lot of content that, in turn, could be re-purposed inexpensively to its Web venture. (p. 234)

Those interactive features that were most prevalent such as news customization primarily through news archives represented economical solutions. Furthermore, investment in expensive high-tech solutions may be unnecessary in any case, if low-tech solutions are sufficient to attract readers and, in turn, advertisers. Indeed, experiments into read-ers' format preferences have indicated that text-based content that is easy to use is preferred over more complicated multimedia sites (Mings, 1997a; Mueller & Kamerer, 1995). Furthermore, readers' overall mem-ory and comprehension of news is not necessarily enhanced by compli-cated multimedia presentation formats—and in fact can be rendered worse by them (Berry, 1999; Mensing, Greer, Gubman, & Louis, 1998; Moon, Ferguson, & Tedder, 1999).

In the Arab world, Alshehri (2000) analyzed 48 online newspapers covering 15 Arab nations. The great majority of these Web publications were in Arabic (85%), whereas the remainder were in English (15%). The format and structure of text presentation on the Internet has been a hin-drance to the establishment of Arab online newspapers. Most Internet applications do not recognize Arabic text unless it has been designed and set-up within an Arabic operating system. Most Arab electronic news-papers (79%) provided archive services to their readers ranging from a 1-to-2-days archive to full searchable archives spanning much longer periods. Four in ten (40%) online Arab newspapers provided a 7 days ar-chive, and around one in eight (13%) had archives extending for up to 1 year. One in five of these electronic newspapers maintained no news ar-chive. There were limited interactive facilities supplied by Arab online newspapers. All newspapers analyzed in this study maintained an e-mail facility for readers to use. Just one newspaper offered a chat room that enabled interaction among readers and journalists and one other newspaper provided a guest book facility. The chat room was ob-served to be silent on most weekdays.

IS IT ALL PLAIN SAILING?

One of the key advantages identified for online news is its interactive ca-pability. However, research evidence has offered contradictory views about this feature. Although some interactive features assist readers to find their way around news issues, others do not. For example, embed-ding hypertext links into a Web-published story has been criticized for giving readers a false sense of interactive control over content (Lasica, 1997). At the same time, it has been supported as a device that has not been given its due.

Augmenting a story with multimedia elements, links to topically rel-evant material, or both, seemingly is the full measure of content interactivity for a number of writers (Lasica, 1996). It is also how the concept of *nonlinear storytelling* is sometimes defined (Friedland & Webb, 1996; Paul, 1995). Fredin (1997) and Meyer (1998) described a process for constructing a nonlinear Web-published news story that is more complex than augmenting a full article that otherwise stays arrayed for linear reading.

Searchable news story archives, direct access to news wires, and technical features that let readers custom order the delivery of only the news they like—all describe a level of interactivity commonly expected with online journalism (Lasica, 1997c). A common thread to these views is the notion that online journalism potentially empowers its readership. Khoo and Gopal (1996) called this "prosumerism" or the act of content producers ceding to content consumers the power to control, to varying degrees, their interaction with the news (Dennis, 1996). Online journalism's contribution therefore is found in its capacity to free readers from the tyranny of linearity and the constraints of news space found in traditional media.

Some writers argued that the chief benefit of online journalism lies in its potential for interpersonal interactivity. Morris and Ogan (1996) suggested that in a general sense, communication by the Net "can be best understood as a continuum" (p. 42). The basic asynchronous act of one-to-one messaging by e-mail and the complex accommodation by a Web site of all sender–receiver iterations are its end points. Between them lies the asynchronous act of one-to-many interaction, followed up one step by those virtual rooms where a person can have a synchronous chat with one, a few, or many other people.

Two broad dimensions of interactive online journalism appear to be taking shape here. One is *content interactivity*, defined generally as the degree to which journalists technologically empower consumers over content. The second is *interpersonal interactivity*, or the extent to which news audiences can have computer-mediated conversations through journalists' technological largesse. But this perspective does little to ease a number of concerns about how the concept of interactivity can be applied reliably to Web news-making. For example, if an online journalist fails to respond to e-mail from readers, then is the provision of e-mail links to the newsroom truly a valid measure of interpersonal activity?

The embedding of hypertext links into a Web-published story has been criticized, for example, for giving readers a false sense of interactive control over content (Lasica, 1997a, 1997b, 1996). At the same time, it has been supported as a device that has not been given its due.

Within the digital electronic environment, a wide range of multimedia presentational opportunities are opened up for news presentation. Object-oriented multimedia can create digital objects in full motion video and audio. This type of advanced Web technology can facilitate the provision of information about an object in visual, audio, and textual form with all three of these formats seamlessly integrated. Hence, a video news report about a politician might be digitized to include additional, multimedia information about his or her background, voting record, special interests, and other relevant facts. Such new communications technologies can enable journalists to create a presentational "atmosphere" that is more involving for news consumers. They do not just passively receive a pre-created and unalterable news package. They can actively engage with stories and seek out further information as they require. The news in this environment is more dynamic because it is updated more frequently and it encourages consumers to seek out more than is initially offered to them. In that sense, the news becomes more personalized. Consumers can choose their own story perspectives. This provision of a customized news service places additional pressures on the skills of the news providers, because they must conceive of news story writing and presentation in a multidimensional fashion (see Pavlik, 2001).

FROM PRESENTATION TO PRACTICE

This chapter examined presentational and content features of online news publications. One of the advantages of going online is that it opens up new opportunities for news presentation that cannot be accommodated by hard-copy publications. Electronic news sites can provide a great deal more depth of coverage than standard newspapers through archiving facilities. They can also be more readily updated than hard copy, hence putting newspapers on the same footing as broadcast media in terms of the rapidity to which they can respond to new developments.

Electronic news can adopt multimedia formats and therefore present news in a variety of ways, using text, spoken narrative, and still and moving images. Online news publishing can also, potentially, empower readers by providing interactive facilities through which the news consumers can gain more direct access to the producers of news. As yet, though, online newspapers have yet to fulfill this promise. Moreover, the complexity of the interactive functionality of a news Web site can cause distraction to users affecting their subsequent recall of its information content (van Oostendorp & van Nimwegen, 1998).

One of the significant implications of the movement to gain an Internet presence is how this will impact on journalism as a profession. Consideration of this issue is vital to the successful future development of online news publishing. Lack of investment and insufficient professional development may account for the failure of so many newspapers' Internet versions to have realized the full potential of this new medium. Will journalism and the work of journalists need a full-scale overhaul to cope with the new demands of Internet publishing, or will a certain amount of "tweaking around the edges" suffice?

By the mid-1990s, surveys of print media editors in the United States were showing that the great majority expected to have electronic versions of their newspapers or magazines in place by 2000 (e.g., Ross & Middleberg, 1997). Many surveys of editors and journalists revealed, however, that although there was widespread recognition of the need to go online, there was concern about the implications of doing so both for newspaper publishing as a business and journalism as a profession (Alexander, 1997; Ruggiero, 1998; Schultz & Voakes, 1999). Some commentators offered a word of comfort by arguing that even though online journalism is destined to become a widespread phenomenon, the publishing of news *print* will not become totally a thing of the past for some time to come (Lawrence, 1993). When journalism experts were invited to engage in futurology, much emphasis was still placed on the continued importance of the traditional skills of journalism as well as the need for computer literacy (Massey, 1996). The next chapter takes up these points in more detail and considers what the online future holds for practicing journalists.

Chapter 5

Implications for Journalism Practice

The transition to the electronic publishing context has implications, not just for the economics of newspaper publishing, but also for its practice. Newspapers are created by journalists—a fact that will remain largely true regardless of whether the distribution medium is print or the Internet. Journalists will therefore remain a vital cog in the wheel even in the technologically advanced context of online publishing. The Internet, however, will bring with it a number of important implications for journalism practices. Journalism in a multimedia environment still requires most of the basic news reporting skills that are found in the hard-copy world. In addition to these skills, however, journalists and their editors need to acquire a new set of working practices. Electronic publishing opens up fresh possibilities for news delivery that require a different perspective in relation to writing and layout. From a different perspective, the Internet provides a news source that can be utilized by journalists themselves. How valuable a news source has the Internet been perceived to be in this respect? Finding out how the practitioners respond to the Internet is therefore a fundamental area of inquiry. Since the mid-1990s, a number of studies have focused on the significance and implications of the Internet for journalists.

In this chapter, we turn our attention to the media professionals involved in electronic news production. By the end of the 20th century, most news organizations had made the Web and other Internet tools available to news researchers, reporters, and others in the newsroom (Garrison, 1998a; L. C. Miller, 1998; Reddick & King, 1997; Ross & Middleberg, 1997). Such developments mirrored wider diffusion of innovation in broadcast, cable, and other related mass communications technologies (Dupagne, 1999; Lin & Jeffries, 1998; Neuendorf, Atkin, &

Jeffries, 1998). One important aspect of these innovations has been the increased adoption of computer technology in various mass communications situations (Atkin, Jeffries, & Neuendorf, 1998; Lin, 1998). Widespread computer adoption and use, accompanied by the spread of Internet access, have been witnessed in corporate and domestic spheres (Chan & Maston, 1999; Hetland, 1999; Vattyam & Lubbers, 1999).

Research attention has been directed in particular toward the investigation of the diffusion of interactive technologies among journalists, such as use of online resources and the Internet. By the close of the 20th century, the use of personal computers for gathering information for news stories, otherwise known as computer-assisted reporting, was being increasingly adopted in newsrooms (Maier, 2000). The precise nature of the computer applications deployed by journalists, however, was also observed to vary markedly across newsrooms. Some news organizations were further ahead than others in their adoption and effective application of these new technologies (Garrison, 2000; Niebauer, Abbott, Corbin, & Niebergall, 2000).

The adoption of computer technologies may have important implications for the working practices of journalists. What new skills requirements accompany the transition to online news publishing? The Internet offers new ways of collecting and reporting information. The integration of Internet access into the newsroom and movement toward more economical news gathering processes will dominate future news production. Journalists will have to learn how to organize stories into structures conducive to interactive reading online. They might need to know not only about writing the basic news story, but also about effective use of audio, video, animation, and databases that may form part of the larger interactive story package available to users.

There is also a whole new set of dilemmas facing journalists and editors, as the division between commercial and editorial information becomes less pronounced online, and is further blurred by new economic models for online publishing. Furthermore, the immediacy of the medium and the need to attract users may be grounds for a different kind of reporting. The model of online publishing brings some of the forces of commercial television to all content publishers: the direct drive to attract "audiences," the short attention span of readers, and the need to produce captivating material.

According to Bierhoff (1999):

> Quality newspapers, with their established tradition of fair and objective reporting, are at the moment forming a necessary counterweight to the more superficial news reporting brought to us by television. This same quality could be brought to the Internet, from which more and more people will gather their main news intake of the day. Once online, however, newspapers with their trusted brand names can play much more innovative roles than has hitherto been the case. They can be the focus for public debate, they can guide their readers through the overwhelming mass of in-

formation that the Internet offers, and they can try to regain their importance among a younger audience. For this option to become effective,
newspapers need to treat their online versions not merely as an experiment
but as a serious part of their publication's business. (p. 8)

How do journalists and editors perceive the transition to Internet
publishing? Past research among electronic newspapers has highlighted
the steep learning curve that many find themselves on once they have
decided to move across to Internet publishing. One of the problems is
that many established newspapers have been tempted to make the transition to online publishing even though they have few, if any, staff with
experience of the new medium (Singer, 1996a). Journalism has to adapt
to the Internet and so too does the business of news publishing. Not all
media professionals in the newspaper business have expressed opti-
mism at the future in electronic publishing, though many have had to
concede, nevertheless, that this is where the future lies (Schultz &
Voakes, 1999).

In many respects, the essential skills of journalism practice will still
be put to good use even in a Web environment. However, the new communications technologies associated with the Internet provide fresh opportunities for information delivery to readers that require the
acquisition of new skills in the spheres principally of information presentation and organization (Alexander, 1997). There is often a temptation when making the initial transition onto the Internet for a
newspaper to try simply reproducing its hard-copy version online.
There is much more to running a successful Internet newspaper than
this, however (Neuberger, Tonnemacher, Biebl, & Duck, 1998).

The uncertainty surrounding how to conceive of Internet editions of
newspapers has been reflected in the internal organization of newsrooms. In the United States, there was initially a separation between
staffs responsible for the hard-copy and online editions, but this gradually changed over time (Lasica, 1998; Ross & Middleberg, 1998). In contrast, European newspapers have continued to regard their online
editions as separate from the hard-copy editions, not just as publications but also in relation to internal production arrangements (Bierhoff,
van Dusseldorp, & Scullion, 1999).

The WWW has opened many new opportunities for journalists. The
Internet offers opportunities for news delivery and also for journalists;
it provides another on-tap source of information that they can call on to
assist with researching stories (McGuire, Stilborne, McAdams, & Hyatt,
1997; Parsons & Johnson, 1996; Koch, 1996; Williams & Nicholas,
1998a). It is visually powerful and not simply text based. The Web allows a wide range of people to become networked and provide information on demand (Branscomb, 1998; Reddick & King, 1997). As with all
new forms of communication in the past, the Internet will be capitalized
on by some early adopters and reluctantly adopted by resentful others
in the longer term. The general signs within newsrooms have been that

information technology is being used increasingly by a steadily grow-ing numbers of journalists. The use of online resources has also become more and more widespread (Garrison, 1998b).

THE USE OF COMPUTER-ASSISTED SOURCES

Journalists have used computers for several decades dating back to the 1950s (Garrison, 1997b). Long before the Internet was in wide public and business use, journalists used online tools for information-seeking purposes. Smith (1980) noted growing use of computer technology in newsrooms and predicted, even at that time, that the use of various on-line databases would change how journalists gather and synthesize news. Since then, online databases have become widely adopted interna-tionally by journalists. News reporters have grown accustomed to searching commercial databases, computerized government records, and the Web sites of other news organizations.

In the United Kingdom, for example, this sort of application can be traced back to the arrival of FT Profile (then called the World Reporter) in libraries and newsrooms in the mid-1980s (Nicholas, Erbach, Pang, & Paalman, 1988; Nicholas & Fenton, 1987). While FT Profile was the dominant service, others such as NEXIS, Dialog, Reuters Textline, and Business Briefing later found niches for themselves. Nexis offered full text of 25 newspapers and wire services, 100 magazines and newsletters and 60 abstracted periodicals by 1984 (see Miller, 1983, 1984). By the early 1980s, other commercial online database operators such as Knight Ridder's VU/TEXT, and the Dow Jones News-Retrieval Service were of-fering full-text coverage of many newspapers and periodicals online. Since then, many other online data sources have become established (De Fleur, 1997).

The acquisition of such databases within journalism followed the classic S-shaped adoption curve noted for other technological innova-tions (Rogers, 1990). In the United States, observations of online data-base uptake by daily newspapers confirmed this pattern with an initial growth period, followed by a tail-off and then further growth (Endres, 1985; Jacobsen & Ullman, 1989; Kerr & Niebauer, 1986).

These online sources did not hold universal appeal. Many journalists preferred to stick with their hard-copy cuttings. Broadsheet newspaper journalists were generally ahead of tabloid journalists in using online sources. Even here, most were fairly ignorant of what was available or of how useful such services could be potentially (Nicholas, 1996). Not-withstanding these British observations, one limited American study in-dicated a significant proportion of newspaper reporters (over 80%) acknowledged regular use of online databases (De Reimer, 1991). Larger studies, run later, showed smaller proportions of online database use among journalists, with around one in four U.S. journalists claiming weekly use of online databases, and ⅔ claiming monthly use (Middleberg & Ross, 1996).

The main purposes of online links were fact finding and browsing for ideas. Searches of journalists were usually short—most taking less than 10 minutes. Simple searches were made. Online users tended to be male, have an interest in computers, and work in certain departments—financial and foreign news, for example. The introduction of online searching, even before the Internet came into wide use, heralded the decline of the "cuttings collection" in newspapers (Nicholas et al., 1998a).

The rise of online commercial host searching and parallel development of public records becoming widely available in digitized form gave birth to computer-assisted journalism/reporting (known interchangeably as CAJ or CAR). Such developments radically altered the way news was delivered and gathered (DeFleur, 1997). By the mid-1990s, more and more newspapers integrated CAR tools into daily reporting (Garrison, 1997b).

CAJ/CAR spawned a number of specialties. Computer-assisted referencing involved the use of online resources such as dictionaries, encyclopedias, newsmen's interpreters, almanacs, and glosseries. Computer-assisted research was used to access databases of reports and articles, online news releases, and Web sites of important institutions, organizations, groups, and individuals. Computer-assisted rendevous embraced the use of newsgroups, bulletin boards, and listservs composed of inputs from people with specific interests or concerns who engaged in electronic discussion groups. One important impact of these technology developments was the blurring of the distinction between the role of news librarians and reporters (Garrison, 1997a; Semonche, 1993). The Internet opened up further online avenues for journalists in their search for information and gave the public similar access to the same primary sources (Nicholas & Frossling, 1996).

Online services gave journalists the tools of the librarian. The Internet has gone beyond that, however. it has achieved a blurring of distinctions between primary and secondary source material. Primary material—personal conversation, witness accounts, letters, and so on—was never the domain of the information system. But all that has now changed. Today, sources can communicate directly with the media or the public via the Internet (Bacard, 1993; Nicholas et al., 1998a). These developments do not simply mean an erosion of the role of the news librarian. They also carry important implications for the working lives of professional journalists (Nicholas & Frossling, 1996).

THE WEB AND DAILY NEWSPAPERS

The Internet and the Web have had a significant impact on journalism. These new communications technologies have changed the role of the journalist in the news-gathering process and introduced new ways of delivering news to the public. Furthermore, online publishing is creating its own brand of journalism (Deuze, 1999). The new technologies have speeded up the processes of news gathering and production and in many ways have proven to be very economical. Technological advances have opened up new formats for news presentation and presented challenges to the creativity of journalists and editors (Bhuiyan, 2000; Pavlik, 1999, 2001). Internet2™, the next generation of networked computing, is expected to have an even more significant effect on news reporting and content delivery (Phipps, 1999a).

In major news markets such as the United States, most newspapers use the Internet and have established their own Web sites. By the latter part of 1998, 4,900 online newspapers had been created throughout the world and about 3,600 of these were in the United States (Pavlik, 1999; Meyer, 1998). Although most began by simply carrying the printed edition online, many have begun to establish a more unique online personality of their own by presenting original content and providing additional services that printed newspapers are unable to provide (Deuze, 1999; Ross & Middleberg, 1997).

The Web as an Information Source

Newsrooms are making a serious commitment to the use of computers and computer training in gathering news (Garrison, 1999c). More and more newspapers are using the Internet to search for news (Garrison, 2000). News reporters are utilizing the Internet to conduct searches themselves that a few years earlier they would have delegated to librarians (Garrison, 1998b). Hundreds of Web search tools have been developed and become available. In 1998, there were approximately 145 major search engines and that number has continued to grow (A. Glossbrenner & E. Glossbrenner, 1998). Ross and Middleberg (1997) found that print and broadcast journalists most often used the Yahoo! search index and their favourite search engines were AltaVista and Netscape Search. Another study reported that Yahoo! and AltaVista were clearly dominant (Garrison, 1998b).

Web users are often frustrated by the sheer volume and complexity of finding authoritative information. The common reaction is to give up and claim there is nothing on the Internet about the subject (A. Glossbrenner & E. Glossbrenner, 1998). Advanced search options are usually indicated by a hypertext link to a different page at the search site. Advanced options offer tools employing the Boolean search strategy for information retrieval to combine user-defined key words. Other approaches of advanced searches include setting inclusive or exclusive dates, search by domain names or categories, and use of quantitative search parameters. Some search engines and indices permit truncated searches that produce results similar to search terms and proximity searches that find terms adjacent to search terms.

Not all search engines are the same. They often vary in the basic software they employ to search at the basic and advanced levels (Brooks, 1997). Selection of a search tool has significant impact in locating information (A. Glossbrenner & E. Glossbrenner, 1998). Paul and Williams (1999) listed selection of resources, site stability, currency, usability, searchability, listing and usage fees, and link descriptions as indicators of quality search sites. The requirement of fees by some Web search sites has become a restrictive factor. With a growing number of sites that charge fees, individuals have greater access to information that was previously not on the Web or was very hard to find (M. E. Bates, 1999).

Because search engines differ in the sizes of their databases, the procedures used to develop the database, the frequency that the databases are updated, their search options, the speed of response, and even basic user interface, users must be aware that search outcomes vary widely (Hock, 1999). Successful searchers employ a variety of strategies (Ward & Hansen, 1997). M. E. Bates (1999) attributed the accomplishments of experienced professional searchers to their curiosity, use of an iterative or repetitive process, personal expertise and knowledge, analytical abilities, background discussion with clients, and a sense of when to end the search.

Journalists may have difficulty, just like other users of the Web, in separating high-quality information from that which is less valuable. This is due to a number of factors: (a) Web designers who seek to disguise information quality; (b) inadequate training of journalists using the Web; and (c) the verification processes involving online content. This may be significant because the Web could eventually become a substitute for other sources of information (Luge, 1999).

In one analysis of online news-gathering problems, the leading concerns expressed by newspaper journalists were verification of information, unreliable information, badly sourced information, and lack of Web site credibility. Technical problems, such as download time or finding site addresses, were not perceived to be as severe (Garrison, 1998b, 1999a, 1999b).

A wide range of new Web technologies has made gathering and delivering information challenging for even experienced online users. Interactivity through various features of Web sites is one of the most distinguishing characteristics of online journalism (Massey & Levy, 1999). Journalists can interact with readers and sources using electronic mail, video, and audio conferencing, instant messaging, chat rooms and similar features.

Despite the new technologies available to enhance interactivity with audiences, critics have argued that newspapers are not using these new technologies to full potential (Outing, 1998). Daily newspapers have not made necessary changes in the way they collect and distribute news (Lasica, 1997). Some have said that newspapers are following the old model of presenting news every 24 hours instead providing continuous updates, that they are just creating *shovelware*—the term used to describe the process of taking the content of a print edition and reproducing it on a Web site (Cochran, 1995; Marlatt, 1999). Experts have also argued that newspapers are not taking advantage of such special features of the Web such as its interactivity, hypertext, and multimedia (Cochran, 1995; Marlatt, 1999).

Dibean and Garrison (1999) found that most online newspapers have adopted Web technology innovations such as links to related information and consumer services such as searchable classified advertising. Emphasis seemed to be on electronic commerce in 1999, they concluded, perhaps at the expense of news content delivery.

Journalists were not using other Internet-related technologies as frequently as they used the Web. Evidence indicates that electronic mail has been commonly employed for communicating with sources and for gathering information (Buckley, 1999). But other potential information retrieval resources on the Internet, such as file transfer protocol, telnet, "push" Web technology, audio and video-based conferencing, telephony, and other multimedia features have been used much less or very little (Garrison, 2000).

Journalists using the Web have expressed concern for the quality of sites when gathering information. One recent German study found that journalists sought well-structured sites with more information on content than graphics and sites that adequately attribute information (Luge, 1999). Journalists perceive success in using the Web when they find information they seek, especially when it has been challenging to locate. They seek background information and what they consider to be difficult-to-find information using online resources.

Journalists also believe extension of government coverage and finding sources were positive aspects of online research (Garrison, 2000). Other research into what makes useful Web content for journalists underlines the value of local information (J. L. Phipps, 1999a, 1999b).

Pavlik (2001) described a number of new tools available to journalists for news gathering. These include software products designed to search for images (e.g., Web SEEK™, Video Q™). These products can search archived video material and identify required images. Other tools have been developed that can automate and speed up the processing of raw data in the form of hand-written reporter's notes or audio-recorded interviews. By electronically encoding written or oral notes via portable note pads or digital audio recorders, such data can be more readily and speedily edited into print and broadcast news stories.

The Web and Public Relations

The development of online technologies has had a bearing on working practices of journalists who work in domains other than newspapers or news magazines. Within the public relations field, online databases can help practitioners become instant experts on an infinite number of subjects (Dorf, 1995). The Internet offers corporate public relations (PR) practitioners an invaluable tool for issue identification and management (Chikrudate, 1996; Ramsey, 1993; Thomsen, 1995). Using online databases, PR practitioners have "real time" access to breaking news often before stories are published in traditional outlets such as newspapers, radio, or television. Consequently, they are able to pursue a proactive or strategic management approach to issue management anticipating rather than reacting to issues.

In one early study of PR use of new information technologies, Anderson and Reagan (1992) surveyed 104 practitioners about their use of desktop publishing, electronic bulletin boards, electronic mail, internal databases and external databases, facsimile, teleconferencing, spreadsheet use, and use of accounting software. Technicians were found to deploy new technologies to enhance their job responsibilities, such as the production of news releases, graphics, and literature searchers, whereas managers used technology for more strategic purposes such as budgeting, and statistical database searchers for market and demographic information. Managers also used new technologies for setting communication goals and new product launches.

Springston (2001) found similar results some years later. Following a content analysis of messages posted to PRFORUM™, an online discussion list with 1,200 to 1,600 members dedicated to Internet PR and related issues, Springston surveyed a national sample of 750 practitioners about new technologies and public relations. In the content analysis, WWW and *online interaction* were the most frequently mentioned concepts. In the survey of practitioners, however, although e-mail and Web use appeared commonplace, the multimedia and interactive features of the Internet were underutilized. Although practitioners reported regular use of the Internet to scan for issues and developing trends, the same individuals were noncommittal about how new media technologies enhance their roles in their organizations. Although most agreed that the Internet holds much potential as a communications tool for practitioners, survey respondents largely disagreed on whether PR practitioners were actually taking advantage of the opportunities.

Porter, Sallot, Cameron, and Shamp (2001) surveyed corporate PR practitioners classified as managers or technicians to reveal that although online databases were having a positive effect on the practice of public relations, most practitioners were not yet taking advantage of these empowering opportunities. Practitioners need to be aware that online databases provide a new avenue for participation in management decision making. Although there was some relationship found between use made of commercial online databases and participation in management decision making, it was clear that use of these databases was not revolutionizing PR. Although an overwhelming majority of PR practitioners had access to the Internet and WWW, most had not yet adopted the use of the information-intensive, online databases in their day-to-day working practices. Even with access to online databases, most of the PR professionals surveyed in this study reported using this resource perhaps less than once a month. Female PR practitioners were less likely to use online tools than were their male counterparts. This was an important finding given that women tend to comprise the majority of PR professionals.

JOURNALISTS' WORKING PRACTICES

Journalists have used telephones, short-wave radios, fax machines, and other new information-gathering technologies to improve their work and to resolve some of the difficulties of gathering information that have emerged as the profession has evolved. Technology based resources can increase speed and, sometimes, the accuracy of information being reported. But technologies have their shortcomings. Sources on the telephone may not be who they say they are. Newer technologies, such as cellular telephones, often provide poor connections, and radio communications are susceptible to interference. Faxes can produce poorly and be unreadable (Garrison, 1992; Mencher, 1997; Izard, Culbertson, & Lambert, 1994).

The latest technological development—the Internet—has been an asset adopted increasingly by journalists. Growing numbers of journalists have shown considerable enthusiasm for using the WWW (Garrison, 1998; Kaye & Medoff, 1999; Reddick & King, 1997; Ross & Middleberg, 1997). Among the most appealing reasons for use of this new resource is its scope and depth of information as well as the speed at which the information may be retrieved.

Resources found on the Internet often enhance coverage of breaking news stories such as an airline or weather disaster (Ward & Hansen, 1997). Journalists use online resources (a) for background for interviews or other purposes, (b) to find or identify sources, (c) to check or verify facts, (d) to "read" their competition, (e) to become informed about current events, and (f) to identify story ideas (Garrison, 1998; Ward & Hansen, 1997; Ross & Middleberg, 1997).

More and more journalists are conducting their own online research. At larger daily newspapers, where the assistance of news researchers and news librarians has been common for decades, news researchers have gradually given up some of this responsibility to reporters, the reporters' supervising editors, copy editors, graphic artists, and others in the newsroom. As journalists find their newsrooms reconfigured with computer networks and access to online resources available on their desktops, the role of the news librarian has moved from background researcher to trainer and archivist. Although librarians continue to assist in background work on major stories and particularly difficult research assignments, they conduct less routine daily background research than they did a decade earlier (Garrison, 1998b).

Although the Web provides an online library, one other significant application of Internet technology is as a communications tool. By the second half of the 1990s, a number of surveys with American journalists showed that most used e-mail (Ross & Middleberg, 1997, 1998). Most journalists used e-mail; however, relatively few perceived e-mail as a useful feedback device, whether from sources or readers (Garrison, 1997a; Ross & Middleberg, 1997). Journalists still preferred to meet with sources face to face, or at least to talk to them over the telephone. While data from Web sources could provide useful background, there remained a strong need to get information directly from the source via more traditional forms of communication (Garrison, 1997b).

In England, e-mail was acknowledged by journalists as a significant aspect of what the Internet is all about. Not only did the Internet, via the Web, open up publication of information, it also provided a channel through which rapid communications could flow, enabling journalists to follow up information sources discovered on the Web. E-mail was useful for keeping in contact with other journalists, for overseas contacts, and for communicating with all contacts. It was especially attractive for communicating with overseas contacts because it overcame time-zone differences (Nicholas, Williams, Cole, & Martin, 1998). Despite these benefits, British journalists did not take up e-mail very widely during the 1990s. Many still had reservations about it. Some believed that it would increase information load and workload. Others believed it lacked the insights that could be gleaned through more traditional forms of communication—face to face or telephone.

Concerns About Online Technologies

Although new technologies have brought certain advantages for journalism practice, there have also been concerns raised about them. When online services first appeared in news rooms in the late 1970s and early 1980s, much concern focused on the cost of these services (Garrison, 1995).

Other concerns have focused on learning to use complex computer equipment and software, and with computer systems that were not user friendly. Such problems have reduced over time as computer software and other equipment have advanced and journalists themselves have become more familiar with such resources. A problem that remains, despite the widening skills base of journalists, lies with the reliability of online sources. There can be significant problems associated with judging the quality of information provided by different Web sites and online databases (Schlossberg, 1999). Government databases have frequently been found to contain errors (Garrison, 1996; Landau, 1994).

The Internet is a conduit for massive amounts of information. Journalists must be able quickly to evaluate this content for its worth in the context of news reporting or feature writing. Without an authoritative source to consult to obtain a trustworthy assessment of the credibility and reliability of content, the Web can prove to be a highly questionable news resource. Certainly the Internet and WWW can represent valuable news gathering tools for journalists, but finding the information needed is not always easy. This can prove to be a serious issue for journalists working against tight deadlines. Journalists who suffer from techno-phobia can experience particularly serious reactions when faced with accessing stories via cyberspace (Garrison, 1998a; Singer, Tharp, & Haruta, 1998; Ward & Hansen, 1997). One solution is to provide jour-nalists with extra training in the use of the Internet (Garrison, 1996; Kovacs, 1995).

Researchers have identified anonymity and online accountability as major problems with online newsgathering (Singer, 1996a, 1996b). Ac-curacy and verification issues arise when discussing online news sources such as Web publications that are often themselves sources for journalists (Evans, 1998a, 1998b; Lasica, ,1997a, 1997b; McGuire et al., 1997; Reddick & King, 1997).

Some experts have warned of a new form of the accuracy problem that is caused by *hackers*, individuals who intentionally break into and alter a site's content (McGuire et al., 1997; Phipps, 1998). Other writers have identified verification to be the most serious problem with online information (Carleton, 1994).

The Internet has changed the way Internet users assess trustworthi-ness. Schlossberg (1999) argued that traditional standards, such as fa-miliar voices or established reputations, are being discarded in favor of technological features, such as availability of useful links to other sites. *Authoritativeness of sources* on the Web is identified as a factor in using online sources (Evans, 1998a, 1998b; McGuire et al., 1997). The timeli-ness, or freshness, of the information offered is a concern of many jour-nalists (McGuire et al., 1997).

Carleton (1994) noted that the fluid nature of the Internet is trouble-some because information found one day may not appear the next. An-drews (1996) said the new technology is to blame for still another problem—surveillance in cyberspace. Reporters using newsgroups and other online resources to find sources often are vulnerable to spying by competitors or corporate PR people.

Pfaffenberger (1996) noted that searching for information on the Internet usually results in finding too much information or finding too little information. There is also need to consider the context of the infor-mation presented on the Web (McGuire et al., 1997). The Internet pres-ents professional users with an information overload problem and this problem has intensified as the Web has grown (A. Glossbrenner & E. Glossbrenner, 1999). The resulting proliferation of search tools has cre-ated a further problem of deciding which search tools to use.

Garrison (1999, 2000) reported surveys with journalists and editors working for newspapers with a circulation of 20,000+ readers in the United States in 1994, 1995, 1996, and 1998. He recorded a rapid increase in the use of online sources (from 57.2% in 1994 to 95.1% in 1998). By 1998, 92.4% of responding newspapers used the WWW or other Internet sources in newsgathering (compared with 25% in 1994). Journalists used state and federal government online services most often. Search tools such as Yahoo! and AltaVista were also popular.

In 1998, 80.5% of respondents sought information from online sources thought to be reputable. Finding valid, accurate information was also viewed to be important (77.8%) as was the ability to search the site for specific information (70.3%). A total of 60.5% sought data that can be transferred from a Web site into an analytic tool such as a spreadsheet program. Ease of access to information was also important (57.8%).

Problems included inaccurate information (81.6%). Useless or bad content (70.3%) was also frequently cited. Bad or outdated links (67.6%) and lack of attribution (61.6%) were also common criticisms. Lack of verification was another problem cited by more than ½ of respondents (54.1%). More than 4 in 10 also referred to unreliable information, badly sourced information, and lack of site credibility.

Endres (1998) conducted an Internet survey with 123 editors of online magazines. Approaching 9 out of 10 of these respondents produced consumer magazines, special interest magazines, or business magazines on the Internet. These magazines covered a wide range of content including arts and entertainment, computers, hobbies and games, science and nature, and business and finance. Over 4 in 10 (44%) had been online under 2 years and just over ½ (51%) had been online for up to 5 years. The editorial department was the key department determining whether to go online. The main reasons for doing so were that the technology was available and the feeling that the Internet promised considerable business potential. Most of the publications that responded had a print edition as well as an online edition. Nearly ½ the editors (49%) viewed their online edition as a distinct entity from the print edition. Slightly fewer (44%) said they reproduced online only what was available in the print magazine. One advantage perceived for online magazines was that their copy could be updated more frequently. Many editors admitted, however, that they still struggled with staffing issues. In many cases, the online edition was produced by print edition staff (30%), A similar number (31%) said they had separate staffs for each edition. The remainder switched staff between print and online editions.

In sum, the Internet offers a range of advantages and positive benefits to journalists, but these are counterbalanced by a number of inherent weaknesses. Among the benefits of the Internet are that the WWW provides a potentially valuable reference source that can provide cheap, easy, and convenient access to large amounts of content on a huge variety of topics, covering the entire globe (Nicholas & Martin, 1997). On the negative side, concerns have been raised that target content is not always easy to find, there are security issues, and there is the issue of establishing source credibility and information veracity (Coy, Hof, & Judge, 1996; Nicholas et al., 1998a). Concerns have also been raised by journalists that rather than saving time, the Internet might serve to increase their workload. Some journalists have argued that they already had lots of information sources at their disposal before the Internet came along. The Web has simply added a further body of content through which they must sift. A lack of experience or training in the use of the Internet also impedes the efficiency with which this communications tool can be used. Verifying Internet sources also adds to workload because it is not always easy to find out the identity of the source (Nicholas et al., 1998a).

The big overriding concern is with how Internet technology might impact in a broader sense of working practices. There were signs from early on that it might affect the relationship between reporters and news librarians if journalists could gain direct access to information sources via the Net, thus cutting librarians out of the loop. Internet technology also tended to raise expectations about speed and amount of productivity. Journalists have displayed genuine concerns that the Internet may be positioned by management as a cost-saving device through which journalists will be expected to become self-sufficient, whereas back-up staff and services to which they were historically accustomed would be gradually eroded and eventually disappear (Nicholas et al., 1998a).

TRANSFORMATION OF JOURNALISM

New media technologies present a profound challenge to the future of journalism. In some sense, journalism is being altered by new computer software. As a natural outgrowth of advances in artificial intelligence, word processing, grammar, spelling, and style-checker software packages, software is now available to actually write news stories. By the mid-1990s, a number of U.S. newspapers and other news organizations had purchased such software packages and were using them to write stories for publication. The presence of this software had even been held responsible for some journalists losing their jobs (Pavlik, 1996). Such software was developed, in particular, in relation to sports and financial reporting, with many stories being written using basic formulae derived from specific, statistical data, such as scores, stock changes, and other routine data.

Software packages could write stories automatically based on electronic data feeds transmitted directly by various news sources. With these packages, there was no need for any human intervention at all. One such package, called Sportswriter™, was produced by Zybrainics Software, Inc., and was created by Roger Helms, a writer. The program grew out of Helms's initial efforts to improve sports coverage of a weekly newspaper he was considering buying. Using an Apple Macintosh computer, he developed a HyperCard stack to train reporters in better newswriting style, but found the approach ineffective. Instead, it appeared that the program could produce pretty good copy all by itself (Bulkeley, 1994). Critics have accused the software of producing rather dry, unimaginative prose, full of cliches. It also allegedly lacks the depth of analysis of a human observer (Thalhimer, 1994). The program bases its decisions and writing on input received from the coaches of the games, who are asked by the newspaper to fill out a form requesting various results, such as the score by period, and the description of key plays. The coaches phone or fax the data, the data are entered into the program, and the program then spits out a story.

Computers at the Bloomberg LP financial news service write hourly stock market reports and foreign market trends. Computers at Individual, Inc., in Cambridge, Massachusetts, sort thousands of wire service, newspaper, and magazine articles and summarize them into customized newsletters faxed daily to 3,000 subscribers (Bulkeley, 1994). Indeed, in the future, such software could cut out the need for the journalistic middleman altogether. News sources could communicate directly with news consumers, via a news writing software package that would turn raw data into a story.

One journalistic practice that has long been taken for granted is whether to let a source preview a story before publication. The answer has always been "no," with a few exceptions, such as on highly technical stories such as science or health reporting, where a source might be asked to preview a quote for accuracy. Reporters and their news organizations have had many reasons for not allowing sources to preview stories, such as not wanting to alert a source to a negative story before it is published, to avoid leaking an exclusive to a competing news organisation, and general principles about standing by the quality of a reporter's work. One practical reason that has probably played a bigger reason than many in the newsroom would admit is that there has not been time to let a source preview a story. Reporters working under deadline pressure have enjoyed little opportunity to send a story to a source, let them review it, and then return the edited copy to the reporter. This might work for a monthly magazine, but not for an investigative reporter working on a 5 o'clock deadline for tomorrow's paper. But in today's world of online communications, this time factor should pose less of a hindrance to obtaining such feedback.

NEWSROOM STRUCTURE IMPLICATIONS

With the movement of journalism to online environments, newsrooms have become increasingly decentralized and flexible. They have also become more experimental in their production practices and employ staff with a different range of skills from those traditionally associated with journalism. Working conditions tend to be more flexible and work forces more transient (Pavlik, 2001).

Many newspapers have launched news Web sites and some have created separate newsrooms for their online businesses. However, online resources tend to be stretched, even within large, established news orga-nizations. Many journalists in the non-online part of the organization may lack Internet access. In the United States, surveys with journalists have indicated a rapid growth in Internet access for news reporters be-tween 1995 and 1999, from about ⅓ with access in 1995 to virtually all having access by 1999 (Middleberg & Ross, 2000). The Internet has come to be regarded as an important tool that no newsroom should be without. Not all journalists, however, have come to accept this new technology at the same pace.

As the Internet takes a hold, other software tools have surfaced that facilitate Web browsing and the processing of content available via the Net. Specialists in the use of these tools have established a foothold in modern newsrooms but frequently lack journalistic credentials (Pavlik, 2001). Hence, there may be important news quality implications of such developments. The need for multiskilling within journalism has not been totally lost on major news organizations. Some, such as *The New York Times*, encourage reporters to contribute stories via a number of channels—traditional print copy, broadcasting, and Internet. Devel-opments in computer technology have given rise to portable products that reporters can carry around with them, enabling stories to be pro-duced in a number of electronic formats available for presentation on different communications platforms—text, audio, and video—facilitat-ing the speed of editorial processing (Powell, 2000).

Wireless, palm-held computers can also provide remote Internet ac-cess, allowing journalists not only to compile stories wherever they are situated, but also to gain access to a huge array of online content rele-vant to their research (Regan, 1999). The introduction of such mobile devices for news reporting represents what has been referred to as the *virtual newsroom*. As Pavlik (2001) explained:

> A virtual newsroom exists without any physical boundaries. Through elec-tronic mail, remote electronic access to databases, and the ability to trans-mit multimedia via existing public telecommunications infrastructure, journalists are able to work entirely from the field without ever needing to enter a central newsroom location and to exchange messages, stories and picture files with editors anchored firmly in cyberspace. (p. 106)

The movement toward digital newsrooms is well underway. Most news editors, directors, and producers recognize the benefits of this evo-lution in news handling. Digital tools allow for greater flexibility in news production, and also mean that news personnel do not all have to be situated in the same location. They can speed up news production, permit more regular news updating around the clock, and generate news packages that can be readily tailored for any delivery plat-form—television, radio, or print. Even so, it will be important for users not to forget traditional values of accuracy, detail, proper identification of sources, and not allowing technology to determine how the story is told (Pavlik, 2001).

PRACTITIONERS' OPINIONS ABOUT ONLINE NEWS

Singer (1996) pointed out that as newspapers by the hundreds spring onto the Internet, publishers have become proficient at telling one another why online is an attractive place to be. However this proficiency does not help the majority of online publishers to make money out of their online product. Singer's (1996a) exploratory and descriptive study tried to explore how reporters and editors regarded technological changes affecting their carrier. A questionnaire survey of 27 reporters and editors found that few had much experience with interactive media, and even fewer perceived new delivery mechanisms as having a fundamental effect on the things important to them: gathering information, interpreting it, and shaping it into a meaningful story.

Yet Singer (1996a) warned that "it is dangerous for journalists, whose job is deemed so crucial to society that it is protected by our nation's highest law, to stand on the sidelines as new media technologies emerge, take shape and spread" (p. 24). So far though, according to Singer's study, they are. Singer also pointed out "that role as spectator is affecting their attitudes, whether they are chafing at the bit, afraid of the unknown, or merely indifferent to the changes taking place" (p. 24). For journalists to maintain, practice, and strengthen their journalistic values in the interactive media environment, they must be equipped both in terms of their "mind set" and their technical skills. The "equipment" must come from two places: One is from the newspaper industry by providing greater access to online media inside the newsroom, for logistical and psychological reasons to help make interactive media seem routine, familiar and simply a part of the journalistic milieu. The second is to seek to integrate more fully the newspaper's own interactive service with the newsroom as such services come online. Singer (1996a) suggested that these steps would help reporters and editors to start thinking seriously about such services. In addition, journalism educators have an obligation to encourage their students to explore online media and think about them in creative ways. The benefit of such an attitude is that "If students with online savvy more readily land jobs, then spread the enthusiasm for new media among their new colleagues, they may help create a widening circle of acceptance and excitement that benefits academy and industry alike" (Singer, 1996, p. 27).

Two years later, Singer, Tharp, and Haruta (1998) conducted a more detailed survey of online and print editors at 466 U.S. newspapers, identifying key online staffing issues such as salary and experience levels, job classifications, and benefits. The overall results indicated that online newspaper staffs remained small, with salaries and benefits roughly commensurate with those paid to print employees in comparable jobs.

Online editors expressed concerns about the pressure to turn a profit, as well as about the perception that they and their staffs were seen as second-class citizens by many of their print colleagues.

The study also showed print managers' most critical concerns in directing their staffs fell into two main categories: news content and staffing issues. Some were concerned about finding, hiring, and keeping qualified people. Online editors main concern was with finding multitalented staffers who understand both technology and journalism. This finding supports the suggestion that new college graduates may have an advantage in finding a job if they are able and willing to work on the online product. The researchers noted two areas, not even mentioned by print editors, that came out in online editors' comments: (1) the relationship between the two staffs and (2) their concerns with their product making money. Online editors also had a different take on content issues. Although accurate, fair local news was a main concern for print editors, online editors commented on the fact that they had a nontraditional, new audience to capture and hold. They also had a totally different sort of space problem from their print counterparts.

Online editors also were troubled by the nonstop demands of everchanging technology, their isolation from print colleagues, and the question of money making. The researchers pointed out that publishers' deep ambiguity about the Web was putting considerable pressure on the people whom they are asking to tackle the job. They warned publishers of the growing perception among online editors that they and their staffs were seen as second-class citizens and asked for immediate management attention before the challenge and excitement of doing something new devolves into a routine of overwork laced with bitterness and, before long, burnout.

The Schultz and Voakes (1999) study provides another perspective about the future of newspapers in general expressed by some pessimistic journalists about their carrier's future in the digital age. They surveyed 1,037 randomly selected full-time journalists from 58 newspapers in the United States. More than half (55%) of these journalists believed that printed newspaper will be less important part of American life in 10 years time, compared with 40% who felt that newspapers will be where they are now. Only a tiny minority (4%) thought newspapers will become more important.

Schultz and Voakes (1999) noted a widespread and growing pessimism about newspapers among journalists. The most interesting finding was that journalists' pessimism about the future extended to online newspapers as well with only a small minority (8%) regarding e-newspapers as having a promising future. The majority (53%) however said that online newspapers would decline in importance over the next 10 years. The three major threats outlined by the study were alienation of readers (readership rates have dropped sharply for number of reasons), market-driven journalism, and new media. The diversification of mass media has increased completion across media and demand is unlikely to expand in concert with supply. In parallel with Internet news sources, news competitors have emerged in the form of round-the-clock news services provided by broadcast radio and television and cable television stations. These other new media are also popular with young people, who have been regarded as the primary target market for electronic publishing.

Despite the increasingly competitive marketplace for news, there is still an argument that many news consumers will continue to turn to tried and trusted news sources. As long as journalists supply information that is credible and useful to readers, changes in technology should pose little threat (Fidler, 1997).

From a more specific perspective, Ruggiero (1998) examined with a critical perspective the perceptions of traditional American journalists toward the Internet as a news source by conducting an analysis of rhetoric about the Internet available in major American newspapers. The researcher's main argument was based on the assumption that because traditional American journalists are socialized both ideologically and professionally into the dominant ideology, many are refusing to share their elite positions as disseminators of news with the Internet. Ruggiero (1998) analyzed data from the Lexis-Nexis™ database and American journalism review magazines and indicated that a concerted effort by traditional American journalists to repair the elite news paradigm against incursion by the Internet is occurring. In the market-driven economy, the same threat discussed earlier face's newspapers. The future of the Internet as an acknowledged disseminator of news, at least for critical scholars, remains unanswered.

The journalistic values and what online journalists say is important to them was the subject of another study (Brill, 1999). The study sought to advance the knowledge and understanding of the roles and values of online journalists by examining the similarities and differences between the online and traditional environments and the journalists working within them. The author circulated a questionnaire to journalists from 12 different selected, online newspapers.

The findings showed that in comparison to daily print journalists, online journalists reported that most of their work was similar to that of their print journalist counterparts. Online journalists ranked traditional journalism skills very high, with news judgment (66.2% rated it very important) topping the list, along with spelling and grammar skills (rated as very important by 62.9%). Print newspaper journalists and the online journalists were also closely aligned in how they viewed the news dissemination function of their profession, with 50% of each group agreeing that it was very important to avoid disseminating unverified facts. Getting information to the public quickly was rated as very important by 70% of the print journalists and by 62% of the online journalists. '

In contrast to the journalists interviewed by Schultz and Voakes (1999), journalists questioned by Brill (1999) viewed the future of online products as *very positive* (52%) or *positive* (38%). In general, although the online journalists surveyed by Brill (1999) adhered to some of the tenets of journalism, especially regarding necessary skills, they also viewed their roles and values somewhat differently from other journalists. The online journalists did seem to identify with the news dissemination function of their profession, as did the daily newspaper journalists. The study also found that neither the print journalists nor online journalists seemed to view the adversarial function of journalism as very important. The functions of letting the public express views, setting the political agenda, and providing entertainment were considered more important by online journalists than by print journalists. Print journalists, however, rated developing the cultural interests of the audience as more important than did online journalists. Reaching the largest possible audience and understanding the audience was considered very important by most of the online journalists surveyed in this study. Brill (1999) concluded that it is critical to understand online journalists and how they view their roles and functions. Indeed, if some media analysts are to be believed, they may be the only journalists to study in the next century.

Commitment to the Internet Edition

One of the key issues in relation to any launch of an online version of a newspaper is the allocation of sufficient resources to run it. This means that adequate staffing must be provided, including personnel with journalistic and information technology skills. One of the major concerns raised by journalists associated with the production of online newspapers is that this commitment to the online version is inadequate.

Alexander (1997) examined online newspapers in New England to assess the benefits, drawbacks, and future of electronic publishing. Alexander used an open-ended survey form sent out to the region's daily and weekly newspapers and received 210 responses. The survey found that most of the benefits cited were related not to producing a better journalistic product, but to business considerations. Using new technologies to change the style and substance of newspaper news was cited as a benefit by only few electronic publications. The study also showed that newspapers said keeping current readers happy was at least as important as attracting new readers. However, an ambivalence toward online publishing was apparent in many responses. Interestingly, the study found that some features that have been lauded as revolutionary in electronic publishing, such as the ability to deliver news instantly and provide immediate updates, are the same elements cited as drawbacks facing electronic newspapers. Respondents also cited lack of staff and training, cost, equipment, and limited payback in terms of revenue potential as the most drawbacks that face electronic publishing. The vast majority of respondents (80%) reported that electronic newspapers may complement, but will never replace, the traditional newspapers. Alexander concluded that one newspaper's opportunity appears to be another one's burden.

Research among electronic newspapers in the Arab world indicated a serious shortage of adequately qualified professionals despite the dramatic growth of online newspapers since 1995 (Alshehri, 2000). One observer estimated that the Arab states would need to create around 7 million skilled workers by 2015 to accommodate the expanding market in Internet content generation (Cisco, 1999). By the close of the 20th century, there were 48 online Arab newspapers. In a survey of their proprietors, 27 replied. Of these, nearly 3 in 4 (74%) said they had assigned staff specifically to work on the Internet edition. Out of the total sample of respondents, more than 4 in 10 (44%) had allocated three or fewer staff to work with the online edition, however, whereas 3 in 10 (30%) allocated 4 or more staff to this job (Alshehri, 2000).

The Internet as a Research Tool

The Internet can provide a potentially valuable research tool for journalists. It is a repository for vast amounts of information that is being constantly updated. Part of the problem is that the WWW contains so much material that it can be difficult to find exactly what is needed. Practice is required to become a skilled exponent of navigational systems on the Net. Another potential problem for the profession of journalism, however, is whether there may develop a temptation to become overreliant on the Internet for research, especially where budget cuts mean fewer journalists in the field.

Garrison (1998b, 1999a, 2000) conducted a series of surveys that reviewed the use of the WWW and other online services by U. S. daily newspapers via mail surveys with a longitudinal design. Newspapers with a circulation of 20,000 or more were selected for analysis over a 4-year period, 1994 to 1998. The study analyzed general computer use, value placed on the Web as a news tool, preferred browsers, search tools used, most widely used sites, site qualities and problems, and online successes and failures. Computer use in newsgathering was found to have grown in two areas: first journalists who become more dependent on the WWW and the Internet as sources of information; and second, the overall use of computers in newsgathering, which increased steadily from 66% in 1994 to 88% in 1997.

The study showed that the daily use of the Net almost doubled across the period analyzed and that about 92% of the newspapers surveyed used the Web by 1997. Furthermore, research by reporters increased to 48% from 25% from 1995 to 1997; their preferred browser (for 67.5%) was Netscape communicator, with AltaVista as the most popular search engine (for 47.2%) in daily newspapers newsroom. The most widely used Web sites (23.9%) were the government sites (both federal and state sites) followed by search-engine sites. However, journalists showed concerns about the quality and validity of the WWW for newsgathering with information verification (cited by 19.6% as the biggest problem). Garrison (1998d, 1999a, 2000) conceded, however, that although journalists seemed to be aware of the usefulness of the WWW, their use of the networked information resources for newsgathering was still in its infancy. He also observed that many newsrooms viewed online resources in the skeptical manner in which they view traditional documents and human sources.

The journalists interviewed in this study described use of their online resources as most helpful in backgrounding stories. In addition, the Internet was useful for locating difficult-to-find information, locating sources, and obtaining government information (Garrison, 2000).

Neuberger et.al. (1998) examined the producers, their products, and the users of German online newspapers by using a standardized mail survey of all 81 daily newspapers with a WWW presence in May, 1997 (response rate: 78%). The users (2,524 respondents) were surveyed via an online questionnaire. The researchers found that almost ½ of the staff on online editorial boards had journalistic duties, and that technical duties were of growing importance. The majority of German online editorial boards surveyed depended on the editorial decisions of the print editors; the news sections in online papers consisted mainly of duplicates of the printed "parent" paper. The study also showed that articles for the online version were rarely edited and that very few external links and no graphic or sound effects were added. In terms of users behavior, the study revealed that about ⅔ of users would have chosen the print newspaper and just under ⅓ would have preferred the online version if only one of the versions had been available.

The impact of print product culture was apparent in that online publishers and users based their activities and/or expectations on the print newspaper. The study revealed that the staff of the German online editorial boards tended to be relatively young. The researchers pointed out that in terms of generating revenue, the publishers need a lot of patience, as users in the long term will have to accept either advertising (and thus, longer download times) or subscription charges.

In the United Kingdom, Williams and Nicholas (1998a) conducted a 1-year research project to examine the "truth about the Internet" by interviewing 247 people from more than 24 (press) organizations. The researchers approached the topic from a perspective of the changing information environment created by the Internet. They justified their choice of journalists as a case study because the journalists are in the information frontline and information is the commodity with which they work.

The results of this in-depth investigation revealed a number of interesting findings. Significantly, the researchers found that the main factors influencing journalists' (lack of) use of the Internet were job (anxiety) role and security, especially among younger journalists working on short-term contracts and with very heavy workloads. The experience factor was also found to be important among the older journalists who had experienced electronic information years prior to the Internet. Accordingly, senior reporters who enjoyed ease of access were found to be heavy users of the Internet. Despite signs of change, young graduates were found to be inadequately trained compared to their older colleagues, as journalism courses had not really paid sufficient attention to training on the Internet.

News services and online newspapers such as *The Washington Post* were found to be the most consulted sites journalists referred to as well as many other official Web sites. Yet the study found that, in overall use, less than one in five national journalists (and fewer in the regional press) benefitted from the Internet in the United Kingdom and that "the Internet was certainly not a panacea for all journalists' communication and retrieval ills" (Williams & Nicholas, 1998a, p.12). Furthermore, those journalists who had taken the Internet route were in their 30s and 40s, contradicting the stereotypical image of the online user as someone just starting out in their career.

One of the important contributions of this study was the categorization of the journalist users of the Internet. Seven user–nonuser groups were determined:

- *New worshippers*. Young generation (often untrained journalists) who have embraced every aspect of the Internet as a means of extending information democracy by weakening the power of large news agencies.
- *The economically driven*. Those skillful people (including freelancers) who used the system to access information that would otherwise be expensive to obtain. Members of this category normally worked in small specialist newspapers or magazines and saw the Internet as a "godsend," with its myriad information sources.
- *The pragmatists*. Those who incorporated the Internet into their array of general information sources.
- *The occasional dippers*. Included a large number of journalists who used the Internet only when other sources did not solve their information problems.
- *Enthusiastic novices*. Those who have never used the Internet, but they are intrigued by what they have heard, although they may not use it much because of lack of time and inadequate training.
- *The nonbelievers*. Those who are not interested in the Internet or may foresee difficulties with authenticating information obtained from it.
- *Resentful dinosaurs*. A small minority who see the Internet as a threat to their privileged access to information.

The overall findings indicated that most journalists believed that it is just a matter of time before they begin to use the Internet. The researchers concluded by stating that the Internet is a more "Jekyll and Hyde" than a "knight in shining armour for the media." From the outcome of their research, Williams and Nicholas (1998a) summed up that "it [the Internet] offers, but it disrupts, it gives and takes away, it provides opportunities, but it also gives competitors the edge" (p. 12). Their conclusion indicated how profound the Internet can be in impacting media and informational working practices.

In a subsequent publication, Nicholas et al. (2000) reported further on their work with journalists' use of the Internet. A combination of methods including closed-question interviews, in-depth, open-ended interviews, group discussions, and observations yielded data on the extent and nature of Internet use. Internet use among journalists was found to occur among a minority only, both among national and regional or local newspapers. There were variations among newspapers, however, in the prevalence of Internet use. For instance, of 50 journalists interviewed at *The Times*, ⅔ did not use the Internet, while of 52 interviewed at *The Guardian*, ⅔ were Internet users.

On this occasion, lack of convenient Internet access emerged as a major factor in the low and uneven Internet take-up across many publications. Nearly one in three journalists interviewed reported having no Internet access at all. More than ½ of the nonusers said they would use the Internet if access was improved. Once again, it was not the youngest journalists who emerged as the major Internet users in their profession, but rather those in their 30s and 40s. There was also a relationship between the seniority of journalists and likelihood that they would use the Internet; more senior personnel had better access to equipment and more autonomy in the way they carried out their jobs.

The Internet was perceived as another tool to assist in doing the job, rather than as a recreation. Among Internet users, favored sites were those provided by other news organizations, especially other newspapers, and sites provided by government departments, universities, and other institutions. The Internet provided another source to consult and represented an extension of traditional sources. Journalists would usually depend to a significant extent on the news-cuttings service supplied by their in-house media library. Thus, the preference for other news sites indicated that the Internet acted like an electronic news-cuttings service.

In addition to using the Internet as a reference source, it is a provided form of communication. Nearly half (48%) of the journalists mentioned the use of e-mail, especially for overseas communication. It offered the advantage of speed and obviated time-zone problems. Journalists based overseas used e-mail because it made them feel in closer touch with the office. E-mail was also used to communicate with established contacts, though this was more common among specialist press, freelancers, and new media journalists.

Information overload proved to be a problem for just over ½ the journalists (51%) interviewed by Nicholas and his colleagues (2000). It was the nonusers, however, who were most likely to perceive this as a problem. Less experienced users of the Internet tended to rely on the default search engine and took minimal care over query terms. Advanced users chose the search engine to fit their query, followed directory subcategories, and used Boolean operators or other advanced search options where available. Where too many articles were obtained, a few were scrutinized for relevance and the search terminated. For regular users of the Internet, information overload was not a problem. Some of these journalists believed it was better to have too much information rather than too little information. Once accustomed to it, the Internet provided for the journalists a ready source of information on lots of subjects—a kind of "one-stop shopping" for news.

Where a problem did arise, even among some of the more experienced Internet users, was in judging the quality of the information on the Net. Because anyone can publish material on the Net, there is an ongoing problem for journalists of authenticating information. How reliable are Internet sources? There is a need for professional judgment here. Greater experience in using the Internet was felt to assist in making this kind of judgment. Experienced users came to recognize sources that they believed could be taken at face value and usually felt able to distinguish such sources from less reliable ones.

CHALLENGES FOR ETHICAL PRACTICE

A central tenet of journalism is that news should be fair, balanced, and objective. Collecting and disseminating information is part of the job; ensuring that information is factually accurate is equally important. Journalism places much emphasis on verification of the facts. In an online environment in which news consumers are empowered with greater control over the reception of news, and where consumers may obtain information from a multitude of sources, there is an increased likelihood that some of those sources may be less than reliable. There is therefore perhaps even more onus than ever on journalists to ensure that information disseminated under their name is accurate.

Responsibility for linked content and chat room content credibility and accuracy, privacy invasion, and separation of advertising and editorial content have been identified as key concerns. One writer noted that "As public records and documents have become increasingly electronic and as journalists have used the Freedom of Information Act and electronic FOIA requests to access those digital records, prickly ethical issues arises" (Pavlik, 2001, p. 84).

Documents previously only available in hard-copy, often rendering them difficult to access, are becoming increasingly available on the Web. This movement toward greater openness of government begs questions about what is appropriate to disclose in this way in the public domain. There is a tension between the drive for greater freedom of information and sensitivities about protection of privacy, particularly where online public records may concern personal details of private citizens.

Pavlik (2001) reported an example of a request by a news organization for access to the financial records of federal judges in the United States. Although records for individual judges had previously been released to newspapers, a request for the records of all judges was denied on the grounds that releasing such information on the Internet might place those judges and their families at risk. The news organization—APB News—launched a successful legal challenge, arguing that personal information about judges' addresses and their families was not part of the records it requested. The reason for the request was to establish that judges had no financial conflict of interest in relation to cases.

There are, however, other pressures that may affect the objectivity of the news on the Internet. The expectations of established Net users that content should be free is one example. As news producers move online, they must find ways of funding the services they provide. If charging consumers for access to content is inconsistent with market practices and expectations, then other sources of revenue must be explored. The most obvious alternatives are advertising and sponsorship. Online advertising has become a growing phenomenon. Although news publishers might seldom run prominent advertisements on the front page of their newspapers, they are quite willing to do this on the home page of their online publication.

The traditional and important distinction between news and advertising has represented a central aspect of the maintenance of objectivity in journalism. Some writers have argued that the emergence of online publishing may undermine this highly significant ethical standard (Williams, 1998). Advertisers have a long history of trying to influence the news agenda and editorial content to their corporate advantage. Normally, journalists would rarely drop or rewrite a story for the benefit of advertisers, although on occasion, their editors or publishers may take a different line. Concern has been voiced that advertisers will continue to try to influence the news in the online environment, and even that they may enjoy greater success in doing so (Zachary, 1992).

The likelihood of this outcome is reinforced by changes that have occurred in news provision, not all of which are a function of the Internet per se. Newspapers have suffered a serious erosion in readership. This has placed them under commercial pressure to undergo changes to their businesses and to modify their products. In parallel with this phenomenon, the news itself has become more dynamic and time sensitive. In a more competitive news environment, it is increasingly important to be the first news agency to break a story or, at least, to avoid being left behind by counterparts operating within the same media environment. This has meant a movement toward the reporting of raw facts about events and reduced attention to placing them in context. There is insufficient time to be reflective. Furthermore, the public have become accustomed to getting the news virtually as it happens. With the growth of news provision, the news has become more fragmented. Increasingly, news providers seek niche markets, unless they have the size to operate effectively with mass markets.

In the online environment, the news is cheap to disseminate. The cost of setting up and running a traditional newspaper or broadcast operation requires significant financial backing because of the organizational infrastructure required to underpin such operations. On the Internet, anyone can become a news provider as well as a news receiver, using equipment that most ordinary citizens can afford to purchase and install at home. The traditional news suppliers are facing a serious challenge to their position as news gatekeepers.

With further enhancements to technology, it will become increasingly difficult to differentiate between print and broadcast news suppliers, because all will operate within a multimedia environment on the Web. The news will be presented in text, sound, and video. Traditional news broadcasters who go online will present text news as well as news on film and video. Print news publishers, in turn, will adopt broadcast formats to run alongside their customary print news formats. News will also become more interactive, allowing readers, listeners, and viewers to have more influence over the way news is presented to them. Indeed, news consumers will acquire a creative and an editorial role in determining the news diet they receive. The news will become tailored to individual needs and interests.

In an online environment where consumers do not expect to pay for much of the content they receive, news publishers will become increasingly dependent on advertisers for revenue. Thus, not only does the Internet present a more competitive business environment, it is one in which customers often do not expect to pay directly for the services they receive; this consumer attitude plays into the hands of the advertisers.

In this electronic environment, advertisers may become content providers themselves. They may offer information (and entertainment) services as vehicles for promoting their brands. Such content may have the outward appearance of authentic news in which the usual ethical standards of journalism have been observed. Yet it may be difficult legally to prove that these services are misleading consumers if their "factual" content cannot be demonstrated to be untrue or harmful. Indeed, the definition of *news* may become more diffuse in cyberspace, with content that is little more than gossip, rumor, or speculation being presented news information. The problem with developments of this sort is that they may lead to a stronger degree of public cynicism about journalists than exists already. This may be especially likely to happen if Internet users are unable to distinguish between content that has been produced by professionals trained to observe high ethical standards of objectivity and content that derives from sources who are not bound by such standards.

In the end, the key questions are whether a strong reliance on advertising and sponsorship to financially sustain news Web sites can exist alongside the maintenance of editorial integrity and independence in news selection and production. Will commercially sponsored news Web sites end up as public relations vehicles for their sponsors? Will the news agenda be affected by sponsors who wish to run their commercial messages alongside only certain types of story?

Pavlik (2001) reported that in the United States, the American Society of Magazine Editors had issued guidelines for the treatment of editorial and advertising content in new media:

[These] guidelines direct editors, publishers, and advertisers to:

- Display clearly the name and logo of the organization that controls the content of the site.
- Distinguish clearly between editorial and advertising content on all pages.
- Label as advertising all special advertising sections, "advertorials," and the like.
- Never allow editors to create content for advertising.
- Put no links to advertising in the table of contents, directory of contents, or in any listing of editorial content of an online publication. (p. 92)

Similar guidelines may, in due course, need to be adopted by other news organizations who move their business onto the Internet.

WHAT IS NEXT FOR JOURNALISM?

The Internet has provided a new medium for journalists to work with and worth through. The migration of newspapers onto the Net has wrought changes to journalism practice and the need to rethink the business of news publishing. It has provided a new interface between newsmakers and news consumers and caused the profession to consider whether the role played by journalists in the future will have to evolve into recognition of the business and user requirements associated with operating through the Internet.

The establishment of the Internet has happened very swiftly and the technology associated with it is advancing all the time. To make maximum use of this new medium, journalists need to develop fresh sets of skills that go beyond the traditional ones at the center of their usual professional practice. Although a good nose for a story and the ability to construct an accurate, informative, and attention-holding narrative are still paramount, the Internet affords fresh opportunities for news presentation. Moreover, regular users of the Net expect facilities to engage with information that goes beyond traditional news media. The Internet affords the opportunity to utilize multimedia formats, links to news archives and other more distant information sources, and a degree of interactivity between news consumers and news providers. All these facilities necessitate a change of mindset on the part of news publishers, editors, and journalists.

The Internet also poses serious challenges to newspapers as businesses and requires a "re-think" of traditional business models. Revenues are not generated in the same way in the online environment as in the offline environment. This factor may have important consequences and implications for professional journalism practice. The significance of advertising revenues in the online environment places advertisers in a more powerful position to influence news agendas and editorial content. News publishers will be under growing pressure to maintain favorable relationships with their principal advertisers because the viability of their online businesses will be significantly dependent on revenues generated by these sources. Some observers have suggested that this could pose a challenge to the integrity of journalists and undermine ethical standards of objectivity in reporting.

It is clear that there is still much to be learned about the usefulness and implications of online technologies in the newsroom, especially as it relates to news-gathering and other journalistic practices. The rapid growth of online editions of newspapers across the last 10 years of the 20th century testifies to the fact that this is a major phenomenon. Given this level of commitment within the news publishing industry, it is vital that news professionals understand as much as possible about the benefits and problems associated with computer technology and the Internet. According to one writer, "Journalists are aware, at some level, of the potential for problems with content on the Web. They must be made aware of new issues and concerns as they evolve to protect their interests in using the Web as the primary newsgathering resource today" (Garrison, 2000, p. 507).

Among the important implications of these developments for news-gathering, there is a particular question mark over the quality of information made available over the Internet. Identifiable data sources, such as government, public records, business corporations, academic institutions, and news agencies have established brands and associated reputations that enable journalists to judge the authority and reliability of the information they generate. However, anyone can "publish" on the Internet and there are significant quantities of information on the Web that derive from unknown sources whose agendas, credibility, and trustworthiness may be difficult, if not impossible, to gauge.

Many journalists themselves remain concerned about the quality of the information on the Internet rather than with the quality of the medium itself (Garrison, 2000). Although journalists may not need to understand how the computer networks they use actually work, they must understand that the capabilities related to how they work may impact on their news-gathering and analysis of information. Search engines may vary in the range and quality of information they supply. Not all engines follow the same checking and updating policies, or the same systems for facilitating access to information sources. Such idiosyncracies could result in significantly different information yields in each case. These are features of which journalists need to be fully aware.

Some journalists have accommodated to this new world more swiftly than others. It is clear that the Internet is not going to disappear and that it will play an increasingly significant role as a news provider. It will be important that the training of journalists incorporates information about how to use the Internet, both from the perspectives of research and the presentation of news. Although some in the profession may lament the passing of the old style journalism through the traditional mass media, the convergence of communications technologies, such as broadcasting, telecommunications, and computing, has opened up a whole new vista for the information industries that is here to stay.

Chapter 6

Online News and Legal Issues

The Internet and online media are raising a number of issues about the regulation of news output. Publishing on the Internet can carry news all over the globe. It can enable local publishers to reach an international audience or readership. Private individuals as well as large news organizations can become purveyors of news. This scenario raises questions about whose legislation is applicable in the case of stories that may be guilty of some offense, such as libel or invasion of privacy, when the content is uplinked in one country and then transported and consumed in a different country. The consideration of the source of liability invokes related questions about who is the publisher in cyberspace. Does liability rest solely with the producer of the content? Or does the carrier of the content—for example, the owner and operator of the computer server from which the content was launched—also have a legal responsibility?

Debates are being conducted around the world about these issues. Different case law has emerged in different parts of the world. But the question remains as to which nation's case law should prevail when two or more countries are involved. One of the core principles linked to these debates is freedom of speech. Societies vary in the centrality of this principle within their prevailing legal and value systems. Other key principles in the debate are the entitlement of individuals to protection of their reputation and their privacy. Once again, legal systems vary in the degree to which they allow for such protection and the conditions under which such protection is provided.

Much Internet news content has originated in the United States and it is here where legal debates about the status of online publishing have been conducted the longest. The Internet was welcomed as a new opportunity for everyone to communicate publicly. In such an open system, however, to which everyone can gain access, not just as consumers but also as producers and publishers of content, there are opportunities for

119

abuse. The Internet as a publishing network has invoked concerns about obscenity, invasion of privacy, the misrepresentation of people, issues, and events, libel, and copyright violation. This has led to calls for protection of consumer interests through appropriate regulation and controls over content. Such calls inevitably create a tension with the principles of the First Amendment to the U.S. Constitution that embodies the key principle of freedom of speech, which includes freedom of the press.

Disputes over conflicting rights of freedom of speech and protection of individuals' reputations, privacy, and intellectual property have been complicated enough in relation to traditional media. In the electronic communications environment, these legal questions have had to be re-defined in some cases when old laws have been found inappropriate for cyberspace.

In countries such as the United States, freedom of speech legislation permits considerable latitude to journalists in what they may write about. Restrictions on freedom of the press may be imposed only where publications or broadcasts can be demonstrated to cause serious harm to another. As this chapter discusses, in the electronic publishing context, confusion can occur over who is responsible for the production and dissemination of offending material, as well as over the site at which "publication" is deemed to have taken place. Is the "publisher" the original author of the material? Or, in the Internet environment, does the service provider carry a degree of responsibility? In a global, electronic publishing situation, where does publication occur—in the country where the server from which the original communication was sent is based or in the location of the offended party who downloaded the content onto their own machine? Determination of the publisher is important, not just from the perspective of deciding who is responsible or liable when the content causes offense, but also from the perspective of ownership of the content as "property," with consequent commercial and professional implications. In the case of defamation, liability may depend on the degree of control different parties have over the content. For example, an Internet service provider (ISP) might not be deemed liable for slander or libel if it acts simply as a conduit, in the same way that a telephone network does for private conversations. In contrast, if the ISP assumes an editorial stance in regard to the content its network conveys, then its legal responsibilities may change (Borden, 1998).

Before discussing these issues in turn, this chapter begins by outlining the core principles relating to public rights and freedom to publish. It is important to be clear which key public rights need to be considered afresh in the context of online journalism.

FREEDOM OF SPEECH

The First Amendment has been the prevailing standard against which all questions of press freedom and control have been judged. For over 200 years, the U.S. courts have interpreted all laws affecting public communication in light of that amendment. In this context, the press has been afforded a considerable degree of latitude to report on matters in the way they see fit. The founding fathers of the United States believed that a free press was essential to democracy.

In a true democracy, ultimate power resides in the hands of the people and not in the hands of some autocratic figure, family, or party. Government should serve the people rather than the other way around. Elected government representatives should be accountable to their constituents who voted them into office. A free press is essential to represent the people's interests as an independent source of evidence about the performance of government and its officials. It is thus crucial that the press should be free to criticize government on behalf of the people. In Britain during the 19th century, the press became known as the "fourth estate of the realm," meaning that it had become equal in power to the political, financial, and religious authorities. In the United States, the press has assumed the same mantle during the 20th century, although here assuming almost equal power to the executive, legislative, and judicial branches of government.

OTHER LEGAL PRINCIPLES

The *freedom of the press* is an overriding principle that governs the way the media can operate in many parts of the world. This principle does not grant the media the right to conduct themselves any way they please. In addition to this central guiding principle, a number of other public rights exist that may, in some instances, serve to restrict the freedom of the press. It is worth outlining these principles in their broadest terms before turning to their implications for online journalism and publishing on the Internet. The focus here is on those public rights that are most relevant to online news.

Important public rights in this context include (a) the right to know; (b) the right to protect one's reputation; (c) the right to privacy; (d) the right to a fair trial; (e) the right to protect sources of information; and (f) the right to ownership of intellectual property (see Hiebert & Gibbons, 2000).

THE RIGHT TO KNOW: FREEDOM OF INFORMATION AND ONLINE DATA RECORDS

Freedom of speech comprises a principle through which the media are enabled to operate openly to discuss matters of public concern and to criticize government without fear of legal retribution. Associated with this principle is the right to know. The principle that enables a free press to perform its social role to the full is the free flow of information around society. The right to know is a sacred principle in journalism and, in the United States, is closely linked to the First Amendment. A basic question is how much does the public have the right to know? Are individuals, who might find themselves the focus of media attention, entitled to protection from having personal details of their lives disclosed? This issue is examined more closely under the right to privacy. Do governments have a right to keep secrets, the disclosure of which might damage national security? When does the public have the right to know and when does it not have that right?

In the United States, this right to know principle, as applied to government disclosures, has been embodied in the Freedom of Information Act (FOIA), first passed in 1967. The aim of this act was to provide an "open society in which the people's right to know is cherished and guarded" (U.S. Senate, 1974). The FOIA created a right of public access to government information, and made that right enforceable.

The FOIA was drafted at a time when most government agencies kept records in paper form. Soon afterward, documents were stored increasingly in electronic form on computer tape. This created problems for the existing legislation that was written to cover access to written paper records, not electronic ones.

The FOIA applied to every agency, department, regulatory commission, government-controlled corporation, and any other establishment in the executive branch of federal government, but not to Congress or to federally funded state agencies. The Act stated that all information, except for nine designated exempted categories from those agencies should be available to the public. The FOIA has been used by journalists to obtain information that government would otherwise have kept hidden. Under the FOIA, anyone not granted access to public records can take the matter up with the U.S. Federal Court.

In 1974, an amendment to the FOIA set time limits for responding to public requests for access to government records. This amendment also allowed a fee rate to become established to cover the cost of locating and duplicating records for consumption outside government agencies. There was a further amendment to the Act in 1986. The FOI Reform Act of 1986 established categories of requesters and granted preferred status to the press, educational, and noncommercial scientific users. Commercial users could be charged for document search, duplication, and review costs. Those with noncommercial status could obtain records usually without charge.

Since FOIA was enacted, the numbers of requests for access to public records in the United States have soared. There are many more records available in electronic form, as all government departments, as a matter of routine, stores their records in this form. By 1991, the federal agencies received a total of 589,391 requests. At this time, dealing with these requests cost the federal government more than 67 million dollars a year to process (Brophy, 1991). With the transition to electronic media, more requests came in for records to be provided in machine-readable form. The law did not require the government to provide them in this form. Government agencies used this loophole as a means of denying access.

DeFleur (1997) identified six issues surrounding the accessibility of government records in the electronic age. The issues were phrased as questions:

1. What is a "record"?
2. In which "formats" can information be obtained?
3. What constitutes a "new" (newly created) record?
4. What is the nature of a "search"?
5. What defines a "reasonable effort" to comply with a request?
6. What is the legal status of software and codebooks used to decipher computerized records? (p. 55)

Defining a record was important to establish the status of information that was electronically stored vis-à-vis information in a paper document. A landmark case was *Long v. Internal Revenue Service* (1979). The Court concluded that FOIA applied to computer tapes as well as paper documents (see Grodsky, 1988). The U.S. Supreme Court addressed the same issue in 1980. In *Forsham v. Harris* (1980), the Court cited the Records Disposal Act, a statute that included machine-readable materials in its definition of agency records, and concluded that this definition also applied to the FOIA.

While information stored in computers is subject to the FOIA, requesters are not guaranteed access to the information in formats other than paper. The decision as to how helpful to be here, rests with the custodian of the agency's records. A landmark case was *Dismukes v. Department of the Interior* (1984). The plaintiff had asked for a nine-track computer tape that listed participants in the Bureau of Land Management's California oil and gas leasing lotteries. The Department of the Interior denied the request saying that the information was available only on microfiche. The court ruled that an agency has no obligation to accommodate the requester's preference for the format of the information; only to provide the information in a "reasonably accessible form" (603 F. Supp. 760 [D. D. C. 1984]). The FOIA does not require agencies to create "new" records for requesters. Agencies are required only to provide access to what are called *records in being*—information that the agency has already prepared in the form in which the agency uses it. The issue has been challenged repeatedly, with some requesters asking for additional explanatory material to basic agency records.

Under the FOIA, a person may ask an agency to search through its files for a specific record. Such requests are common. An agency can comply with paper files by manually searching through them for the requested record. In the electronic environment, however, the position is somewhat different. It may be necessary for someone within the agency to write a computer program to facilitate the search for a specific record. Although citizen groups have argued that writing a program to search electronic records is no different from sending someone manually to search through paper records, not all government agencies agree. Indeed, one position is that the development of a computer program to conduct an electronic search represents the creation of a new document in its own right. If that is the case, then earlier court findings on creation of new documents would suggest that government agencies are legally entitled to deny such requests.

This position has been challenged in the courts. In *Public Citizen v. Occupational Safety and Health Administration* (OSHA), the public interest group asked for information concerning specific companies that was contained in OSHA's computerized database. The agency responded that even though the records were contained in the database, to retrieve them would require a new computer program to be written. Public Citizen argued that this was no different from conducting a manual search. The matter was settled out of court with the agency providing the information. In another case—*Clarke v. U.S. Department of Treasury*—the court ruled that the creation of a special computer program to extract information exceeded the agency's obligations under FOIA.

Disputes also arise over what constitutes "reasonable effort" to find a record on the part of an agency. Courts have ruled in favor of plaintiffs and agencies on different occasions, depending on the nature of the effort required. Hence, making certain minor adjustments to record formats or contents may be regarded as reasonable effort and as something less than creation of a new document (*Long v. IRS*, 1979). In contrast, reorganization of records to facilitate a search system by attributes different from those normally used to facilitate such searches might be seen as new document creation and therefore as beyond what is required under FOIA (*Yeager v. Drug Enforcement Agency*, 1982).

Senator Patrick Leahy (D–VT) introduced a bill in the U.S. Senate in 1991 to amend Title 5 of the U.S. Code. This bill, called the Electronic Freedom of Information Act of 1991, was to ensure public access to information in an electronic format (Leahy, 1991). The bill also attempted to get a requirement placed on government agencies that even if records were kept in nonelectronic form, the specific agency should make a reasonable effort to supply them in electronic form if requested to do so. However, it was not passed.

Senator Leahy introduced another bill to amend the FOIA in 1995. The Electronic Freedom of Information Improvement Act clarified the definition of a "record" to mean "all books, papers, maps, photographs, machine-readable materials, or other information or documentary materials, regardless of physical form or characteristics." The bill instructed agencies to provide records in any form requested.

RIGHT TO PROTECT ONE'S REPUTATION: ONLINE DEFAMATION

This principle is regarded as an important right in many societies. *Defamation* is any public communication that damages a person's reputation causing them to be held in lower esteem by their peers, usually in a business or professional context, or exposes them more widely to hatred or ridicule. The courts in many countries regard defamation as a serious offense.

Defamation can occur through spoken communication (*slander*) or published or broadcast communication (*libel*). Of these two forms, libel is generally regarded as more serious because it reaches many more people. In fact, libel can be considered as so serious an offense that a plaintiff may sue for significant financial damages. Libel cases can be expensive for media organizations when they are found guilty of publishing libelous material. In some parts of the world, libel is treated as a criminal offense and punishment can include imprisonment.

It is possible, however, to defend successfully against accusations of libel if the allegedly defamatory material can be proven to be true. In some countries, such as the United States, truth is an absolute defense in libel cases. A plaintiff cannot recover damages if the offending communication is shown to be true. In other countries, however, defamation may be punished even when a story about the plaintiff is truthful.

Another complicating factor in relation to the need to protect reputation is that certain documents may be classified as privileged. A fair and accurate report about police records, court transactions, or legislative proceedings can be published or broadcast without causing liability for a libel suit. Most of the potentially libelous news each day is based on information from such privileged documents or proceedings, so actionable libel is never a question.

The concept of *fair comment* can also be a defense for publishing or broadcasting words that might be considered defamatory without resulting in a libel suit. This long-standing precedent permits journalists to express opinions on matters of public interest, as long as those opinions have some basis in truth and are not published or broadcast with malicious intent to injure. An example might be that of a sports journalist who criticizes the poor performance of a football team and questions the competence and decisions of the team's manager. The manager might believe that his reputation has been defiled, but the journalist might argue in defense that the team performs in public and they have played badly. Someone must be held responsible for this and the manager must carry some of this burden.

Internet and Defamation

An early instance of a defamation suit being brought in connection with the Internet was the case in Australia of *Rindos v. Hardwick* (1994). An archaeologist, David Rindos brought a libel action against Professor Gilbert Hardwick over allegedly defamatory material the latter published about the plaintiff on a computer bulletin board. Hardwick had alleged that Rindos was a pedophile, a racist, and a drunk. The court rejected some of the libel action claims but agreed that the accusations about sexual conduct and lack of professional competence were defamatory. The court consequently awarded Rindos damages of A$40,000 (Borden, 1998).

A small number of Internet-related defamation cases occurred during the 1990s. The outcomes of these tended to turn on the defendant's status as either a publisher or a distributor of information. A more detailed discussion of this issue follows in a later section.

Protecting an individual's reputation lies at the heart of defamation law. Defamation occurs when a communication has a deleterious effect on the individual's reputation in the eyes of the community or when it may deter others from dealing with that person (W. P. Keeton, Dobbs, R. E. Keeton, & Owen, 1984). In the United States, for example, defamation cases are heard by state courts. People bringing libel action in such cases are heard in civil courts and seek monetary damages. Some states operate criminal libel laws, but these are rarely invoked (Tedford, 1993). The law is designed to maintain the individual's good reputation. This emphasis changed with the U.S. Supreme Court's ruling in the case of *The New York Times v. Sullivan* (1964), before the days of online publishing. In this case, *The Times* ran a full page advertisement signed by the Committee to Defend Martin Luther King, who protested about terror tactics being used against Black people by authorities in the south who were involved in nonviolent demonstrations about racial equality. Sullivan, an elected commissioner of police in Alabama, sued for libel. The Alabama courts awarded him $500,000 in damages. This ruling was overturned by the U.S. Supreme Court, who offered a constitutional privilege to media libel defendants to publish and disseminate information of public concern. The Alabama issue was one of public concern and public officials were required to prove that defamatory statements were made with *actual malice*—that is, advance knowledge that statements were false or a reckless disregard for checking the truthfulness of the statements.

As Borden (1998) observed:

> Before 1964, the common law's interest in protecting reputation was one of strict liability, requiring only that the plaintiff establish defamatory communication (i.e., that the defamation was intentionally communicated by the defendant to a third person). The defamatory statement was viewed as false unless the defendant proved truth or called upon a complex structure of privileges, such as reporting on public meetings or commenting on matters of public concern. The issue of fault was irrelevant. (p. 93)

This ruling shifted attention away from reputational harm and truth or falsity of defamatory statements to the motivation of the media defendant. The central factor here was whether there was malice behind the statement. The burden of proof shifted from the defendant onto the plaintiff. The Court in *The New York Times* case created a standard linked to what constitutes a "public" speech. For the law to work in this way, it is necessary to establish what Borden (1998) called the "publicness" of individuals and speech. In this context, public officials might expect to be challenged more while wearing their public hats and hence may have less recourse to protection by the courts. The concept of speech of "public concern" is paramount here. A private plaintiff could be readily expect to recover damages for a defamatory falsehood, without a showing of actual malice, if the speech is judged to be not a matter of public concern.

The Internet causes serious problems for the operation of defamation laws because of the ease with which it facilitates the flow of publications across national boundaries. It is easy for someone to make a defamatory remark about someone else in this environment. The issue of the consequences of defamation goes beyond the originator of the communication. Internet Service Providers may also be found liable.

One early case that drew attention to this issue concerned an anonymous user of the interactive online service, Prodigy, who posted messages on Money Talk™, an electronic bulletin board in October, 1994. The messages accused investment banking firm Stratton Oakmont, Inc. and its president of criminal fraud and dishonesty. Stratton Oakmont's response was to bring a 200 million dollar libel suit against Prodigy and the anonymous "flamer," alleging the message had caused the firm humiliation and public disgrace throughout its online network (*Stratton Oakmont v. Prodigy*, 1995). The central issue here was the responsibility of Prodigy. Was it a "publisher" of information or simply a "distributor" of information. The liability standards are different in each case.

Four years earlier, U.S. courts had defined another online service provider that had been sued for libel as a "distributor" of information. In *Cubby v. Compuserve* (1991), the court held that Compuserve had little or no editorial control over the content of messages on its bulletin boards and that, as a result, it should be deemed a distributor (or secondary publisher) of news—more like a library than a newspaper. It should therefore be absolved from liability for defamatory speech, unless it distributed such material knowing it was false or with reckless disregard of its truth. In contrast, the court found that Prodigy employed strict content controls by utilizing software that screened its system for taste and etiquette and by relying on system operators (or editors) to screen posted messages. The court therefore ruled that Prodigy should be elevated to the status of a primary publisher. The case was eventually settled out of court with Prodigy's public apology to Stratton Oakmont.

Further early American instances of cyberspace defamation served to contribute toward case law. In *Medphone Corp. v. Denigris* (1992), Peter Denigris logged onto Prodigy's Money Talk bulletin board and posted a message urging investors to be wary of the Medphone Corporation because the company appeared to be engaged in fraudulent practices. Medphone responded by bringing a libel action in the federal district court in New Jersey, arguing that Denigris's comments damaged its reputation and caused the company irreparable harm. Before a court could decide, however, the parties settled out of court.

In *Suarez v. Meeks* (1994), Brock R. Meeks, editor of an electronic newsletter called *Cyberwire Dispatch*, posted two messages accusing Suarez Industries of running an electronic postal service scam. Through online research and follow-up confirmation through authorities, Meeks discovered that the State of Washington had sued Suarez for similar violations of various computer protection laws and had enjoined Suarez from continuing its mass mailing solicitations. Meeks posted these findings in his Internet newsletter.

Suarez sued Meeks for defamation directly, alleging that two portions of the articles were false and defamatory. Meeks argued, in a motion for summary judgment, that Suarez should be subject to *The Times* fault standard: proof of actual malice. Meeks argued that Suarez was a public figure, not because of his position in society, but because of his company's mass mailing solicitation on the Internet, he voluntarily exposed himself to scrutiny by the Internet public. Meeks further argued that like any other Internet user, Suarez had ample opportunity to respond to the criticism by posting a reply rather than suing for libel. Eventually, the parties settled out of court before a court judgment was reached.

In another American case of Alexander Lunney against Prodigy, the U.S. Supreme Court gave ISPs full protection against any libelous or abusive message sent over the Web (Martinson, 2000). Lunney sued Prodigy after an imposter used his name to send threatening and profane messages to some of his neighbors in Westchester County in New York. At the time, in 1994, Mr. Lunney was 15 years old. One of the e-mails sent to a local Boy Scout troop leader, was headlined: "HOW I'M GOING TO KILL YOU." Following complaints from the recipients, Prodigy told Mr. Lunney it was terminating his account "due to the transmission of obscene, abusive, threatening and sexually explicit material." But Lunney was not even a Prodigy member. A ruling by the New York Court of Appeals supported Prodigy's defense that it was not liable for messages sent over its system.

England heard its first online defamation case in *Godfrey v. Demon Internet Ltd.* (1999). Laurence Godfrey was a lecturer in physics, mathematics, and computer science. On January 13, 1997, someone unknown made a posting in the United States in the newsgroup, "soc.culture.thai." The posting followed a path from its American originating ISP to Godfrey's news server in England. This posting contained allegedly obscene and defamatory remarks about the plaintiff. It also invited replies, giving the plaintiff's e-mail address. The posting was a forgery. On January 17, 1997, the plaintiff sent a letter to the managing director of Demon Internet, informing him that the posting was a forgery, that he was not responsible for it and requested that it should be removed from Demon's Usenet server. Despite receiving this request, the posting was not removed until its expiration on January 27, 1997. The defendant did not dispute that the posting should have been removed after receiving the plaintiff's request. In July, 1998, a second posting from one of Demon's customers, under the pseudonym "Iniquity," appeared in the uk.legal newsgroup and made further defamatory and personal allegations about Dr. Godfrey (Woodward, 2000).

The question was who was responsible for publication in this case and was Demon Internet liable? The judge concluded that the defamatory material was published by the Usenet supplier. Given that they were made aware of the defamatory content of the posting from January 17, 1997, and could not seek defense under Section 1 of the Defamation Act, 1996, through which they could claim guilt only of innocent dissemination, the plaintiff therefore had a legitimate case against the ISP. Even so, any award of damages to the plaintiff in this case was likely to be small. In the end, the case was settled out of court when Demon Internet agreed to pay £15,000 damages and court costs of around £230,000 to Laurence Godfrey.

The case appeared to establish in England that Internet service providers are subject to the same libel laws as newspapers and other media. Some lawyers argued that the settlement amounted to unacceptable censorship of the Internet, although this was disputed by others. It was felt that the ruling could herald a run of libel actions in England where libel laws are much tighter than in the United States, over allegedly defamatory statements on the Net.

In July, 2001, another England court ruling, again involving Demon Internet, effectively indicated that ISPs would not be held responsible for content they carried. This case concerned the disclosure of the whereabouts or new identities of Jon Venables and Robert Thompson , two 18 year olds, who several years earlier had been found guilty of the murder of 2-year old James Bulger in Liverpool. A previous court injunction had ruled that the media should not disclose the whereabouts of Venables and Thompson after their release from imprisonment because of concerns about reprisals against them. In the later ruling, however, the same judge stipulated that her earlier judgement was inappropriate as regards the Internet, and that ISPs were protected if contemptuous material was posted on Web pages, as long as they took "all reasonable steps" to prevent the publication of such material (Dunne, 2001).

Demon wanted the judge to specify the steps that would be reasonable for ISPs to take to stop offending material reaching Web pages. But she said changing technology would make it impossible to cover all eventualities and it was better to leave the injunction in more general terms.

Shortly after this case, the first victim of tighter ISP controls over content providers occurred. English ISP Netbenefit closed the Web site of a radical magazine called *Outcast*, which branded itself as a "queer current affairs" publication, after a threatened libel suit concerning material posted there from the more mainstream gay *Pink Paper* (Wells, 2000a, 2000b).

These cases underscore the complexities of defamation in cyberspace. First, it is necessary to prove that defendants are primary publishers. Second, it is necessary to demonstrate the "publicness" of the plaintiff in the context of the defamation suit being brought. Is the plaintiff a public figure (e.g., a celebrity), a public official acting in a public capacity, or a private figure? Third, is the speech at issue a matter of public concern or private concern? These issues can become cloudy in the online environment. Individuals who might otherwise regard themselves as private figures, could become reclassified as public figures when posting messages on the Internet, where they can be read by potentially millions of people. Equally, users of online communications may have better and more immediate opportunities to counteract online defamation than is the case in relation to defamation in traditional mass media, through which access to legal recourse or even voluntary apology are often less immediate and less forthcoming. The position is neatly summed up again by Borden (1998):

> "Unlike traditional mass media, online communications are relatively unmediated, and the resulting freedom to speak whatever is on one's mind often leads to flame wars, the hurling of argumentative and inflammatory statements, often designed for hastened reputational gain. Online, this source of conflict is called "baiting" or "posting flame bait." Often, the practice involves the deliberate posting of a message that is a clear violation of cyberspatial conventions; or it may involve posting a message that tries to "sucker" as many people as possible. (p. 104)

Steps have been taken to provide measures designed to defuse inflammatory and potentially costly actions. One aim has been to encourage parties involved in cyber defamation disputes to settle out of court and to avoid long and expensive legal battles. As already indicated, the Internet allows parties to place corrections or clarifications more swiftly than older media. The medium could be used as effectively to douse as well as to fan the flames in defamation cases.

Although liability for defamation for ISPs has been eased within some countries—most notably the United States and England—it remains a thorny issue in other countries (Wall, 1999). This means that individuals may be exposed to legal action against them even though they themselves operate out of a country in which such action is fairly rare.

Some countries protect free speech more rigorously than do others and have more open media systems (R. L. Weaver, 2000). Restrictive jurisdictions may be especially likely to launch defamation cases and may pose a genuine threat to news publishers whose outputs cross many national boundaries.

One center of contention is the position taken by a jurisdiction about where the place of publication resides in cyberspace. Is it the location of the server on which a story was first posted or is it the location of the machine on which the plaintiff downloaded the story? The answer to this question can vary from one place to the next. It is important though because it may determine where the defamation case is heard.

Some writers have argued that defamation cases across international boundaries are unlikely to be successful unless the defendant has a significant physical presence in the locality where the plaintiff resides. Thus, a global business with offices and employees in many countries may be more vulnerable than a company that operates only in one locality (Goldsmith, 1998).

There are variations between nations in the extent to which the onus is on the plaintiff to prove their case or the defendant to prove their innocence in particular cases. This is a significant point when considering that the great majority of all Internet content originates in the United States. U.S. constitutional guarantees of freedom of the press run counter to the values of other jurisdictions—including those in countries such as England and Australia. The tort of *defamation* has been defined in different degrees within different countries (R. L. Weaver, 2000).

In some countries where internal states have distinct laws, complicated issues have arisen where cases cross state boundaries and the same legal framework does not apply. In one Internet defamation case in Australia (*Macquarie Bank Limited & Anor v. Berg*, 1999), the New South Wales (NSW) Supreme Court refused to restrain the publication of material over the Internet on the basis that to do so would be to superimpose the NSW law relating to defamation on every other state, territory, and country in the world. An injunction to restrain defamation must comply with the laws of NSW. It is not designed to impose the laws of NSW on other jurisdictions. Because the defamatory material clearly originated outside the state, the judge was unable to pronounce a judgment on it.

Determining the Status of Publisher

Jurisdictional issues are not the only problems posed by the Internet. It also poses challenges to the notion of publication. Who is the publisher on the Internet? Is it the author, the publication, or the ISP? Fixing responsibility is important in determining who is liable for obscenity and libel and in establishing individual freedoms in electronic publishing. The Internet creates opportunities for more people to become publishers of material. This opens up the possibility for widespread production and dissemination of defamatory material. Internet communications involve new and different kinds of intermediaries than those involved in the publication of print or broadcast matter (Lindsay, 2000).

There is also the question of hyperlinks. Although the case law on this is far from clear, there is a possibility that content associated with defamatory material through such links could render the content provider liable even though they were not responsible for the production of the offending material.

The traditional principles of print media may not apply when publishing on the Internet (Schiel, 1996). In some jurisdictions, Internet publishing has been treated similarly to broadcasting on television or radio. The key question, in the context of defamation, is whether receipt in one location of a message originated in another location is regarded simply as reception or as a further act of publication (Perritt, 1997).

Some writers have argued for the Internet to be treated differently from television and radio broadcasts. Mere accessibility of broadcasts has been held to equate with publication such that publication is presumed to occur in all areas in which broadcasts are received. On the Internet, in contrast, it cannot be presumed that every Web site is accessed in every jurisdiction where it can theoretically be accessed (Kohl, 2000).

In the United States, ISPs have varied in the degree to which they have taken on responsibilities as publishers of content flowing through their systems. Prodigy took responsibility for mail and discussion communications, censoring users who abused the system and denying them further access. The issue went to court in a case involving Compuserve and Don Fitzpatrick Associates, publishers of an electronic newspaper called *Rumorville*. Compuserve claimed that its contract with Fitzpatrick gave Fitzpatrick total responsibility for the contents of this electronic publication. The court found for Compuserve.

In Australia, McNamara (1998) contended that "There is no significant case law in Australia dealing with the subject of defamation on the Internet" (p. 37). Case law has become established in Western Australia and New South Wales such that a person accused of defamation on the Internet in those two states would be regarded as the publisher and a plaintiff could take action against that person in those states. In other states, though, it is less clear how the courts would proceed with such cases.

Most defamation cases have occurred in the United States and most have centered on ISP liability in instances of anonymous defamation (Crombie, 2000). In the United States, Guenther (1998) argued that the closest traditional media analogy that can be made to the Internet is the handbill. Guenther noted, "Courts across the country are struggling to apply the already complex law of defamation to online communications. The medieval tort of defamation has not adapted readily to new media, and no single media analogy has proven to be a good fit" (p. 55).

In Australia, Grant (2002) reported that case law has both found that content providers can be liable for defamation and yet courts also place great weight on the public's ability to access political information. Australian cases of *Theophanous v. The Herald and Weekly Times Ltd.* (1994) and *Stephens v. Western Australian Newspapers* (1994), the High Court "defined the right of speech to include protections against defamatory liability" (Gilhooly, 1998, p. 189). In *Theophanus v. The Herald and Weekly Times Ltd.* (1994) the High Court included a modified version of the U.S. "actual malice" standard adopted in *The New York Times v. Sullivan* (1964), which shifted the burden of proof so that recovery was not permitted unless the defendant was aware of the falsity of the material; or published the material recklessly without concern for whether the material was true or false; or publication was unreasonable under the circumstances (Weaver, 2000).

Grant (2002) argued that a universal approach to Internet law is desirable to ensure that outdated laws are not misapplied in relation to a communications environment that has advanced technologically in significant ways within a short space of time. In Australia, defamation laws were already under review before the Internet era because of conflicting state laws. No uniform defamation law has emerged yet, in part because of the requirement for a referendum to give power to the commonwealth to legislate. With the advent of online distribution of newspapers, a debate has arisen over whether electronic publications are telecommunications and therefore fall within the realm of the commonwealth's postal and telegraphic jurisdiction.

The threat of legal action against Internet content distributors in the international arena can lead some to take drastic action. Hence, Compuserve blocked access to more than 200 news groups for its 4 million subscribers worldwide in response to a threat of prosecution for its violation of Germany's antipornography laws (Kohl, 2000). In effect, in this case, Germany superimposed its moral and legal standards on the rest of the world.

Under current Australian law, it is the place of publication where defamation occurs (*Jenner v. Sun Oil Co. Ltd.*, 1952). The problem for the Internet is that once an item is published on the Web, it is difficult to restrict its distribution; it reaches all around the world. In a defamation case, it is important also to establish that the offending material was seen or read by a third party, other than the defendant or plaintiff. The plaintiff's concern, after all, is that defamatory material that was published by the defendant could be read by others, hence damaging the plaintiff's reputation. It is not always easy to establish who has visited and read material on a particular Web site. Although software has emerged that can monitor not just visits to Web sites but also who the visitors were, there remain methodological problems with such research.

According to Grant (2002), "the unique character of the Internet may warrant new approaches to remedies for defamation in on online context" (p. 128). Roberts (1996) argued that new approaches to remedies may be needed that take advantage of the technological capabilities of the Internet. Roberts called for a reexamination of self-help options, such as greater emphasis on the right of reply, as well as the establishment of virtual online courts to hear disputes.

Guenther (1998) observed that "[defamation] law is designed to protect people who have no ability to reply. But the rules do change in cyberspace where everyone has the ability to respond" (p. 96). In contrast, Weaver (2000) pointed out that "it may be difficult or impossible for a defamed person to know of all the places to which a defamatory messages was sent" (p. 32). But the existing remedies for defamation, such as injunctions and damages, may be unsuitable for the Internet (Roberts, 1996).

One important legal precedent regarding the source of liability on the Internet emerged from a German case. A Munich court convicted a former executive of an online service provider for aiding and abetting the spread of child pornography. Felix Somm, former head of Compuserve online service in Germany, was given a 2-year suspended sentence. This was believed to be the first time anywhere in the world that a representative of a firm providing access to the Internet had been criminalized because of the content of the material available in cyberspace (Traynor, 1998).

The judge found Somm guilty on 13 counts of helping to peddle child and animal pornography despite arguments from both the defense and the prosecution for an acquittal and despite new multimedia legislation in Germany that all but absolves Internet access providers of responsibility for criminally offensive material on the Internet.

In the case it mounted against Somm, the Bavarian state prosecutors argued that Somm had knowingly facilitated the spread of child and animal pornography in newsgroups on the WWW to which Compuserve subscribers have access. Late in the case, the prosecution called for an acquittal, revising its views and agreeing with the defense that Somm could not have been expected to control the content of the huge volume of material on the Web.

The Bavarian court, however, found that Somm should be held personally responsible for the ISP's actions in allowing open access to Usenet. Earlier, the Bavarian government had accused Compuserve of breaking the law by allowing German online users access to illegal material on the Internet in 1995. This move resulted in Compuserve having to "regionalize" its access facilities to ensure its ability to meet local legal requirements.

In the end, it is important to recognize that given the unique qualities of the Internet, anyone can become a publisher and they can publish on a global scale by placing material on the WWW. Once the material is out there in cyberspace, it is difficult to know who may read it. This medium provides a significant platform for promoting free speech, but equally it is an environment in which a person could be also defamed globally—even though the originating publisher would normally operate only on a local basis. There must therefore be an appropriate recourse for individuals who have been defamed in this way. The question remains however as to the degree to which it is appropriate or even possible to impose artificial boundaries on the Internet.

THE RIGHT TO PRIVACY AND ONLINE PUBLISHING

This right is more difficult to define than libel. Invasion of privacy can result in legal action for a number of reasons. Hiebert and Gibbons (2000) gave four principal justifications for legal action in this context:

> 1. The use of an individual's name or likeness for commercial purposes without first getting consent; 2. The intrusion on a person's solitude; 3. The publication of private information about a person; 4. The publication of false information about a person, or putting someone in a false light. (p. 86)

When using a person's name, image, or likeness in an advertisement, permission must be sought beforehand to do so. Failure to comply with this rule is an actionable offense. In the other instance, newsworthiness is usually an acceptable defense. The courts may regard the public's right to know about a newsworthy situation as more important than the privacy of the individual(s) involved. Thus, a person who becomes part of an event that is of public interest may lose the right to privacy in that context. An individual might have recourse to legal defense if the media knowingly published inaccurate or false information about them. Where no prior malice can be proven, however, this defense may not be acceptable.

In the context of Internet publishing, further privacy issues arise in connection with who might be ultimately responsible for content. It was noted earlier that fixing responsibility for content in terms of who is legally deemed to be the publisher is central to attributing liability in defamation cases. If ISPs have a degree of legal responsibility to monitor content to ensure that it does not cause offense to users, this may raise questions about the extent to which users as publishers have a right to privacy in their electronic publications, or if system operators have a right to examine and censor content prior to publication as part of their responsibilities as "broadcasters."

THE RIGHT TO A FAIR TRIAL: CONTEMPT AND ONLINE PUBLISHING

In the United States, the right to a fair trial is guaranteed in the Sixth Amendment to the Constitution. This right can come into direct conflict with the rights in the First Amendment when news media coverage might jeopardize the fairness of judicial proceedings. Can you have a fair trial if jurors are getting information about the trial from the press as well as from court proceedings?

In the United Kingdom, a similar legal principle applies under Contempt of Court Law. The media are forbidden from publishing news about court actions until the case has been decided. Once a person has been arrested, no news about the legal proceedings can be published or broadcast until the court has rendered its verdict (Wells, 2002).

This practice has not prevailed in the United States because of the fear of secret trials. The belief is that by opening up trials to full public scrutiny, defendants are protected against corruption of the judicial process. Even so, the possibility of an impact of press freedom on trial proceedings can be alleviated by the courts that may decide to move a trial to a new location, and away from one where extensive media coverage has occurred. The judge can advise members of a jury not to read the newspapers or watch television during the trial in cases of unusual media interest; the judge can also issue gag orders preventing jurors from speaking to the press themselves while the trial is in progress.

Within journalism, there is another public right connected to contempt legislation. Journalists may get information that is central to their stories from sources who do not wish to be identified. Although some in the profession have argued that sources should not be used unless they are prepared to be named, there are others who acknowledge that use of an anonymous source may be justified if the story and the public's need to know are important enough. There are occasions when anonymous information is essential to a case in court. Under these circumstances, journalists may be called upon to reveal their sources. Refusal to do so may lead to a journalist being held in contempt of court. Some journalists have spent time in prison rather than reveal the identities of their sources to a court.

In the context of Internet publishing, case law is still being established in relation to contempt of court issues. However, some recent court rulings in England have caused some concern for newspapers with online archives and may have implications further afield.

In 2001, a trial was held in Scotland with reference to a horrific murder case. During the trial, the judge made an historic ruling that has profound implications for newspapers that maintain a publicly accessible Internet archive. The effect of the ruling was to lay newspaper publishers and editors open to contempt of court charges if they do not remove online material relating to previous convictions of anyone facing criminal proceedings and other relevant background information.

In 1987, William Beggs was jailed for life for the murder and attempted dismemberment of a young man in northern England. He was later freed on a technicality. In 1991, he was jailed again after slashing a young man in Glasgow, Scotland. This information was carried in newspaper reports at the time of the trials, which could be routinely accessed by anyone who looked in paper archives contained in public libraries. This would not raise an issue of contempt. But the trial judge took a different view of the Internet archive, ruling that online information was, in effect, "published anew" every time someone accessed it.

It would seem that similar principles might apply in England and Wales. The court of appeal in London, as part of a case between *The Times* and a Russian businessman, Grigori Loutchansky, relied on an 1849 precedent to make a similar ruling in the Beggs case. Loutchansky successfully sued for libel over articles that were kept on *The Times*'s Internet archive. He claimed that they portrayed him as the head of a Russian criminal organization. *The Times* argued that the Internet publication was protected by the paper's duty to keep the archive as a service and the public's interest in accessing it (Kennedy, 2001a). *The Times* won its appeal against Lutchansky when the Court of Appeal ruled that the libel trial judge had wrongly interpreted law relating to freedom of the press. Notwithstanding the appeal court's overall ruling, the law lords also ruled that *The Times* had no defense for letting the articles about Loutchansky remain unaltered on its Web site archive after the Russian had threatened to sue (Kennedy, 2001b). The appeal court rejected *The Times*'s argument that a "single publication rule" should be established—that an article on the Internet would be deemed to have been published on the day it was posted.

The Loutchansky case related to defamation, but there is every possibility that the principle could be applied to contempt. The logical extension of both rulings is that newspaper editors would have to monitor every single criminal case the length and breadth of the land (a case becomes "active" for the purposes of contempt as soon as someone is arrested) and remove offending material from their archives. If this happened a valuable resource for historians and researchers would be lost.

The court's concern rests on the risk that such archive material might serve to prejudice juries if the juries could readily look up past information about defendants on the Internet. Search engines ensure that obscure information is easily accessed on an Internet archive, whereas such material might not be so readily accessed via a standard newspaper library archive unless the searcher knew where to look.

There is some comfort for editors though. Material is not held to be in contempt unless it creates a "substantial risk of serious prejudice." A newspaper could hope to defend a contempt charge by arguing that the maintenance of an archive, with its relatively limited family of users, was not as serious a risk as "broadcasting the same material on the news." Nonetheless, newspapers are placed in an invidious position.

One fundamental obligation of journalism that may bring journalists in contempt of court is to protect the confidentiality of their sources. In fact, many journalists would be unable to work effectively without the degree of trust between journalists and sources that this principle provides. In Britain, until the enactment of the Contempt of Court Act in 1981, journalists who sought to keep the identity of a source confidential were viewed by the court no differently from others who considered themselves bound by obligations of confidence. However, the European Convention on Human Rights and the right to freedom of expression enshrined in Article 10 prompted the United Kingdom's parliament to provide additional protection for journalists and their sources. It was acknowledged that protection of sources was a basic condition for press freedom and without it, sources could be deterred from informing the press on matters of public interest. For the first time, journalists were given a statutory right to protect their sources.

There may, however, be exceptions to this rule. Indeed, Section 10 of the Contempt of Court Act (1981) provides that

> No court may require a person to disclose, nor is any person guilty of contempt of court for refusing to disclose, the source of information contained in a publication for which he is responsible, unless it be established to the satisfaction of the court that disclosure is necessary in the interests of justice or national security or for the prevention of disorder or crime. (p. ?)

The protection of section 10 can only be overturned if a party satisfies the court on various matters. A party must show that an order for disclosure is "necessary." The courts have viewed this as setting a high threshold and will only make such an order if the party's case is so important that it overrides the public interest in protecting journalistic sources. A party must show that an order is truly necessary by demonstrating he or she has tried other ways to identify the source before resorting to court.

If a court therefore decides that disclosure of sources is necessary, and the journalist fails to comply, as the British National Union of Journalists' own code of conduct would require, he or she may face a charge of contempt, which is punishable by imprisonment of a maximum of 2 years or a fine (Moncrieff, 2000).

Turning to the Internet, a landmark case occurred in Britain in 2001 involving an ISP—Totalise™—and Web site providers. Finance sites, Motley Fool™ and Interactive Investor™, were forced to reveal the identity of an anonymous user of their services who, according to the ISP, had defamed the company and its employees. In other words, the court decided that the Web sites could not protect their sources as newspapers can because they imposed no editorial control over their forums. In effect, this meant that, under English law, Web sites could be sued for libel because they are publishers *and* be compelled to hand over personal details of sources. Motley Fool originated in the United States (Gold, 2001).

The case could have set a precedent following which most other ISPs could be open to legal action from potential litigants out to discover the identity of users who defame other people or organizations on their services.

RIGHT TO OWNERSHIP OF INTELLECTUAL PROPERTY

This right is important to individuals who produce creative work. This might include journalists, creative writers, artists, musicians, composers, and photographers. *Copyright* is the legal instrument used to protect one person's intellectual property from other persons who would exploit it for their own gain. The Internet has made it easy to distribute information. Supporters of the Internet see this as a positive step for free speech, while opponents believe that it affords too much freedom to those who would abuse the privilege. There is a further battle in debates about the Internet over the issue of copyright. The entertainment and software industries have been most sensitive to this matter fearing that Internet-led piracy of their copyright material is a major threat to their existence (C. Evans, 2002).

The concept of copyright began with the Statute of Anne in Britain in 1710. This law was designed to bring the early printing monopolies under control (Samuelson, 1995). The first statute limited printers' market power by restricting copyright ownership to 14 years, after which the original producer no longer held exclusive rights over its production and distribution. This law also ensured that authors would receive some degree of recompense for their work by granting ownership of copyright to them rather than only to the printers.

Current copyright law states that authors can protect ownership of their work for their lifetime, plus 50 years. Facts cannot be copyrighted, but the style in which those facts are organized can be. Infringements of copyright law are not pursued through criminal courts, but through the bringing of civil cases in the courts by those whose intellectual property ownership rights have been violated.

Turning to Internet content, discussion earlier in this chapter highlighted the difficulties that have emerged in defining the status of the "publisher" in relation to online communications. Although this issue was demonstrated to have significance in the context of attribution of liability when content caused offense, it is also important in determining who has ownership over content as "property." Material that is protected by copyright assigns ownership to its original producer, who may then subsequently continue to benefit financially or in terms of reputation from its repeated use. Although there are debates over publisher status in the Internet context, there may also be confusion over who owns the copyright to content in that environment.

The World Intellectual Property Organization (WIPO) was introduced in 1996 with a mission to clean up copyright law as it relates to the Internet. Its job was to sort out proposals for international legislation on who owns what on the Internet. A central difficulty with holding information electronically is that it is easy to breach copyright unintentionally.

The WIPO initiative was challenged by other organizations such as the Ad Hoc Copyright Coalition, which included companies such as America Online and MCI. They warned that the WIPO proposals could jeopardize the future of electronic commerce and communication. The initial fear was if new laws were drawn up in line with WIPOs views that copyright on the Internet should be treated in the same way as elsewhere, trade on the net would be halted by making it illegal for Internet service providers to hold data on their servers. WIPO dismissed these criticisms as being based on misunderstandings about what it was try-ing to achieve. Although believing that the Internet should be subject to some sort of regulation of its content, WIPO acknowledged that it would be unreasonable to expect service providers to check every in-coming upload for copyright content (Clapperton, 1996).

On the contemporary scene, ISPs often remove content that is alleged to be illegal, without recourse to the courts and without consulting the content provider. The area where such unaccountable self-regulation is becoming most institutionalized is copyright, where *notice and takedown* (notice of infringement is given to the ISP by the copyright owner, and then the ISP takes the material down) is now common practice.

There is an ongoing debate about the regulation of Internet content in this context. Within this debate are further arguments about the merits of self-regulation versus regulation through the courts. The Digital Mil-lennium Copyright Act (DMCA) in the United States has been designed to expedite self-regulatory control over Internet content and circum-vent costly and time consuming court action. Users who repeatedly in-fringe copyright can have their access terminated by ISPs.

In Europe, RightsWatch™ represents an initiative which aims to create a standardized set of pan-European procedures for the notice and takedown of infringing content and oversee all self-regulation of copy-right-infringing content on the Internet (Starr, 2002). It is a United King-dom-based, nonprofit company run by a consortium of major layers in the telecoms market (including British Telecom and Sweden-based Telia) and providers of copyright enforcement services (e.g., the Mechanical Copyright Protection Society, and the Performing Rights Society).

RightsWatch has made much of its neutrality and openness, claiming that it conducts wide-ranging consultation with all major stake-holders. Proactive efforts are made to ensure that all interested parties are able to have their views reflected in its regulatory practices and their implementation.

The RightsWatch approach to Internet content control has not received a universally warm welcome (see Starr, 2002). Critics have serious con-cerns about the independence of such self-regulatory practices in copy-right disputes. Although more costly and time consuming, the courts are seen as being more likely to offer a fair hearing to someone accused of copyright infringement than would be true of industry regulation.

The shift from court regulation of the Internet to industry is a contin-uing trend. It has been encouraged by the extension of traditional copy-right law to Internet content, and enshrined in the WIPO Copyright Treaty (1996). The Treaty says that authors of literary and artistic works shall enjoy the exclusive right of authorizing any communica-tion to the public of their works, by wire or wireless means (WIPO Copyright Treaty, 1996). This seems a fair system in terms of traditional intellectual property (IP) law, but it does nothing to address the essential difference between "wire" and "wireless" means of communication—namely the ease with which material can be reproduced and distributed online, which makes it very difficult technically to enforce IP law on the Internet through the courts.

When the WIPO Copyright Treaty (1996) was implemented as national legislation in the United States, in the form of the DMCA, regulation was ushered in from outside the courts. The DMCA states that an ISP "shall not be liable for monetary relief," provided that "upon obtaining ... knowledge or awareness" of content that infringes copyright, it "acts expeditiously to remove, or disable access to, the material" (Digital Millennium Copyright Act, 2000, pp. 20–21). This forced ISPs to remove material based on notification alone without the prior involvement of a court.

A similar self-regulatory system was implemented in Europe as part of the European Parliament and Council Directive on Certain Legal Aspects of Electronic Commerce in the Internal Market (2000/31/EC), commonly known as the E-commerce Directive. Using similar wording to the DMCA, the E-commerce Directive states: "Member States shall ensure that the service provider is not liable for the information stored at the request of a recipient of a service," provided that "upon obtaining ... knowledge or awareness" of illegal content, the ISP "acts expeditiously to remove or disable access to the information" (European Parliament and Council, 2000).

The DMCA and the E-commerce Directive both place on ISPs the responsibility for removing all allegedly copyright-infringing content of which they are notified. ISPs never asked for this responsibility. When the U.K. government held a consultation on the E-commerce directive, it reported that the ISP liability was "the biggest stumbling block" among respondents and that both ISPs and content providers objected to "ISPs acting as 'judge and jury'" (DTI consultation on implementation of the Directive on Electronic Commerce, Department of Trade and Industry). A WIPO study of ISP liability also acknowledged that "the liability of online service providers is perhaps the most controversial legal issue to emerge from cyberspace" (Koelman & Hugenholtz, 1999).

Despite this, the DMCA and the E-commerce Directive are now used on a regular basis to enforce ISPs to accept complaints of copyright infringement on faith.

An early test case of breach of copyright on the Internet that was heard in court involved the *Shetland News* and was heard in the Scottish courts. The *Shetland News* was an electronic publication that went out daily on the WWW, and published links with Web pages managed by its hard-copy counterpart, the *Shetland Times*. The *Shetland Times* unexpectedly sued for breach of copyright and the Court of Session in Edinburgh granted an interdict—the Scottish equivalent of an injunction—to the *Shetland Times* in October 1996. This meant that the *Shetland News* was no longer able to publish links onto the *Shetland Times* (Clapperton, 1996).

CONCLUSION

Publishing on the Internet presents news providers with a whole new set of considerations within a legal context. These concerns will interplay with other professional practice issues that have arisen with the emergence of online journalism. Journalists working in the older mass media have required training in media law as an integral part of their professional skills. The establishment of the Internet as a news medium, however, has lead to a "re-think" about the validity and application of certain laws associated with publishing. A fresh approach to defining the legal status of online publishing, as compared with more traditional forms of publishing, has implications for the regulation and control of news media that stretch beyond national boundaries.

The online environment provides opportunities for publishing that go far beyond the earlier media. The Internet has provided wider and easier access to mass audiences. Virtually anyone with basic computing equipment and knowledge of how to use it can become a publisher. For established news media, the Internet offers the potential to present news to bigger markets at modest cost and to utilize more elaborate ways of presenting information. In taking advantage of these communication opportunities, however, news publishers must realize that they may find themselves operating in markets with significantly different value systems and legal systems from those in which they have customarily operated closer to home. They must therefore ensure that they are aware of the implications of such market expansion for their business—beyond the potential financial benefits that might accrue from reaching more people.

For publishers who engage with a wider array of potential information suppliers through the Internet, there must be an awareness of the liabilities this arrangement may carry, especially where they may exert less control over the content that is eventually transmitted. For organizations whose businesses are built upon the provision of online communications systems, the organizations must be clear about their legal status as publishers or mere distributors of content. This distinction may be crucial to their liability for any problematic content that flows through their networks.

Chapter 7

Readers and Electronic Newspapers

An examination of readers of electronic news sites is a vitally important part of establishing the credentials of this new news medium. Electronic newspapers have been a rapidly expanding phenomenon the world over. In the United States, for instance, there were more than 3,400 U.S. on-line newspapers and 2,000 non-U.S. online newspapers being produced by the end of the 20th century. As recently as 1990, there were only seven newspapers that were accessed mostly via bulletin board systems. In the Arab world, daily electronic newspapers grew from a zero point in 1994 to 65 publications on the Internet in the year 2000 (Alshehri, 2000).

In many instances, this growth has been technology driven. Because the technology exists to produce newspapers in this way, some publishers have decided that they need to jump on this communications bandwagon. There is also a view that Internet publishing is where the future lies and that it is necessary to establish a toehold in that market as early as possible. There remain doubts about the performance of Internet newspapers, however. As with many developments in communications technology, the needs and interests of consumers are often not considered as fully as they should be.

Internet newspapers, in principle, are expected to offer additional services beyond what traditional hard-copy newspapers can provide. Electronic newspapers can provide readers with greater amounts of information, access to news archives, and more up-to-date information. At present though, the jury is out on whether they have actually delivered on these promises to readers' satisfaction. Electronic newspaper publishers probably need to understand their markets much more than they do.

A NEW PRIMARY NEWS SOURCE

The emergence of the Internet is the latest in a line of major news sources that have become established over the past 200 years. Newspapers became established as the primary news medium in the 19th century and remained prominent until well into the 20th century. Then along came radio and then television, and the position of newspapers changed. Between the mid-1950s and mid-1980s, television evolved as the primary news medium (Robinson & Levy, 1986). On average, around ⅔ of people in modern industrialized societies claimed television as their main source of national and international news (Independent Broadcasting Authority [IBA], 1985; Roper Organization, 1983).

Although television continued to move ahead of newspapers as the claimed source of "most world news" during the 1990s, newspapers retained their customary prominence as the major source of local news (Independent Television Commission [ITC], 1998). But by the end of the 1990s, television had caught up with newspapers as the claimed source of most local news (ITC, 1999). From the mid-1990s in England, electronic news text began to emerge as a nominated source of world and local news. Teletext information received via the television set was identified by small percentages of British television viewers as their primary news source (ITC, 1998, 1999, 2000).

During the early years of the new millennium, it is likely that the Internet will also begin to emerge as a major nominated news source among national publics. When *Advertising Age* announced the results of its sixth annual interactive media study in the United States, gathering news or information was the most frequently reported activity (by 93% of a national random sample; Maddox, 1998). In another study of media consumption in the United States, a marked increase was observed in the proportion of adults who went online at least once a week between 1995 (4%) and 1998 (20%). Men (25%) were more likely than women (15%) to go online this often, with young adults (30% going online at least once a week) emerging as the biggest users in 1998 (Pew Research Center, 2000). The same study revealed that Internet users were an information-hungry group. Internet users went online most often for information about hobbies, movies, and restaurants (82%), science and health news (64%), online forums, discussion lists or chat groups (61%), technology news (60%), financial information or stocks and bond trades (52%), and weather information (48%). More than half of Internet users (54%) said they had gone online to get more information about a story they first saw or heard about from a more traditional news source. Two in three (66%) of those who went online for news said they followed the national news most of the time. Hence, a clear pattern emerged of Internet users as people with strong appetites for news.

In another U.S. study, news ranked as the fourth most popular activity on the Internet after Web surfing, e-mail, and finding hobby information (UCLA Center for Communication Policy, 2000). According to this research, 57% of Internet users read news online.

Research among readers of Arab electronic newspapers showed that the most popularly mentioned reason for using the Internet was to obtain news information (Alshehri, 2000). Further, it is not just young people who are interested in getting online to receive news. In the United States, the fastest growing age segment in online buyers are those 65 years and over (American Association of Retired Persons [AARP], 1999). Indeed, nearly eight out of ten (78%) of American elderly Internet users have made an online purchase (Greenfield Online, 1999). Because this group also ranks as important among the major news consumers in the population, it is likely the demand for Internet based news will grow.

Research has shown that the Internet has become the medium of choice for many news consumers. For instance Jupiter Communications (JUP.COM) surveyed more than 2,200 online consumers about their attitudes toward news online. The results showed that more than 80% of U.S. online consumers trust online news as much as they trust newspapers, broadcast television, and cable news outlets. An additional seven percent view online news as more reliable than other media (Jupiter Communications, 1999).

Readers' opinions about electronic newspapers are vital aspects of the future success of such news publishing enterprises. There is a need for newspaper publishers to rethink their business strategies when operating on the Internet because the nature of the relationship between media product and media consumer is different in the context of the Internet, as compared with, say, a hard copy newspaper. The principal economic reasons for this change of approach are linked to the conditioning of Internet users to expect a lot of the Web-based information they access to be supplied free of charge.

Another set of factors are associated with the changes to traditional news consumption habits that are facilitated by the new communication technologies of the Internet. The Internet, as a medium, has been labeled *nonlinear* (Friedland & Webb, 1996; Paul, 1995), although this is probably only partly true. This means that information can be provided and consumed in a nonsequential fashion by readers. With a hard-copy newspaper, finite information is prepared that a reader consumers by starting at the top of the page and reading down. With an electronic newspaper, the reader may be able to switch from the story halfway through to pursue more detailed information on a point that is archived elsewhere. Thus, there are additional complexities in the writing and presentation of news stories on the Internet (Fredin, 1997; Meyer, 1999).

These evolutionary changes to news publishing on the Internet also invoke a different kind of response from readers. News consumers are encouraged by the Internet to become interactive consumers who are also more demanding of the news provider. News consumers are empowered by electronic publishing, when it is done properly, introducing a new form of "prosumerism" in which content producers cede power to the consumers to control the way news is received (Dennis, 1996; Khoo & Gopal, 1996).

The new and emerging concept of *interactive journalism* requires new skills and a fresh approach on the part of news producers and news consumers if both are to reap benefits from Web-based activity. Increasingly, communication on the Web is not a one-way process such as that associated with the older, established media of newspapers, radio, and television. The Internet opens up possibilities for sender–receiver interactions and even for receiver–receiver interactions related to what the sender has transmitted (see Morris & Ogan, 1996).

Newspaper publishers therefore need to be not just aware of these developments, but also to understand the full extent of their implications for their news businesses. Simple transference of the hard-copy version of the newspaper onto a Web site may serve the initial purpose of attaining a presence on the Internet, but is a far cry from the kind of news service of which the Internet is capable and which increasingly experienced Internet users have come to expect.

THE NATURE OF USER INTERACTIVITY

Businesses and organizations have been jockeying for position on the WWW. A presence on the Web has attained paramount significance for many bodies. Businesses use Web pages to promote their products and services, politicians use them to urge voters to support them. Relatively little is known about how users interact with this new medium.

The integration of audio, video, graphic, and textual information through hypermedia links is conceived to give the new medium significant advantages over older established media. The links that can be provided between electronic pages such as links connecting a news story with other related stories or news archives with more detailed background information of relevance, represent a particularly important development.

Thus, users can access massive repositories of information within a few mouse clicks. This process underlines the other significant enhancement of the Internet—interactivity. Understanding interactivity and how it works is fundamental to understanding the likely success of Internet services. Fredin and David (1998) provided a model to help conceptualize the main elements of what they called the "Hypermedia Interaction Cycle." In particular, they were concerned with the form of interactivity known as *browsing*. Browsing is important with hypermedia systems because of their structure—a network of links among many articles or Web pages that users can traverse (Conklin, 1987). Fredin and David (1998) focused on the browsing of the Web for information.

Browsing has been defined as "a kind of searching, in which the initial search criteria or goals are only partly defined or known in advance" (Chang & Rice, 1993, p. 232). Browsing is an activity that has been increasingly recognized as important in library and information science, as well as in consumer behavior (Chang & Rice, 1993). Different types of browsing have been identified, particularly in library and information science, and many of these are based on the narrowness and specificity of the goals toward which the browsing is directed (Belkin, Marchetti, & Cool, 1993). The behavioral features of browsing alone are not sufficient to understand it; it is also important to consider the internal states of the user while browsing.

Fredin and David (1998) developed a model called the Hypermedia Interaction Cycle (HIC). Each cycle has three stages: namely, preparation, exploration, and consolidation. During a typical session on the Web, the user encounters a home page, which serves as a starting point. Most home pages offer a menu of choices. The *preparation* phase of the cycle refers to the process of making a choice from a menu of options. During this phase, the user makes an estimate or guess of a best choice, or at least a good one. In making the selection, the goals of the user may be many and vague, although at times they may be quite specific and detailed. The preparation phase basically occurs before the user leaves a starting point such as a main menu. Once the choice is made, the user is presented with a variety of information related to the menu choice, which marks the beginning of the *exploration* phase of the cycle. Typically, the information is in multimedia format with integrated text, graphics, audio, and video. Sampling of information occurs during the exploration stage when the user peeks under the various menu choices and buttons before perhaps deciding to focus on a few items.

The exploration phase is terminated by the *consolidation* phase, which occurs because the user either found something of interest, or failed to, and has decided to try different options. The cycle then starts again. What occurs during the exploration phase is enormously varied depending upon both the user and the medium, and the success or failure of a cycle largely depends on what happens during the exploration phase.

The HIC model has two dimensions: cycle stages and motivational components. There are two key motivational components: goals and self-efficacy. Goals are further broken down into two elements: *goal foreshadowing* and *goal evaluation*. The self-efficacy component of the model is divided into *global* and *local* self-efficacy.

Self-efficacy is a sense or conviction that one can do what is required to accomplish a particular outcome. Self-efficacy is not just a mechanical knowledge of procedures or some mechanical amassing of past experience (Bandura, 1982). It involves the sense that one can integrate knowledge, affect, and skills to devise goals and to meet challenges in changing, ambiguous, unpredictable situations (Bandura, & Schunk, 1981). Self-efficacy is involved when a person establishes immediate goals in specific situations, which underscores its importance in browsing. In turn, the outcomes of action in a particular situation are evaluated with regard to goals established. Local efficacy represents the ability to perform an immediate task of a particular nature. Global efficacy is the confidence one has about finding useful information about a general topic within the hypermedia environment. Global self-efficacy operates during the preparation phase, whereas local self-efficacy operates more during the later phases. Self-efficacy is also associated with the amount of surprise experienced with the material found. Surprise can affect the individual's confidence in finding the content he or she is seeking. It can also result in the development of new trains of thought about searching for information (Iran-Nejad, 1987) and greater depth of processing and improved recall of information once found (Hastie, 1984).

Goals arise through forethought—through prediction and inference, and through the assessment of potential consequences. Action is motivated in part by mentally represented goals. Such goals represent a source of motivation by providing the potential for satisfaction or dissatisfaction (Bandura, & Schunk, 1981). Thus, while motivation is driven partly by cognitive processes involved with goals, motivation is affect-laden as well because of the potential satisfaction or dissatisfaction involved. According to Fredin and David (1998; see also Table 7.1):

> Goal evaluation … involves the interpretation of selected portions of the feedback obtained during the exploration phase of the HIC. The feedback itself is the material found during exploration as a result of the choices made during the preparation phase of the HIC. (p. 40)

This model was confirmed in a study with students from an introductory news-writing class who took part in 90-minute laboratory sessions. They were instructed to imagine that they worked on a newspaper and that their editor had assigned them the task of developing story ideas for a special section about the aftermath of the disastrous earthquake in Kobe, Japan. They were asked to imagine they were revisiting the topic a few months after the quake to look for ideas, picture essays, news, or feature stories. The students were directed to look for material that sparked ideas about stories and to collect supporting evidence from the Web to convince an editor that they had located potential

TABLE 7.1
Two-Dimensional Layout of the Hypermedia Interaction Cycle

	Cycle Stages	
Motivational components	*Preparation*	*Consolidation*
Efficacy factors	Global efficacy	Local efficacy
Goal conditions	Goal foreshadowing	Goal evaluation

Note. From "Browsing and the Hypermedia Interaction Cycle: A Model of Self-Efficacy and Goal Dynamics," by E.S. Fredin and P. David, 1998, *Journalism and Mass Communication Quarterly*, 75, (1), pp. 35–54. Copyright © 1998. Reprinted with permission.

stories. Evidence could be presented as pictures or text. Participants were also instructed to bookmark important evidence. They were further told that the editor was interested in three types of story: the quake itself, recovery from the quake, and information about the city of Kobe. At end of search, they were given a consolidation phase questionnaire with questions regarding goal evaluation and efficacy factors.

USER CHARACTERISTICS

It is important for any news publishers with plans to migrate their business onto the Web to establish a solid background knowledge about users or potential users of the Internet. To assume that readers of hard copy publications will automatically move across to consume an electronic version without some marketing evidence would be naive. Reviews of the adoption of innovations literature have indicated that demography is associated with new media adoption and usage behaviors (Atkin & LaRose, 1994a; Dutton, Rogers, & Jun, 1987a, 1987b; Krugman, 1985). Early adopters tended to be from a higher income and better educated strata of society and are younger than nonadopters. In addition to early adoption of new television services and home video technology, this pattern has been reported in relation to early adopters of home computers (Dickerson & Gentry, 1983; Lin, 1998).

Constant monitoring of consumption of new media is required as new communications technologies spread. Usage patterns and consumer market composition and needs change as new media become more widely established. In the United States by the mid-1990s, it was observed that demographic differences between adopters and nonadopters of new media were diminishing, as cable, home video, and other technologies reached the flat part of their diffusion curve (Atkin & LaRose, 1994a; Lin, 1994a; Rogers, 1995). The same market development can probably be expected of Internet-related services. Indeed, the use of the Internet for electronic mail and placing retail orders has exhibited a fairly weak relationship to consumer education and income levels (Jeffres & Atkin, 1996). Clearly, such market information is very relevant to online news publishers.

Research has indicated that the adoption of new text services is related to the adoption of other innovations (Ettema, 1984; Jeffres & Atkin, 1996; Lin, 1994b). Thus, early experience with technology is linked to early take-up of cable, audiotext, and computer media services (e.g., Atkin & LaRose, 1994a, 1994b; Reagan, 1989). Indeed, adoption of a given media innovation is related most powerfully to adoption of other technologies (Reagan, 1987). Atkin and LaRose (1994b) found that the adoption of telephone-delivered information services, including the use of audiotext, was related to functionally similar information services such as videotext and "1-900" numbers. Subsequently, Lin (1998) noted that computer adoption was related to Internet adoption intentions as well as a technology adoption index that comprised 14 telecommunications media. In their analysis of audience demand for popular online services, Jeffres and Atkin (1996) maintained that researchers should shift their focus away from technological hardware and toward communication needs.

Although some inconsistent findings on adopter profiles may be due to varying methodologies and service packages studied, it is likely that demographics are imperfect surrogates for deeper motivational variables that drive Internet adoption. Indeed, Rogers (1995) noted that demographic differences between adopters and nonadopters of new media technologies were leveling off for the more mature media such as cable and video-recorders. Perhaps during the early part of its adoption cycle, uptake of the Internet might be expected to be more prevalent among socially and economically upscale individuals. Over time, however, this pattern could be expected to change, if Internet adoption displays the same socioeconomic profile as other new media technologies before it (Jeffres & Atkin, 1996).

USER HABITS AND ELECTRONIC NEWSPAPERS

Motives to Use the Internet. Researchers have long been interested in the reasons why people use different media. With the traditional print and broadcast media, a number of specific functions have been identified that include needs for information, entertainment, escape or distraction, companionship, and to pass the time (E. Katz, Blumler, & Gurevitch, 1974; Rubin, 1981, 1983). Newspapers, in particular, have been found helpful in providing information about and building confidence in society, in overcoming loneliness, and in strengthening social stability (Katz, Gurevitch, and Haas, 1973). Print media, however, has been rated as most successful in gratifying information needs, rather than personal or interpersonal needs, such as overcoming loneliness and maintaining social networks (Elliott & Quattlebaum, 1979).

Investigating technology adoption in light of user needs, Ettema's (1984) study of agricultural videotext found that adopters were more interested in market updates than in news. Lin (1994b) uncovered interest in a somewhat wider scope of videotext services (ranging from voting, to energy management and games). A later study of computer service adoption discovered a "likely adopter" profile involving young, computer-literate innovators who, despite deferred adoption due to financial limitations, will likely become adopters when earnings increase (Lin, 1998).

The needs associated with the use of communications media—whether mass or interpersonal—can vary among individual users who often form their own idiosyncratic opinions about communications channels on the basis of their personal experience (Atkin, Jeffres, & Neuendorf, 1998). Furthermore, the needs satisfied by communications media can vary with the specific context in which they are being used (Lichtenstein & Rosenfeld, 1983, 1984).

Switching attention to newer media, researchers have sought to find out if they serve overlapping gratifications with traditional media (Cohen, Levy, & Golden, 1988). The inherent characteristics of newer technologies suggest that they should be regarded differently from older media. The newer media are marked by increased user control, more specialized content, greater speed of transmission, and nonlinear access (F. Williams, Phillips, & Lum, 1985; F. Williams, Rice, & Rogers, 1988). But do new communications technologies serve different functions or do they represent functional alternatives to the needs gratified by traditional media?

Research among American students revealed that books, film, recorded music, and friends provided for overlapping entertainment functions, as did radio, television, magazines and newspapers (Lichtenstein & Rosenfeld, 1983). In the early 1980s, again, American college students regarded the newer media of cable television and video recorders as filling similar needs as the older medium of television (F. Williams & Rice, 1983). Similar comparisons were made between established media and the newer online media, such as computers and the Internet, in the 1990s. In this context, computers were rated significantly lower (by a student and nonstudent sample) than audio entertainment media, video, print, and interpersonal communication for fulfilling relaxation and escapist needs or to pass time. Video and audio media were ranked highest for entertainment and interpersonal communication for overcoming loneliness (Perse & Courtright, 1993).

Focusing specifically on home computer use, Perse and Dunn (1998) reported that American adults displayed a clear ritualistic character in their involvement with computers in the domestic environment. Regular users of computers were apparently attracted to the medium itself, rather than by any content-specific motives. Home computer users were likely to be heavier users of other relatively newer media, such as video-recorder usage, but lighter users of older established media, such as broadcast or cable television. Computer use was significantly greater for those users who perceived that computers were useful for keeping busy and to use out of habit.

Computer use is an essential prerequisite for Internet connectivity. Knowledge of the nature of the market for the Internet, in terms of characteristics of use and of motives for use, is of vital significance to online newspaper publishers. In a longitudinal study, Kraut et al. (1998) reported that greater Internet use was related to reduced communication in the household, smaller social circles, and a greater sense of depression and loneliness. However, to what extent the Internet was a causal agent in connection with these sociopsychological states and was driven by them, remains unclear. What such research does indicate, however, is that a person's sociopsychological state is intimately tied to their use of the Internet. This means that such details about Internet consumers may form an important part of understanding their online behavior.

More direct studies of the motives underpinning online behavior have revealed a number of different gratifications served by online content. Garramone, Harris, and Anderson (1986) used open-ended questions to assess gratifications sought from political electronic bulletin boards and four gratifications: surveillance, personal identity, diversion, and technological access to legislators. Later research revealed five types of motives associated with Internet use: interpersonal utility, pass time, information seeking, convenience, and entertainment (Papacharissi & Rubin, 2000). The *pass time* and *entertainment* motives are fairly self-explanatory. The *interpersonal utility* motive embraced such features as using the Internet to participate in discussions, to belong to a group, to get others' points of view, to express oneself freely, and to meet new people. The *convenience* motive included such desires as communicating with family and friends, and e-mailing people. The *information-seeking* function is probably most important in relation to online news publishing. However, it is insightful to look at its key defining items. Apart from to desire to look for information, there was a novelty factor here, a feeling that it is easy to use, and also the attraction of getting information for free. The information seeking motive was the second most significant factor in accounting for Internet related motives. The most important, by a long way, however, was the *interpersonal utility* function. This motivational factor was the only significant predictor, out of all the motives, of overall level of use of the Internet. This finding was also linked to a further observation that Internet users were less satisfied with their lives, use the Internet for social contact, and do so perhaps because they also disclosed less satisfaction with the quality of social interaction in their own lives. Such users sought socially oriented gratification from the Internet. In contrast, Internet users who indicated that they felt valued by their friends and family used the Internet for information purposes and were generally satisfied with what they got from the "Net."

Ultimately, the measure of whether a new medium usurps the position of an older one is found in changes in actual media usage patterns. The *media substitution hypothesis* suggests that the introduction of a new medium encourages a restructuring in the way consumers use established media (Jeffres & Atkin, 1996; Krugman, 1985; Lin, 1994a). In line with this view, James, Wotring, and Forrest (1995) found that the use of electronic bulletin boards reduced time spent with television viewing, reading books, and telephone use. Vitalari, Venkatesh, and Gronhaug (1985) found that computer users spent less time with television, books, telephones, and other leisure pursuits. Focusing on functionally similar videotext services, Heikinnen and Reese (1986) discovered that newspaper reading did not discriminate degree of interest in potential videotext service adoption. Lin (1994b) found a similar pattern of non-effects for videotext use on other media. Jeffres and

Atkin (1996) reported that use of online services was generally unrelated to use of other media, although positive relationships with television viewing emerged.

Expectations of Electronic Newspapers. The Internet is a source of a variety of gratifications for users. Researchers who have explored Internet use within a uses and gratifications framework developed to explain general communications-related behavior have found some overlap of motives for using old and newer media. Although such research has indicated that the Internet is regarded as an important information source among some users, it has not investigated the images the public hold of online newspapers. Further, it is of importance also to know how users respond to specific content and format features of electronic newspapers.

Vargo et. al. (1998) conducted a focus group study that provided important insights into how initial summary and link presentation might affect electronic publications' usefulness and appeal to readers. One interesting point to emerge from this research is that despite the image of newspaper publishing as a change resistant business, it was remarkably brisk in its adoption of the Internet and WWW. Even so, the researchers suggested, newspaper publishers need to give more attention to the needs and abilities of their readers, especially where electronic news publishing is concerned.

The researchers examined readers' comments about specific features of e-newspapers. The actual test began with respondents seeing three story summaries stacked in a column in different format. Some groups saw short summaries of the stories (a simple headline), some saw medium-length summaries (a headline plus deck), and some saw long summaries (a headline plus a three-sentence abstract of the story). The questions were about whether the news summary gave them enough information so that they could make a decision to continue reading, and what that decision would be, how interested participants were in the story topics, the attraction of news links and sidebar links, and similar questions.

It was found that the initial summaries and the links to the sidebars could be too long as well as too short. Readers' opinions about these aspects of e-newspapers could be crucial to future market development. However it is difficult to say exactly where the boundaries ought to be in regard to some format elements. Even though a clear majority of subjects chose the headline-plus-deck option as the preferred summary length, other statistics from the study suggest it may not be the most useful length. Specifically, many respondents said the longer abstracts gave too much information and therefore would keep them from wanting to read the stories. But the statistics do not support this argument. In fact, the numbers show that the varying summary lengths had no effect on whether subjects wanted to read the stories commented researchers. Nor did the amount of information in the links to the sidebars significantly affect whether respondents reported wanting to read the sidebars.

In all groups, across all three stories, more respondents said they would read the story after they saw it than said they wanted to read the story after just seeing the initial summary. This was surprising, commented the researchers, because it would seem more likely for readers to be hooked by a good headline or summary, then turn to the full story before deciding they had seen enough and did not need to read about all the details. As expected, respondents were more likely to agree they felt informed in the abstract condition than in the headline alone or head-plus-deck conditions. Overall, 90% to 100% of subjects were able to locate the links to the various sidebars. The most common cause for distraction with the words-in-text and headline links was placement, whereas placement and length were both a problem for the abstract link. When asked if they would like to read news presented in layers and links, almost all respondents (93%) thought they would like to see a summary without having to see the full text of a story.

Mueller and Kamerer (1995) found that Internet newspapers were preferred by readers for global information and traditional newspapers were preferred for localized information. Ulrika Wiss (1996) from the Center for Distance-Spanning Technology University of Luleå Sweden examined readers of a test local newspaper put on the Internet by conducting online questionnaires. The researcher also analyzed the requests that were logged by the Hypertext Transfer Protocol (HTTP) server, by grouping these into "coherent reading groups." During the test period, 783 coherent reading groups were identified, coming from 270 different hosts. In total, 79 questionnaire replies were received.

Results were analyzed for numbers of readers, reading habits, opinions on electronic newspapers, attitudes toward paying for an electronic newspaper, and factors important for reading an electronic newspaper. The study found that it was not possible to get an exact count of the readers during the test period. Two groups of potential readers for the electronic local newspaper, emigrants and people with nontraditional reading habits, were clearly identified by the study. In terms of paying for access to electronic newspapers, the study found that readers were rather reluctant to pay for an electronic newspaper.

It was also found that people had different reading habits for local hard-copy newspapers and electronic newspapers. Hard-copy newspapers were read in the mornings at home, whereas the electronic newspaper were read during the day or evening at work or at school. Also, most reading of electronic news was conducted in short sequences, indicating that the reader took a short look at the paper every now and then during the work day. One important category of reader for local electronic newspapers was the *emigrant*, persons that have moved away from the part of Sweden in which the study was carried out. These individuals therefore found it difficult or impossible to get a hold of the local paper newspaper for that area in hard-copy form. Wiss saw this as a special niche for local newspapers, because they have a content (local news) that with a hard-copy publication is available in a limited geographic area, and the people presumably interested in this information are becoming increasingly mobile.

In an Internet survey covering 800 readers of Arab electronic newspapers, placed all round the world, more than one in two (55%) claimed to read an electronic newspaper every day. More than one in three (36%) said they read an online newspaper at least once or twice a week (Alshehri, 2000). The same survey showed that the online newspapers nominated as read most often coincided with the rankings for hard-copy newspapers. Thus, the Internet versions of the most popular printed Arab daily newspapers have so far proven to be the most accessed electronic newspapers in the Arab world. At the time of the survey, however (in 1999), the electronic versions were not read to the extent that the printed versions were.

USER PERCEPTIONS OF INTERNET NEWS

There are many evaluation criterion for news. Mencher (1994) defined news in terms of news values such as timeliness, potential impact, prominence of people involved, proximity to audience, and novelty of the event. Other important factors included *accuracy* (whereby all published information is verified), *attribution* (proper identification of information sources), *balance, fairness, objectivity, brevity,* and *clarity* (Brooks, Kennedy, Moen, & Ranly, 1992). These criteria emerged as a consequence of the social responsibility era of the press, which began with the Hutchins Commission on Freedom of the Press (1947), stating that what a free society needs from journalists is "a truthful, comprehensive and intelligent account of the day's events in a context which gives them meaning" (p. 2).

In the context of digital, online news provision, there has been fairly limited research on readers' perceptions of digital versus traditional newspapers or preferences among different approaches to news delivery. Osborne and Holton (1988) found no differences in either reading speed or comprehension between screen and paper, but did not test for preferences. M. L. DeFleur, Davenport, Cronin, and M. DeFleur (1992) found that facts from news stories read from a computer screen were recalled at a higher rate than the same facts from radio or television, but not at a higher rate than the same facts read from a traditional newspaper.

Thompson (1995) examined reactions to stories and pictures presented on paper, on a computer screen, and on a computer screen with a 5- to 8-second sound bite. All three conditions used the same design. Seventy-five individuals were asked to evaluate the perceived simplicity, interestingness, and pleasingness of the three formats and found that the multimedia format (with sound bite) rated higher than the other two conditions, which were not significantly different from one another.

In another study, Mueller and Kamerer (1995) asked 62 individuals to rate their preferences between an electronic newspaper (a Web site) and traditional newspapers and found that they preferred the electronic version for topic searches. They believed the information in the electronic newspaper to be more current. However, they also found the electronic version unappealing to browse and more difficult to read than a traditional newspaper. A survey of politically interested Web users during the 1996 U.S. presidential campaign indicated that they saw online newspapers as significantly more credible sources of campaign information than their print counterparts (Johnson & Kaye, 1998).

Appearance and ease of navigation around a Web site are essential attributes that have been recognized in many areas of e-commerce and are not unique to online news publishing (Rosen, 2000). An American investigation examined preferences for a print newspapers, a Web format of the same publication, and a Portable Document Viewer (PDV) format (C. Schierhorn, Weardon, A. B. Schierhorn, Taber, & Andrews, 1998). Participants were college students and the publication under scrutiny was a student newspaper. The PDV version of the newspaper was rated superior to the other two versions on virtually all measures of navigability. It was found to be easier to look through, easier to browse, and easier to switch from one article to a related article compared to the Web version and printed version. The PDV version was also generally rated as superior to the Web version on measures of how easy it was to find the information the user wanted. It was also seen as better than the print version on most of these measures. The Web version was rated as better than the print version in allowing readers to come across articles they might not ordinarily have looked for, whereas the print version was preferred in terms of feeling adequately informed after a quick skim through the paper.

Academic research has also focused on the social responsibility role of news. Self (1988) classified news in terms of its task: to give facts objectively, to explain the facts, to report all sides of an issue fairly. Others have looked into particular aspects of news like accuracy, objectivity, believability, sincerity, bias, informativeness, readability, fairness, truthfulness, and writing quality (Austin & Dong, 1994; M. Burgoon, J. K. Burgoon, & Wilkinson, 1981; Carter & Greenberg, 1965; Sargent, 1965; Slater & Rouner, 1996; Weaver, Hopkins, Billings, & Cole, 1974).

These qualities of news are typically used (in their adjectival form) as dependent variables administered to respondents on quantitative scales ranging from 3 to 10 points. In addition to variables eliciting evaluations of stories, some studies have used variables that describe the self-reported effect of news stories upon respondents—variables such as *happy, sad, interesting, pleasing,* and *disturbing* (LeBouef & Matre, 1977; Slater & Rouner, 1996). Most studies involving receivers' evaluations of credibility and equality of news stories do not administer an open-ended questionnaire to their respondents. They often use adjectives (which are synonymous with credibility or quality or both) anchored in Likert-type or semantic differential scales (Gunther, 1988; Robinson & Kohut, 1988).

Chaffee (1986) pointed out, however, that people may not always carry values in their heads for all the measures that interest researchers, even though participants in an empirical study may produce specific values when asked. Thus, the values obtained by researchers on particular measures are at least in part a function of the fact that the researchers elicited participants' values and not necessarily an indication of the relevant psychological dimensions along which participants varied in response to such stimuli.

Sundar (1999) investigated the structure of receivers' perceptions of news content, comparing news stories presented in a hard-copy newspaper format and news stories presented online. Communications researchers are interested in news as a concept distinct from other types of content. It is therefore important to understand the criteria underlying receivers' perceptions of news. Along what measurable dimensions do human receivers of communication differ in their consideration of news as a function of a variety of variables used in communication research?

Sundar (1999) had college students evaluate print news stories along 21 evaluative scales developed through pretesting and literature review. These scales were: *accurate, believable, biased, boring, clear, coherent, comprehensive, concise, disturbing, enjoyable, fair, important, informative, interesting, lively, objective, pleasing, relevant, sensationalistic, timely,* and *well written.* These measures were in the form of adjectives placed at the left-hand side of a 10-point scale anchored between *describes very poorly* and *describes very well.* In one part of the study, a sample of students evaluated news stories presented online.

Responses were factor analyzed to find out how evaluations were structured. Four factors emerged for ratings of print stories: *credibility* (biased, fair, objective), *liking* (boring, enjoyable, interesting, lively, pleasing), *quality* (accurate, believable, clear, coherent, comprehensive, concise and well written), and *representativeness* (disturbing, important, relevant and timely). The same four factors emerged for evaluations of online news stories. On this occasion though, the accurate and believable items did not form part of the quality factor and the disturbing item fell away from the representativeness factor. Otherwise, the structure of ratings for print and online news stories was similar. The more disturbing the content of a news story in print, the more newsworthy it became. In online news, however, the disturbing nature of the story not only contributed to its perceived newsworthiness, but also detracted from its credibility. Indeed, the accurate and believable ratings also linked to more than one dimension in the context of online news.

Alshehri and Gunter (2002) reported a survey of readers opinions about Arab electronic newspapers. This survey was conducted online with Arab e-newspaper readers worldwide. Although Arab readers were broadly satisfied with the early efforts made by their newspapers in venturing online, there were problems experienced with ease of downloading and browsing. Most readers were unwilling to consider having to pay for their favorite online publication. Stepwise multiple regression analysis revealed that more frequent reading of Arab online newspapers was predicted by (a) being older, (b) frequency of accessing the Internet, (c) significance of the Internet to respondent, (d) giving electronic Arab newspapers a high rating for navigation and updating of copy, and (e) overall satisfaction with the content and format of online newspapers. Higher overall satisfaction with Arab e-newspapers was predicted in turn by (a) readers being male, (b) frequency of accessing the Internet, and (c) favorable opinions about ease of navigation and updating of content. The latter two factors were the most important of all to Arab readers' general satisfaction with electronic newspapers.

PERCEIVED CREDIBILITY OF INFORMATION

Although information obtained via the Internet is abundant, easily available and often comprehensive, it can differ from information obtained via other media sources in several respects. For instance, Web-based information typically undergoes an editorial process prior to publication that may differ greatly from that of other media content. In addition, people are still experimenting with strategies to make sense of Web-based information. Central to this activity is judging whether Web-based information is accurate, unbiased, or misleading. Because the Internet is designed not to be centrally controlled and to facilitate the free flow of information, there may often be a question mark as to from where its information derives. What or who are the sources? Are the sources credible and trustworthy?

Users often make sense of traditional communication and information sources by identifying the genre of the medium and then applying embedded knowledge appropriate to that genre in order to interpret information accordingly. For example, it is likely that newspaper readers make distinctions between *The New York Times* and *New York Post* in terms of their expectations about credibility, sensationalism, and objectivity. These distinctions are based on the genre of the source that, in turn, guides readers' interpretations of content.

The editorial processes that confirm the information delivered through mass media sources provide a certain level of security to information consumers. The use of multiple sources for obtaining information, relatively objective standards of reporting, and fact-checking procedures all help to ensure a degree of information reliability. Users rely on these checks and balances at the editorial level to help them evaluate information effectively.

The relative newness of the Internet, the lack of clearly established genres, and the scarcity of explicit editorial policies for most Web sites suggest that information obtained via the Internet might be dubious or difficult to appraise. Users who are new to the Internet may have an especially difficult time evaluating Internet information accurately. In addition, the rapidly changing nature of Web-based information makes the application of specific genre rules difficult for users, at least in the early stages of the Internet's development. Finally, editorial policies in regard to the majority of information on the Internet are nonexistent, unknown, or ambiguous. Only with Web sites that parallel their more conventional counterparts are editorial policies firmly established (e.g., *The New York Times* online) and are found to positively affect users' perceptions of information credibility (Pew Research Center, 2000).

Studies of media credibility show that as usage of a particular medium increases, so do credibility ratings of that medium (Carter & Greenberg, 1965; Greenberg, 1966; Rimmer & Weaver, 1987; Shaw, 1973; Wanta & Hu, 1994.) There is also evidence that regular users, or users who have more experience with a medium, apply a higher level of scrutiny to the information they obtain from that medium. For example, in a study of people's understanding and attention to source attributions in news stories, Culbertson and Somerick (1977) found that people with a *print orientation* (i.e., greater use of, and preference for, print news sources over other media) noticed sources of quotes in stories more than people who were not regular newspaper or news magazine readers. Furthermore, respondents used source information in their evaluations of the news stories.

Flanagin and Metzger (2000) surveyed student and nonstudent samples to ascertain their perceptions of the credibility of the Internet as an information source. In this respect, the Internet was compared with magazines, newspapers, radio, and television. Comparisons of credibility were also made in connection with different information types—news and current affairs, entertainment information, reference or factual information, and commercial or product information. Overall newspapers were rated significantly higher in credibility than the other media. The other media did not differ significantly from one another on this dimension. Within different information categories, the same result emerged. More experienced Internet users perceived it as more credible than did less experienced users and felt that information was more likely to be verified on the Internet. These results contradicted previous research that had found that the credibility of news information is typically highest on television. However, the highly educated sample used in this study could have had a bias toward print media.

Newhagen and Nass (1989) argued that discrepancies in newspaper and television credibility ratings are a result of people using different levels of analysis when assessing credibility of these two media. People determine newspaper credibility on the basis of their evaluation of the newspaper as an institution whereas television news credibility assessments are based on people's evaluations of the individuals presenting the information (i.e., reporters or anchor persons).

ONLINE NEWS SOURCES AND USER PERCEPTIONS

With the emergence of online news and increased volume of content, there is a greater need than ever for users to know where the content comes from. An identifiable source, such as an established newspaper and news broadcaster, is integral to news consumers' judgments about the quality and reliability of news. In the online news environment, it is often uncertain who or what is the source of a particular piece of information.

Online news that is provided by established news titles has presumably been selected and checked by that news service. Whatever perceptions attach to that news source will become associated with the online service. In the case of Internet news groups, users themselves are able collectively to choose stories for consumption. Thus, audience members become news editors. Even so, they do not have total control because they are still dependent on a primary source to place the news menu online for them to use.

The source credibility literature is quite broad in its interpretation of the term, *source*. A message source may be a person, a group, an organization or institution, a political party, or the government. Any such source could have favorable or unfavourable connotations for the message recipient (Austin & Dong, 1994). With the arrival of new communication technologies, there is yet another contender for the title of source—namely, the physical manifestation of the technology itself. Reeves and Nass (1996) noted that the receivers of messages sometimes treat the medium itself (i.e., the computer box or television set) as an autonomous source worthy of human social attributions. Individuals have been found to react socially to computers. They apply social rules when interacting with computers just as they do with other individuals (Nass & Steuer, 1993). Reasons for this include the computer's use of language, vocal facilities, and interactivity (Nass & Moon, 2000; Nass, Steuer, Henriksen, & Dryer, 1994). Thus, individuals respond to computers much as they respond to humans (Reeves & Nass, 1996).

Sundar and Nass (2001) conducted an experiment that investigated the effects of different types of source attributions on receivers' perception of online news content. Participants read six identical news stories each through an online service. They were told that the stories were selected by one of four sources: news editors, the computer terminal on which they were accessing the stories, other audience members (or users) of the online news service, or (using a pseudo-selection task) the individual user (self).

After reading each online news story, all participants filled out a paper-and-pencil questionnaire indicating their perceptions of the story they had just read. Attribution of identical content to four different types of online sources was associated with significant variation in news story perception. The apparent selection of stories by other users or by the computer led participants to rate stories as higher in quality as compared to the self-selection condition. When other users apparently selected news stories, they were rated as more newsworthy than in the self-selection condition. Although the perceived quality or newsworthiness of news was affected by source attribution, perceived credibility of news did not vary significantly in the same way. In sum, news selected by other users was the favorite psychological condition, with self-selected stories being rated in least positive terms. In addition, participants gave lower liking and quality ratings to stories selected by news editors than to identical stories selected by other users of the online service. There were, however, no significant differences in ratings between stories selected by news editors and news selected by participants themselves. According to Sundar and Nass (2001), this last finding could indicate a confusion in the minds of users about the identity of news editors in the context of online news. The instructions to participants referred only to "professional news editors" but did not indicate whether these editors were in the traditional sense of a newspaper gatekeeper, or in the more modern sense of a bulletin-board manager who might not be accorded the same status by online users.

INFORMATION UPTAKE BY AUDIENCES

Investigating the differences between media in terms of audience learning and recall is a traditional theme in mass communication research (Neuman, Just, & Crigler, 1992; Stauffer, Frost, & Rybolt, 1981). A few studies have examined the effects of differences between computer-based news presentations and other media. One such study compared audience recall of information from news presented by newspaper, television, radio, and computer. The results indicated that exposure to newspaper and computer-based news produced roughly equivalent learning and that both were superior to radio and television (DeFleur et al., 1992).

Edwardson, Kent, and McConnell (1985) compared information gain from television news and videotext stories. They reported that participants exposed to videotext delivered via television recalled more information from a story than did participants exposed to a television version of the same story.

Fico, Heeter, Soffin, and Stanley (1987) compared the differences between reading an indexed version of a newspaper (similar to a menu-based layout) and reading one with a traditional layout. They found that readers of an indexed paper were less likely to read stories about local, national, and international current events. Participants in the study considered the indexed paper to be most useful for goal-directed reading, whereas the traditional layout was better for headline scanning and for its ease of use.

Initially the Web was text only. As it has evolved, it has incorporated other modalities such as audio and visuals (Jankowski & Hanssen,

1996). Although these new additions represent true technical accomplishments, much still needs to be learned about the psychological importance of them to online communications. Does multimedia help or hinder cognitive processing of news and information on Web sites? It would be unwise to assume, uncritically, that multimedia formats have invariably benevolent cognitive effects (Hoogeveen, 1997).

Theories of Multimedia Effects

Several theories shed some light on memory processes pertaining to multiple modalities of presentation. The *dual coding theory* assumes that there are two cognitive subsystems—one specialized in processing verbal stimuli and the other specialized in nonverbal or image stimuli—that operate independently as far as encoding into memory is concerned. This theory would predict that delivering information in two modalities (instead of one) acts as a "double dose," thereby enhancing the storage potential of that information (Paivio, 1986).

The *cue summation theory* posits that when textual information is presented along with images, it provides additional learning cues, particularly at the time of retrieval from memory (Severin, 1967). It has been shown that the addition of pictures and graphics serves to enhance memory for print news (Griffin & Stevenson, 1992, 1994) and broadcast news (Findahl & Hoijer, 1981).

The *limited capacity information processing theory* (Lang, 2000) and the *multiple resource theory* (Leigh, 1991) argue that media messages delivered simultaneously in a number of modalities are cognitively complex and serve to overload the processing system. This theoretical perspective posits that the availability of resources for encoding, rehearsal, and storage tasks are finite, and that formal features of media messages will eat into this resource base by commanding more resources for encoding at the cost of thorough rehearsal and storage. In this formulation, recognition measures of memory indicate how much information was encoded, whereas recall measures index how much information was stored and is available for retrieval (Lang, 2000). According to this perspective, the addition of multimedia to text-only systems should result in superior recognition memory but inferior recall memory.

Sundar (2000) conducted a five-condition experiment to examine the effects of multimedia features of news Web sites on users' memory for news and for embedded advertising. Each study participant read three news stories from a news Web site created for the experiment. He or she was given either (a) a text-only version of the news site; (b) a version with text and pictures; (c) one with text and audio; (d) one with text, pictures and audio; or (e) one with text, pictures and video.

Following exposure, participants filled out a paper-and-pencil questionnaire assessing their memory and perceptions. Results suggested that pictures and audio were particularly powerful psychological cues. In general multimedia tended to hinder memory for story content and led to negative evaluations of the site and its content, but improved memory for advertisements. The text-only and text-with-picture conditions in this study were the psychological favorites. The addition of pictures to text appeared to have a positive effect overall—pictorial cues had memory enhancing effects and were subjectively positively received. However, contrary to the prediction of dual coding theory, the addition of newer modalities such as audio and video appeared to take away the advantage offered by pictures. When the two modalities—picture and audio—were directly compared, the results strongly suggested that audio downloads reduced memory for news story content, while at the same time increasing memory for embedded advertising content, especially when pictures were present on the site. Audio downloads resulted in more negative evaluations of the site's coherence and the journalistic quality of stories featured on the site. Furthermore, it appears that the interplay of audio and picture can have significant effects on the user's perception of the site and its content. The addition of pictures, in general, served to exaggerate the negative evaluations caused by the presence of audio downloads.

Sundar (2000) noted that the results sent contradictory messages to news organizations. Adding multimedia could hinder users' memory of news. At the same time, though, it positively impacted upon their memory for advertising on the site. A balance will therefore have to be struck between designing a site with features that will make it attractive for advertisers, while not impeding its news value for users.

CATERING FOR USERS IN THE FUTURE

In this chapter, we have examined what is known about readers' reactions to electronic newspapers. The rapid expansion of the Internet has been largely technology driven and the rate of advancement in technology has left many users—whether businesses or consumers—trailing behind. Many newspapers have established a presence on the Web, but have frequently given insufficient attention to how to make the most effective use of this new medium. The Internet empowers consumers to a much greater extent than the longer established news media of print and broadcasting. Internet users have greater choice of content and greater control over its consumption—or at least, they expect such facilities to be present. In addition, the Internet is expected to provide a greater quantity and depth of information on specific topics and users anticipate being able to "mine" this great library at their own pace. Whereas they are restricted to whatever appears on the printed pages of a hard-copy newspaper, with electronic newspapers, it is expected that there will be links to much more than that made readily available, should they wish to explore.

Keeping the customers satisfied has always been important in the context of any successful business, but is perhaps more important than ever in the world of e-commerce. The range of choice available to Internet users means that if one news site fails to provide a service that lives up to expectations, there are many more to choose from. Few studies have so far attempted to explore the factors that predict user satisfaction in the electronic news context. Research with users of electronic newspapers in the Arab world has yielded some initial insights.

Principal sources of complaint were about slow downloading, difficulty browsing, and problems relating to content quality and rate of updating. Ease of navigating around a news site and the extent to which it is updated proved to be key predictors of overall frequency of reading electronic newspapers and overall satisfaction with the service they provided. Other predictors were linked to measures of wider Internet involvement (Alshehri, 2000; Alshehri & Gunter, 2002). Of course, this study was conducted in one region and in a part of the world where Internet access was not as widespread and technology not as advanced as in the West. Even so, these findings are indicative of the kinds of elements to which news providers must pay careful attention when operating on the Internet. Readers of electronic newspapers want more than they get from a hard copy newspaper. If the Internet versions fail to deliver these "value-added" extras or only do so in a half-hearted way, the reactions of users are likely to be severe.

Chapter 8

The Future of News Online

This book has examined journalism on the Internet. It has considered the implications of the Internet for news publishing, journalism practice, news presentation, and news consumption. The presence of news sites on the WWW grew dramatically over the last decade of the 20th century. Established news organizations migrated their businesses or key publications onto the Net, whereas start-up news suppliers emerged via this new medium in a marketplace where traditionally it can be difficult to gain a foothold. Despite the importance attached to establishing an online presence among news organizations, many have frequently failed to make the necessary investment or have lacked the technical skills needed to do so effectively. Thus, online news publishing as a business is experiencing a steep learning curve as it comes to terms with the fact that electronic commerce is not the same as the environment in which it is accustomed to doing business.

WHY GO ONLINE?

There has been much hype about the Internet. This hype has played a significant part in the pressure many organizations have experienced to establish a Web presence. This phenomenon has been especially true of organizations whose business involves trading in content (e.g., news organizations that buy and sell news). Migration onto the Internet is often done as a matter of urgency, in the absence of a clear business strategy. Indeed, many large organizations seem to be particularly vulnerable to this phenomenon, especially when they perceive their major competitors establishing an online presence (Flanagin, 2000; Scott, 1995; Scott & Christensen, 1995). Many companies therefore finish up investing in going online without having first taken the time to think through the way this alternative marketplace works. Bandwagon pressures can cause companies to adopt inefficient Web sites that may do them more harm than good (Abrahamson & Rosenkopf, 1993). Business gurus evangelize about the fruits waiting to be plucked from the Internet for companies with the foresight to recognize the potential it holds for their businesses (e.g., Siegel, 1999; Slywotsky & Morrison, 2000). At the same time, though, closer reading of these works indicates that companies must be prepared to alter their entire corporate culture and undergo a major overhaul of their core value systems to accommodate to the needs and requirements of successful Web practice.

Before going online, organizations should consider whether there is any real strategic advantage to being on the Internet. If there is, how can this advantage best be realized? Does the company need to adopt a new business model? Has it determined (a) what this new model is, and (b) whether it is ready to undergo the changes required? Thus, prior to launching itself on the Web, any organization should ask itself what it hopes to achieve by doing so. What degree of success can be expected? What types and levels of investment are needed to ensure that its online services operate effectively? If there are any doubts that the organization is ready to embrace fully the corporate culture changes and changes to working practices entailed, then it should delay any Web launch until such doubts have been allayed.

THE PROMISE OF ONLINE NEWS PUBLISHING

The promise of the Internet for news publishers arose as newspaper publishers were already struggling to redefine newspapers in the pre-Net era in which circulation figures and advertising revenues were in decline. There was special concern about the failure to attract or retain younger readers (Denton & Kurtz, 1993; Ungaro, 1991). This decline appeared to be connected to changing ideas among readers about what they wanted and needed from newspapers (Aufderheide, 1998). Some newspapers responded to the changing market by attempting to be more entertaining or more demographically targeted. Others used the newspaper's resources to create public spaces in which community life could be promoted by organizing events and projects (Austin, 1994; Rosen, 1992). As such, newspapers were already gearing up for radical rethinking of their businesses and their product in response, not simply to technological change, but more especially to cultural shifts (Aufderheide, 1998).

What then does the future hold for online news? What changes to news provision are likely to be wrought by the Internet? How is journalism likely to change in this new environment? Will the role of journalists radically alter? How important will the traditional skills remain in cyber-journalism? In this final chapter, we consider these and other questions about the online future of journalism. The implications of Internet news publishing extend beyond simply how the job of journalists might change. There are important issues that must be considered concerning the definition of news, the regulation of content, and ways in which the interests of news consumers will need to be protected.

EVERYONE IS A JOURNALIST

In the online environment, news is cheap to disseminate, whereas it is getting more expensive to produce news on paper or in broadcast form. Potentially, this means that anyone can be a journalist or a news provider. In the past, the sheer cost of publishing a newspaper or owning and operating a television station kept news production in the hands of a relatively small number of companies and journalists. As information moves online, many more people, groups, and companies will be able to afford to tell their own version of events. Anyone with Internet access, a personal computer, and the right software can set up his or her own home page on the WWW to advertise or disseminate information. One of the best examples of this phenomenon has been the emergence of *blog* Web sites—news commentaries published on the Internet by individuals that are produced through cheap and easy to use, off-the-shelf Web software (Sullivan, 2002).

In a world where everyone, potentially, can become a publisher, journalists are vulnerable to losing their franchise as gatekeepers of the news. Journalists may thus develop more of a guiding role, helping people find and make links among the different kinds of information they are searching through (W. S. Williams, 1998). Indeed, the sense of authorship in hypertext can become clouded by the ability of the Internet to create authors out of readers (Warnick, 1997). The blurring of the distinction between reporter and reader was observed in the context of a year-long investigation by the *San Jose Mercury News* into links between the spread of crack cocaine in the United States and fundraising for the CIA-backed contra rebels in Central America. The story was the first investigative report to achieve national prominence primarily via Internet dissemination. Readers were invited to post their views of reporters' accounts. The contents of these "posts" were then subsequently featured in later reports and discussions of the story. Such cross-referral led at times to an almost indistinguishable merging of reporter- and reader-originated content (McCoy, 2001).

The news is fragmented in the online environment. The Internet can provide vast amounts of information, far greater than is normally available via traditional news media such as hard-copy newspapers or radio and television broadcasts. This fragmentation can mean that, without help, finding the particular information the individual is most interested in can become a difficult and time-consuming task. However, the technology associated with the Net means that it is possible to link specific news fragments with other fragments in the online environment. Journalists could therefore play an important role is helping to build a framework of links among different news sources, providing routes for readers to follow.

The ease of access to Internet publishing means that virtually anyone with a little know-how, can post anything on the Web. The downside to this is that it may not always be clear-cut to judge the credibility and quality of information on the Net. This observation is particularly relevant where the sources have unknown or questionable reputation. It may also apply to content produced by established news organizations that are encouraged by the pace of the Internet to release and update stories before the normal, quality control checks have been made.

ENHANCED DEMOCRACY?

The accessibility of the Internet to producers and receivers of content has been trumpeted as a tool for enhanced democracy (Whillock, 1997). Citizens can gain direct access to other citizens without going through the intermediary of the news media. This new communications channel can bring people together in new cyber communities (Preece, 2000). The Internet can empower ordinary citizens to participate more directly in the political system (Grossman, 1996). The Internet has been the site of the growth of civic networks across the United States and Europe (Tambini, 1999). City-based experiments in electronic democracy have been established to provide members of the community with access to public information, for a discussion of political and social issues, and e-mail links (Dutton, 1996; Schuler, 1996; Schwarz, 1998).

The Internet also provides a medium through which politicians and political parties can communicate directly to the electorate without having their words modified and filtered by journalists. Since the mid-1990s, political Web sites have become increasingly prominent and elaborate (Bimber, 1997; Browning & Weitzner, 1996).

NEWS OR ENTERTAINMENT OR ADVERTISING?

The selection of news is becoming more driven by commercial interests. The pressure for this is coming from advertisers and the companies that own the media. Although not always directly influenced by specific advertising interests, competitive commercial pressures are squeezing news companies and threatening traditional journalistic standards. In an effort to make the news more attractive, the dividing line between entertainment and news can become blurred—especially on television, although also in newspaper newsrooms. Simultaneously, the line between news and opinion has become blurred. Hard news veers closer to opinion as reporters try to capture the essence of an event and interpret it for the public. Journalists are also increasingly interviewed as "experts" on trials and events they have covered, in effect giving them the option of writing both traditional coverage in the newspaper and then later, on television or a radio talk show, giving their opinions about the issues at hand.

Advertising is changing with the advent of media technology developments as well as news. Advertising is becoming more fragmented and better targeted to individual buyers. Advertisers have progressed from targeting small communities of people with shared interests and buying habits to collecting information about individual consumers.

Advertising is also becoming connected with other, traditionally nonmarketing vehicles. There are commercial tie-ins with movies and television series, and with more subtle kinds of advertising in the form of sponsorship and product placement. At the same time, technological innovations are enabling consumers to avoid traditional forms of advertising (see Pavlou & Stewart, 2000). The remote control device can be used on video recordings to fast forward through advertising breaks, and some modern video-recorders are capable of sensing and skipping these breaks altogether.

Advertisers also try to mimic news by sponsoring features or news-style presentations in which their brands are mentioned. This plays on the public sense that the news is objective, balanced, and truthful in the hope that such attributes will rub off on the product or service being advertised. In the online environment, advertising can become interactive. Links can be provided from an advertising banner to other sites where information can be found alongside further mentions of the brand. This system is analogous to hyperlink frameworks that connect different news sites or news sites and news archives.

The breakdown of a clear distinction between news and advertising may be problematic in the context of the legal framework that ensures a protected space for news. News or "noncommercial speech" receives protection from freedom of speech legislation (e.g., the First Amendment in the United States, the European Directive on Human Rights in Europe), whereas advertising or "commercial speech" may still experience regulatory restrictions that can overrule freedom of speech privileges. This framework can work perfectly well provided it is clear when speech is noncommercial or commercial. Problems can arise where the distinction between the two becomes cloudy.

Already, in some newspapers and magazines, advertising can appear in the form of "news." News features or entire supplements can be sponsored by advertisers. Although they may provide accurate and authoritative information on a subject, the advertiser's name, brand, or logo may repeatedly appear either adorning the edges of an article or as actual mentions within the body of the news narrative. Information about products or services such as property, cars, fashion, and travel may indeed provider readers with useful news on subjects that are important to them. At the same time, this information is "branded" by the sponsor and has the additional purpose of raising awareness of the sponsor's products or services and enhancing their credibility.

One concern about the growing role of advertisers that may be further facilitated by the Internet is that it could threaten the position of serious, investigative journalism, especially if the latter posed a challenge to or criticized the advertiser. With pressure to seek new revenues to support their online publications, news organizations may entertain the idea of reaching arrangements with commercial sponsors that might place editorial integrity in question. Concerns have been raised that financial imperatives faced by news organizations in the online environment could encourage executive level decisions about content and format that compromise journalistic standards of independence and objectivity (Pavlik, 2001).

The expansion of cyberspace as an information medium has also led to the emergence of a variety of concepts of what constitutes news. For online news site users, the interactive capability of the Net opens up the possibility of becoming more involved in the news production process. Web sites may provide chat rooms where online discussions can be held. Users may engage in rumor-mongering and speculation about events of their own making. However, such online gossip may become wrapped up with the wider provision of news and come to be seen as news in its own right. At the same time, nonmedia organizations with their own public relations apparatus will be able to utilize the Internet to reach the public with news releases of their own, cutting out the middle man in the form of journalists and the traditional media.

This plethora of news sources could cause difficulties for users in verifying the factual accuracy and impartiality of news stories. News values could be further undermined by commercial imperatives, especially for those online publications that are heavily dependent on sponsor support. These are attributes that are central to good journalism. Verification gives journalistic communication credibility and believability (Newhagen & Levy, 1998). In the Internet context, this form of verification may prove to be increasingly difficult. Vast amounts of information are channeled through the WWW from a multitude of sources. With established newspapers, there are attached attributes, such as their political affiliations or leanings, that define the identity and authority of the publication. Its readers know what to expect, not just in terms of layout, but also in the way issues are represented and the kinds of perspectives that are taken. In the mass of information provision on the Net, such insights may be lost, unless specific Web sites stand out as having special credibility. There may be additional fuzziness about the authenticity of news sources on the Internet as audiovisual forms of presentation supersede purely textual forms of presentation. Television has consistently been rated as the most trusted news medium (Robinson & Levy, 1986). A key reason for this is that television news film allows viewers to assume the position of eyewitnesses to events as they happen, and seeing is believing (Newhagen & Nass, 1989).

DO-IT-YOURSELF GATEKEEPING

As intelligent online search agents develop, Internet users will become more empowered to select for themselves the news they wish to consume. Although they may still need journalists to produce digestible copy, they will not need journalists to select what they should consume. Hyperlinks will enable Internet users to move directly from a story to other sites with relevant or related information. Journalists may have a role in the development of these connections between news sites (W. S. Williams, 1998).

This do-it-yourself news selection process is fraught with other complications for users, however. The hyperlinks may direct users to sites produced by advertisers or producers with their own agenda. This could pose ethical and legal problems, particularly if users are seriously misled.

REVISED CONNECTIONS BETWEEN JOURNALISTS AND NEWS CONSUMERS

Online journalism restructures relationships, redefining who is a client and what is a product. Changes will occur in journalism upon its migration to cyberspace, but it is not technology alone that will invoke these changes, but the way in which the technology is deployed. The Internet will present a different kind of marketplace for journalists, through which they will encounter different kinds of relationships with their readers or viewers. One of the most difficult challenges for journalists will be to accept the partial loss of their gatekeeper status. The *top–down model* of the journalistic process associated with the traditional news media will not always apply in cyberspace. Traditionally, sources speak to journalists who then communicate what they have to say to the public, via an editorial gate-keeping mechanism operated within news organizations. With the Internet, sources can communicate directly to the public and the public can communicate directly to sources and to other members of the public, cutting out the requirement for a journalistic mediator.

Even in the early days of the Internet, the potential for a shift in the social role of journalism was noted, whereby news sites would not simply represent information sources, but also a public space within which virtual communities could become established and interact (Rosen, 1992). Although whether these communities comprise truly empowered news consumers is a debatable point. Some writers would argue that the agenda for news consumers will simply be set by corporate systems with commercial interests rather than by journalists (Gandy, 1993; Schiller, 1989).

NEWS RECEIVERS BECOMES NEWS PRODUCERS

Internet technology has enabled news consumers to become news creators. The interactive nature of the Internet means that ordinary citizens can become content publishers in their own right, provided they have access to the required computing hardware and software and possess the skills to produce their own Web sites or use interactive communications networks available on the Internet. The Internet has created online communities linked by common content interests. Indeed, even if a person does not possess the computing skills themselves, they can purchase Web site templates that are easy to install or they can engage with *Web homesteaders*, that is Web companies that allow people to create their own electronic communities on ready-made Web sites (Preece, 2000).

A number of options exist for creating or joining an online community. Primary services include *list servers* and *news groups*. List servers are comprised of a group of subscribers with a common interest and the software coordinates e-mail delivery to the group of users. It thus serves as an information exchange on the specialist topic it was set up to deal with. News groups take the form of online discussions or read-only information built around subjects of interest. UseNet News, for example, is a collection of discussions on various topics, usually hosted on Internet-connected servers. Most are *open communities*, meaning that anyone can join in. UseNet groups exist that deal with science topics, business, social issues and current affairs. Others specialize in more recreational topics or general gossip and chit-chat. However, as noted, some of these sites are founded on an established interest in news issues. As such they represent alternative news sources to the mainstream news agencies.

Other online news and information is available through bulletin boards, Web sites established by commercial and noncommercial organizations, and subscription news services produced by specialist agencies (e.g., Bloomberg, Dow Jones, Reuters). Although the latter agencies are used as "feeds" by mainstream news publishers, private corporations and individuals can also gain direct access to them. Hence, there are opportunities for news consumers to cut out the usual middleman, that is, the newspaper or news broadcaster they would otherwise use.

ARE CONSUMERS REALLY THE GATEKEEPERS?

The new electronic media have been trumpeted as launching a new age of consumer sovereignty. Certainly the traditional media structures have broken down in tandem with the new configurations that became available with technological developments in communications over the last 20 years of the 20th century. The established divisions between media sectors were broken down as mergers and takeovers among major media institutions in broadcasting and publishing became commonplace. In addition, the evolution of new forms of electronic communication facilitated mergers between mass media, telecommunications, and computing. Telephone companies began to conceive of themselves as content providers in the same way that publishers and broadcasters present themselves. Computer corporations realized that they needed to get involved in content provision as well, and not simply restrict their business interests to the construction of technologies to facilitate the passage of content.

The emergence of a fairly small number of very large multinational corporations who dominate the communications, information, and entertainment markets, however, means that content provision is determined by the business agendas of just a few companies. The advent of cable television promised viewers greater choice and control over consumption. In the event, however, viewers found themselves faced with more of the same rather than with a greater variety of content. In multichannel television markets, just a few channels attract very large market shares and a tolerance for premium subscription fees.

The Internet may hold the promise of breaking this business mold. As during earlier periods of media history, whether this promise is fulfilled depends on who owns the infrastructure and determines the provision of content. Certainly, Internet users may find a wealth of content on the WWW, but increasingly, a few well-known, strongly branded sites may come to dominate the market and the information or entertainment agenda of the public.

THE EVOLUTION OF NEWS PRESENTATION

The Internet opens up many exciting and challenging possibilities for news presentation. New forms of news presentation are likely to evolve as the use of the Internet as a news conduit becomes more adventurous. In consequence, the traditional news divides between print and broadcast will dissolve as the established presentation practice takes on a fully multimedia format. Online newspapers have already been observed to include formats traditionally associated with broadcast journalism, such as audio and video clips, to support purely textual reports (McCoy, 2001).

At present, much site design is crude, at least compared to what it will eventually become. Site design is nonetheless a crucial, even now, to the success of an Internet news operation. The Web is a dynamic place. Online publishing can deliver fast-changing information. Furthermore, users of the Internet are conditioned to expect regularly updated information. They do not want to read the same information every time they visit an online site. With news publishing, of course, news changes all the time anyway. But whereas readers will settle for seeing one hard-copy edition per day, the same may not be true when accessing the news online. Here, they may expect to see hourly updates. The provision of this type of service requires considerable investment and resources.

A Web site must also be easy to use. The Web is about communication. Information must be readily accessible and easy to digest. A further part of the online experience is that a site must add a personal touch in its dealings with users. Users like Web sites to respond to them personally. Hence, Web design is not solely an alternative route to mass marketing, it also needs to regard and treat users as individuals. Personalizing Web sites is not easy, but with the right software tools and server systems, it is increasingly possible to achieve. At the simplest level, customization of this kind means that visitors to a site are welcomed with a personal message and a range of suggestions as to what they may like to access based on their previous visits and the interests they displayed during those visits. At more sophisticated levels, sites will increasingly offer fully filtered and bespoke information services. Such developments have little in common with the traditional notion of static analog content. To accommodate the requirements of a successful Web site the nature of content presentation may have to be rethought. Traditional content delivery styles may no longer be adequate for the Internet. Understanding how users interact with sites is vital to building a Web presence that will attract a viable market.

The preferred format for online news publishing is a multimedia one. A multimedia environment allows for the presentation of information in text, audio, and video. It is the environment in which newspapers and broadcasters will go head to head. Written articles will be accompanied by voice synthesis, music, color photographs, animated charts, and moving video footage. Using multimedia technology, online newspapers could provide highly detailed maps that describe the area being talked about in a story. It would be possible to transmit more numeric information in graphics and use animated formats to add dynamism. In a multimedia environment, newspapers will no longer lag behind the broadcast media in terms of immediacy.

The implications of such developments for journalists are profound. Certainly, the fundamental story-telling and writing skills will still be essential. In addition, however, it will be necessary for journalists to have computing, multimedia, and Web design skills to compose news "packets" in a multimedia format and take full advantage of the presentation alternatives offered by these new technologies. Because software can be used by members of the Internet audience to manipulate content to produce preferred and personalized news packages, it could be important for journalists to appreciate and understand the predominant tastes of news consumers and to offer news provision that provides the choices the market demands.

Multimedia is an open-ended proposition (Elderkin, 1996). The limits are set by the resources news producers commit to news production in this environment rather than by technological capability. In all likelihood, the practical solution will be to provide users with a limited range of options for choosing their own content and the format within which it is presented. As online news consumers become more sophisticated in terms of computing skills, such news service options will have to evolve.

Online newspapers of the future will need hypertext software in order to maximize the multimedia benefits to news consumers. Hypertext and hypermedia allow people to branch out in different directions in different kinds of media. Hypertext allows each user to roam freely through the content of an online newspaper. Electronic newspapers will not only offer what is immediate and happening in the world, but also provide links to more detailed, historical background information in archives and also connections to related information sources elsewhere in cyberspace. Such links will allow news consumers to delve as deeply into a subject as they wish.

IMMERSED IN NEWS

One ultimate futuristic scenario envisages news consumers becoming totally immersed in the news, courtesy of virtual reality (VR) technology. VR will enable users to read newspapers electronically almost as they would read newsprint. A system in which users wear a helmet that controls visual and audio input is the one most usually associated with a fully immersive environment. However, alternative systems are feasible using computer screens or high definition television that do not require the user to wear a helmet. Interactive computing is possible with screens so close to the user's eyes that they take up the entire spectrum of what the person can see. With earphones, this technology can give the person the impression that they are in a different world. In a virtual news setting, instead of the user watching an anchor person on screen, the anchor may be shown sitting at a desk in a three dimensional format as if they were physically present in the user's home. Playing on the aspect of human perception known as "presence," such technology has the capability of creating an entirely new communications experience, in which news audiences are not merely passive consumers, but can interact with news presenters and position themselves as if physically present at the site of a news event (Freeman, Lessiter, & Ijsselsteijn, 2001).

THE REVISED STATUS OF NEWS

The provision of news in most advanced countries is protected by freedom of speech legislation. This regulatory framework permits the news media to operate freely and to ask probing questions of individuals, organizations, institutions, and most especially of governments and those in power. Limitations on this freedom of the press are most likely to occur in connection with the legal protection that may be afforded individuals to protect their privacy and their reputation. Thus, the media may find themselves involved in legal action for defamation when accused of publishing remarks about individuals that could damage their professional or social standing, particularly where there is evidence that this outcome was motivated out of malice.

The problem faced by online publishing is that rules developed from old media—especially print media—may be deemed inappropriate for the Internet. Furthermore, because of the access the Internet can provide local publishers to global markets, content that crosses national boundaries may be judged by different jurisdictions. Even more seriously, different jurisdictions may hold varying views about the sanctity of freedom of speech rights in defamation or invasion of privacy cases. At present, insufficient case law or international agreements have emerged to determine which jurisdiction's ruling may take precedence. Matters can become even more complicated in regard to where liability in such cases may reside. Determination of this matter is dependent crucially on deciding who has the status of "publisher" on the Internet. In some cyberspace defamation cases already, ISPs have been tagged as *primary publisher*. In other instances, they have been categorized as *secondary publisher*. This is an important distinction because a primary publisher may be deemed to have liability for content, while a secondary publisher does not. Online news operators who provide increased access to readers to contribute comment on current issues must become increasingly vigilant to ensure they are not permitting content through their news filters that might cause offense in a receiving jurisdiction, even though unlikely to cause legal problems within their own jurisdiction.

MAKING THE RIGHT DECISIONS

The need for newspapers to explore new markets and the prospect of losing ground to competitors, not only from their sector, but also from broadcasting and the news agencies, this led many print news publishers to migrate their publications onto the Internet. Organizational Web sites have been regarded as an essential area of progression for many businesses. In the future, if projections for news distribution of multimedia presentation formats and interactive capability are accurate, then newspapers must become part of this new business environment or suffer the eventual economic consequences. Notwithstanding the implications of the futuristic scenario, newspapers should avoid being panicked into the establishment of electronic publications. Research has shown that social pressures, operating at the interorganizational level, can act as critical determinants of early adoption of new technological innovations before organizations have fully prepared themselves (Flanagin, 2000). For many years, it has been known that high uncertainty often inhibits rational organizational decision making (March & Simon, 1958). Such uncertainty and the observation that competitors are adopting innovations can produce a "band-wagon" effect, with other organizations following suit before undertaking a rational cost-benefit analysis of the likely consequences of pursuing such a course of action (Contractor & Eisenberg, 1990). Because organizations are often deeply influenced by those around them, institutional pressures arise to confirm to the behavior of others, whether or not it has been determined to be the best course of action (DiMaggio & Powell,

1983; Scott, 1995; Scott & Christensen, 1994). Fads and fashions can lead to the adoption of inefficient innovations as well as to the nonadoption of efficient ones (Abrahamson, 1991). For newspapers, therefore, the future may be online, multimedia, and interactive.

Ultimately, this may be a non-negotiable choice in a market environment in which business and consumer transactions are increasingly conducted online. Migration into cyberspace will bring newspapers into direct competition with news suppliers who have traditionally operated in different markets (e.g., broadcasters) and with ones that have not previously aimed their services directly at consumers (e.g., news agencies). To survive, news organizations will need to learn quickly how to operate effectively in this new business environment where consumer expectations are different. Success will depend on a corporate willingness to embrace change. The study of innovation adoption by organizations has shown that it is important to think through the business implications and the corporate culture implications before going online, and to consider how radical must be the restructuring of internal and external operations to ensure that the business thrives in the new electronic news marketplace.

References

Abrahamson, E. (1991). Managerial fads and fashions: The diffusion and rejection of innovations. *Academy of Management Review, 16,* 586–612.

Abrahamson, E., & Rosenkopf, L. (1993). Institutional and competitive bandwagons: Using mathematical modeling as a tool to explore innovation diffusion. *Academy of Management Review, 18,* 487–517.

Ackerman, L. (1993). Is enof enough? Design and evaluation of an electronic newspaper of the future. Masters thesis, Technology and Human Affairs, Washington University, Seattle.

Akinfe, A. (1997). Printing: Spreading the news [Internet]. Available from: http://www.dotprint.com/newspapers/newslist.htm. Accessed 5 May 1999.

Alexander, M. J. (1997, August). *Net Gain? New England's online newspapers assess benefits and drawbacks of their electronic editing.* Paper presented at the Association for Education in Journalism & Mass Communication conference. Chicago, IL.

Alshehri, F. (1997). *The Internet as a source of news and information: An analytical study of the news and information about Saudi Arabia on the World Wide Web.* Masters thesis, Department of Journalism Studies, University of Sheffield, England.

Alshehri, F. (2000). *Electronic newspapers on the Internet: A study of the production and consumption of Arab dailies on the World Wide Web.* Unpublished doctoral dissertation, Department of Journalism Studies, University of Sheffield, England.

Alshehri, F., & Gunter, B. (2002). The market for electronic newspapers in the Arab world. *Aslib Proceedings, 54*(1), 56–70.

Alterman, J. (1998). *New Media, New Politics: From Satellite Television to the Internet in the Arab World.* Washington, D: The Washington Institute for Near East Policy.

American Association of Retired Persons. (1999). A profile of older Americans, 1999. Washington, DC: Author.

Anderson, R., & Reagan, J. (1992). Practitioner roles and uses of new technologies. *Journalism Quarterly, 69,* 156–165.

Andrews, W. (1996). Surveillance in cyberspace. *American Journalism Review, 18,* 12.

Angevine, K., Salido, L., Yarri, E., & Zapfel, P. (1996). *The personalized electronic newspaper.* Class project, Harvard Business School and John F. Kennedy School of Government.

Arant, M. D., Jr. (1996). *The use of online resources in teaching journalism and mass communication.* Paper presented at the Annual Meeting of AEJMC Communication Technology and Policy Division, November, Los Angeles, California.

Arbitron.com (1999). *Radio and e-commerce* [Internet]. Available at: http://www.arbitron.com/article3.htm

Arlen, G. H. (1994, March). Washington Post picks Ziff Interactive to publish its online newspaper. *Information & Interaction Services Report, 25.*

Atkin, D. J., Jeffries, L. W., & Neuendorf, K. A. (1998). Understanding Internet adoption as telecommunications behavior. *Journal of Broadcasting & Electronic Media, 42,* 475–490.

Atkin, D., & LaRose, R. (1994a). An analysis of the information services adoption literature. In J. Hanson (Ed.), *Advances in telematics* (Vol. 2, pp. 91–110). New York: Ablex.

Atkin, D., & LaRose, R. (1994b). Profiling call-in poll users. *Journal of Broadcasting & Electronic Media, 38,* 217–227.

Aufderheide, P. (1998). Niche-market culture, off and online. In D. L. Borden & K. Harvey (Eds.), *The electronic grapevine: Rumor, reputation, and reporting in the new online environment* (pp. 43–57). Mahwah, NJ: Lawrence Erlbaum Associates.

Austin, E. W., & Dong, Q. (1994). Source vs. content effects on judgments of news believability. *Journalism Quarterly, 71,* 973–983.

Bacard, A. (1993, July/August). Electronic democracy: Can we retake our nation? *The Humanist,* 42–43.

Bandura, A. (1982). Self-efficacy mechanism in human agency. *American Psychologist, 37,* 122–147.

Bandura, A., & Schunk, D. H. (1981). Cultivating competence, self-efficacy and intrinsic interest through proximal self motivation. *Journal of Personality and Social Psychology, 41,* 586–598.

Barlow, M. H., Barlow, D. E., & Chiricos, T. G. (1994). Economic conditions and ideologies of crime in the media: A content analysis of crime news. *Crime and Delinquency, 41,* 3–19.

Baron, N. (1984). Computer-mediated communication as a force in language change. *Visible Language, 18*(2), 118–141.

Bates, B. J., Chambers, L. T., Emery, M., Jones, M., McClung, S., & Park, J. (1997). Television on the Web, 1996: Local television stations' use of the World Wide Web. Paper presented at the meeting of the Association for Education in Journalism & Mass Communication, Chicago, IL.

Bates, M. E. (1999). *Super searchers do business: The online secrets of top business researchers.* Medford, NJ: CyberAge Books.

Batty, M., & Barr, B. (1994). The electronic frontier: Exploring and mapping cyberspace. *Futures, 26*(3), 699–712.

Beckett, A. (1994). From press To click. *Independent, 6.*

Belkin, N. J., Marchetti, P. G., & Cool, C. (1993). BRAQUE: Design of an interface to support user interaction in information retrieval. *Information Processing and Management, 29,* 325–344.

Bellafonte, G. (1995). Strange sounds and sights. *Time, 145*(12), 14–16.

Bender, W. (1993, May). Riding the digital highway. *Presstime,* 54–55.

Bennett, R. (1996, March). *Newspapers and the Internet.* Paper presented to Newspaper Association of America meeting, Houston, TX.

Berry, D. L. (1999). *Comprehension and recall of Internet news: A quantitative study of Web page design.* Paper submitted to the Communication Technology & Policy Division, Jung-Sook Lee Competition of the AEJMC National Convention, New Orleans, LA.

Berthon, P., Pitt, G., & Watson, G. (1997). The World Wide Web as an advertising medium: toward an understanding of conversion efficiency. *Journal of Advertising Research, 36,* 43–58.

Bhuiyanh, S. I. (2000, February). *Media in the new millennium: Online communications and the transformation of journalism.* Unpublished paper presented to the Communication Technology and Policy Division, Association for Education in Journalism and Mass Communication, mid-year meeting, Denver, CO.

Bierhoff, J. (1999). *The future of the printed press: Challenges in a digital world.* Research report, European Journalism Centre, Maastricht, The Netherlands.

Bierhoff, J., van Dusseldorp, M., & Scullion, M. (1999). *The future of the printed press. Challenges in a digital world.* Maastricht, Belgium: European Journalism Center.

Bimber, B. (1997, August). *The Internet and political participation: The 1996 election season.* Paper presented at the 1997 annual meeting of the American Political Science Association, Washington, DC.

Bitta, N. (2001, March 28) Is cyberspace bad news? *The Australian–Media,* 6.

Bjorner, S. (Ed.). (1995). *Newspapers online* (3rd ed.). Needham Heights, MA: BiblioData.

Blumer, J. (1939). *The crowd, the public, the news.* In A. M. Lee (Ed.), New online of the principles of sociology (pp. 1850–1899). New York: Barnes & Noble.

Blumler, J. G. (1964). British television: The outline of a research strategy. *British Journal of Sociology, 15*(3), 223–233.

Boedewijk, J. L., & van Kaam, B. (1986). Towards a new classification of tele-information services. *Intermedia, 14,* 16–21.

Borden, D. L. (1998). Cyberlibel: Time to flame the Times standard. In D. L. Borden & K. Harvey (Eds.), *The electronic grapevine: Rumor, reputation, and reporting in the new online environment* (pp. 91–110). Mahwah, NJ: Lawrence Erlbaum Associates.

Boulter, J. (1995). Online publishing: The past, present, and future of electronic distribution. Available at: http://netpressence.com/boulter/, Reflist

Boutin, P. (1997, April 2). Look before you push. *Wired News* [Online]. Available at: http://www.wired.dom/news/technology/story/2905.html

Brand, S. (1988). *The media lab: Inventing the future at M.I.T.* New York: Penguin Books.

Branscomb, H. E. (1998). *Cashing your net: A student's guide to research on the Internet.* Boston: Allyn & Bacon.

Breznick, A. (1999, October, 4). ABC launches live video newscast on the Web. *Cableworld,* 10.

Brill, A. (1999, August). *New media, old values. What online journalists say is important to them.* Paper presented to the Association for Education in Journalism & Mass Communication conference, Chicago, IL.

Brooks, B. S. (1997). *Journalism in the information age: A guide to computers for reporters and editors.* Boston: Allyn & Bacon.

Brooks, B. S., Kennedy, G., Moen, D. R., & Ranly, D. (1992). *News reporting and writing.* New York: St. Martin's Press.

Brophy, K. J. (1991, March) Sharing secrets on how to keep them. *Inform,* 42.

Browning, G., & Weitzner, D. J. (1996). *Electronic democracy: Using the Internet to influence American politics.* Wilton, CT: Online.

Buckley, S. (1999, March). *E-mail use by newspaper editors*. Paper presented to the Creativity and Consumption Conference, University of Luton, England.

Bulkeley, W. M. (1994, March 29). Semi-prose, perhaps, but sportswriting by software is a hit. *Wall Street Journal*, 1.

Burgoon, M., Burgoon, J. K., & Wilkinson, M. (1981). Newspaper image and evaluation. *Journalism Quarterly, 58*, 411–419, 433.

Carey, J. (1978). The ambiguity of policy research. *Journal of Communication, 25*(2), 114–119.

Carleton, G. (1994, September). Internet robust but unreliable. *Uplink, 6*(7), 8.

Carlson, D. (1996). Interactive newspaper publishing: The state of the market interactive newspaper European conference. London: The Hammond Organisation Ltd.: Interactive Newspaper Europe.

Carter, R. F., & Greenberg, B. S. (1965). Newspaper or television: Which do you believe? *Journalism Quarterly, 42*, 29–34.

Chaffee, S. H. (1986). *Issues in inferring media effects from surveys*. Keynote address at the College of Communications Research Symposium, University of Tennessee, Knoxville.

Chan, A. P., & Maston, T. (1999, August). Internet use and issue knowledge of the college-age population. Paper presented at the annual meeting of Association of Education in Journalism and Mass Communication, New Orleans, LA.

Chan-Olmsted, S. M., & Park, J. S. (2000). From on-air to online world: Examining the content and structures of broadcast TV stations' Web sites. *Journalism & Mass Communication Quarterly, 77*(2), 321–339.

Chang, S.-J., & Rice, R. E. (1993). Browsing: A multidimensional framework. *Annual Review of Information Science and Technology*, Vol. 6, 231–276.

Charon, J. M. (1987). *Les paradis informationels*. [The information paradise]. Paris: Masson.

Chikrudate, N. (1996). Communicating through on-line database systems. In F. J. Richter (Ed.), *The dynamics of Japanese organizations* (pp. 179–188). New York: Routledge.

Chisolm, J. (1998, February). The threat from within. *IDEAS*. New York: International Newspaper Marketing Association.

Cho, C. (1999). How advertising works on the WWW: Modified elaboration likelihood model. *Journal of Current Issues and Research in Advertising, 21*, 33–50.

Cho, C.-H., & Leckenby, J. D. (1997). Internet-related programming technology and advertising. In M. C. Macklin (Ed.), *Proceedings of the 1997 Conference of the American Academy of Advertising*. Cincinnati, OH: University of Cincinnati.

Chyi, H. I. (1998, February). *Access, use and preference: Online newspapers as a new medium from users' perspective*. Paper presented at the Mid-Winter Conference of the Association for Education in Journalism and Mass Communication, Dallas, TX.

Chyi, H. I., & Sylvie, G. (1998). Competing with whom? Where? And how? A structural analysis of the electronic newspaper market. *The Journal of Media Economics, 2*, 1–18.

Chyi, H. I., & Sylvie, G. (1999, August). Opening the umbrella: An economic analysis of online newspaper geography. Paper presented to the Association for Education in Journalism & Mass Communication, New Orleans, LA.

Cisco (1999, May 2). Networking skills shortage could add to Gulf's economic turmoil. *Cisco Middle East News, 2*, 2.

Clapperton, G. (1996, November). Game of the name … a roulette of rights. *The Guardian Online, 28*, 2–3.

Clarke, R. (1999). *Key issues in electronic commerce and electronic publishing.* Proceedings of the Ninth Australasian Information Online & On Disc Conference and Exhibition, Sydney Convention and Exhibition Center, Sydney, Australia. Sydney, Australia: Convention & Exhibition Center, Darling Harbour.

Cochran, W. (1995, May). Searching for right mixture: Online newspapers seek own identities to compete with ink-stained brethren. *Quill, 36.*

Cohen, A. A., Levy, M. R., & Golden, K. (1988). Children's uses and gratifications of home VCRs. *Communication Research, 15,* 772–780.

Conklin, J. (1987). Hypertext: An introduction and survey. *Computer, 20,* 17–41.

Contempt of Court Act. (1981). London: Her Majesty's Stationary Office.

Contractor, N. S., & Eisenberg, E. M. (1990). Communication networks in organizations. In J. Fulk & C. W. Steinfield (Eds.), *Organizations and communication technology* (pp. 143–172.) Newbury Park, CA: Sage.

Cooper, R., Potter, W. J., & Dupagne, M. (1994). A status report on methods used in mass communication research. *Journalism Education, 48*(4), 54–61.

Cornell Library (1998). *The current status of the Internet in the Arab World.* Available at: http://www.library.cornell.edu/colldev/mideast

Coy, P., Hof, R. D., & Judge, P. C. (1996, August). Has the Net finally reached the wall? *Business Week,* 15.

Christopher, L. C. (1994). Closing the gap: Anxiety rises as news organizations scramble to fill electronic niches. *Quill, 1*(82), 27–29.

Crombie, K. F. (2000). Scots law defamation on the Internet: A consideration of new issues, problems and solutions for Scots law. *Scots Law Student Journal, 11*(1). Available at: www.scottishlaw.org.uk/journal/oct2000/def.pdf

Cubby Inc. v. Compuserve Inc. (1991). New York District Court 776 F. Supp. 135. Available at: www.epic.org/free_speech/cubby v compuserve.html.

Culbertson, H. M., & Somerick, N. (1977). Variables affect how persons view unnamed news sources. *Journalism Quarterly, 54,* 58–69.

Daft, R. L., Lengel, R. H., & Trevino, L. K. (1987). Message equivocality, media selection, and manager performance: Implications for manager performance. *MIS Quarterly, 11,* 355–366.

Damanpour, F. (1991). Organizational innovation: A meta-analysis of effects of determinants and moderators. *Academy of Management Journal, 34,* 555–590.

Damanpour, F. (1998). Innovation type, radicalness, and the adoption process. *Communication Research, 15,* 545–567.

December, J. (1996). Units of analysis for Internet communication. *Journal of Communication, 46,* 14–38.

December, J., & Randall, N. (1995). *The World Wide Wen unleashed* (2nd.ed.). Indianapolis, IN: Sams.Net.

DeFleur, M. H. (1997). *Computer-assisted investigative reporting: Development and methodology.* Mahwah, NJ: Lawrence Erlbaum Associates.

DeFleur, M. L. (1998). Where have all the milestones gone? The decline of significant research on the process and effects of mass communication. *Mass Communication & Society 1,* 85–98.

DeFleur, M. L., & Ball-Rokeach, S. (1989). *Theories of mass communication* (5th ed.). New York: Longman.

DeFleur, M. L., Davenport, L., Cronin, M., & De Fleur, M. (1992). Audience recall of news stories presented by newspaper, computer, television and radio. *Journalism Quarterly, 69,* 1010–1022.

Degen, D. , & Sparks, K. (1997). The future of newspaper journalism. Available at: http://clara.franuniv.edu/fusfolder/com323/sp1997/scan/index.html

Dennis, E. E. (1996). Values and value-added for the new electronic journalism: Public debate and the democratic dialogue. *Media Asia, 23*(2), 107–110.

Denton, F., & Kurtz, H. (1993). *Reinventing the newspaper.* New York: Twentieth Century Fund.

De Reimer, C. (1991, March). *Commercial database use in the newsroom.* Paper presented at the annual meeting of the Association for Education in Journalism and Mass Communication, Boston.

Deuze, M. (1999). The Webcommunicators: Issues in research into online journalism and journalists. *First Monday, 3* [Peer reviewed journal on the Internet]. Available at: Firstmonday.com

Deuze, M. (1999). Journalism and the Web: An analysis of skills and standards in an online environment. *Gazette, 61*(5), 373–390.

Dewar, R. D., & Dutton, J. W. (1986). The adoption of radical and incremental innovations. *Management Science, 132*, 1422–1433.

Dickerson, M. D., & Gentry, J. W. (1983). Characteristics of adopters and non-adopters of home computers. *Journal of Consumer Research, 10*, 225–235.

Dibean, W., & Garrison, B. (1999, October). Online newspaper market size and use of World Wide Web technologies. Paper presented to the Media in Transition Conference, Massachusetts Institute of technology, Cambridge.

Digital Millennium Copyright Act. (2000). (.pdf 318 KB).

DiMaggio, P. J., & Powell, W. W. (1983). The iron cage revisited: Institutional isomorphism and collective rationality in organizational fields. *American Sociological Review, 48*, 147–160.

Disminkes v. Department of the Interior, 603 F. Supp. 760 (D.D.C. 1984).

Dorf, P. (1995). High-tech firms launching clients into cyberspace. *Public Relations Journal, 51*(1), 28–31.

Downs, G. W., & Mohr, L. B. (1976). Conceptual issues in the study of innovation. *Administrative Science Quarterly, 21*, 700–714.

Ducey, R.V. (1996). *Multimedia broadcasting and the Internet.* In Proceedings of The Inet '96 Conference, Montreal, Canada , June, 1996. Internet Society.

Dunne, S. (2001, July 16). Nobody rules OK? *The Guardian*, 50.

Dupagne, M. (1999). Exploring the characteristics of potential high-definition television adopters. *The Journal of Media Economics, 12*, 35–50.

Dusseldorp, M. (1998). The future of the printed press: Challenges in a digital world. Maastricht, The Netherlands: European Journalism Center.

Dutton, W. H. (1996). Network rules of order: Regulating speech in public electronic fora. *Media, Culture & Society, 18*, 269–290.

Dutton, W. H., Rogers, E. M., & Jun, S. H. (1987a). The diffusion and impacts of information technology in households. In *Oxford surveys in information technology* (Vol. 4, pp. 133–193). New York: Oxford University Press.

Dutton, W. H., Rogers, E. M., & Jun, S. H. (1987b). Diffusion and social impacts of personal computers. *Communication Research, 14*, 219–250.

Editor & Publisher. (1998). *Editor & Publisher International Yearbook 1998.* New York: Author.

Edwardson, M., Kent, K., & McConnell, M. (1985). Television news information gain: Videotex versus talking head. *Journal of Broadcasting & Electronic Media, 29*, 367–378.

Elderkin, K. (1996). *The future of newspaper industry: How electronic newspapers will outrun their competition.* Bloomington, IN: Elderkin Associates.

Elliott, C. W. (1999). The Asian online newspaper: A media richness evaluation. *Media Asia, 26*(3), 123–131.

Elliott, W. R., & Quattelbaum, C. P. (1979). Similarities in patterns of media use: A cluster analysis of media gratifications. *Western Journal of Speech Communication, 43*, 61–72.

Endres, F. F. (1985). Daily newspaper utilization of computer data bases. *Newspaper Research Journal, 7*(1), 29–35.

Endres, K. L. (1998, August). *Zine but not heard? Editors talk about publishing online.* Paper presented to the Magazine Division of the Association for Education in Journalism and Mass Communication, Boston.

Erlindson, M. (Ed.). (1995). *Online newspapers: The newspaper industry's dive into cyberspace.*

Ettema, J. S. (1984). Three phases in the creation of information inequities: An empirical assessment of a prototype videotex system. *Journal of Broadcasting & Electronic Media, 30*, 325–329.

European Commission (1995). Admedia Project report: The future of media and advertising . Brussels: Author..

European Commission (1997). *Information market observatory (IMO) European information trends, 1996.* Luxemburg: The Policy Studies Institute.

European Parliament and Council (2000). *Directive on certain legal aspects of electronic commerce in the Internet market* [2000/31/EC]. Brussels: Author.

Evans, C. (2002). *Copyright and wrongs. Sp!ked-IT.* Available at: http://www.spiked-online.com/articles/00000002D415.htm

Evans, J. (1998a). *Government on the Net.* Berkeley, CA: Nolo Press

Evans, J. (1998b, October 22). Losing $21.5 million: As easy as ABCNews.com. *The Industry Standard.*

Fang, I. (1997). *A history of mass communication: Six information revolutions.* Oxford, England: Focal Press.

Felder, F., & Counts, T. (1981). Variations in attribution affect readers' evaluations of stories. *Newspaper Research Journal, 2*, 25–34.

Ferrara, K., Brunner, H., & Whittemore, G. (1991). Interactive written discourse as an emergent register. *Written Communication, 8*(1), 8–34.

Fico, F., Heeter, C., Soffin, S., & Stanley, C. (1987). New wave gatekeeping: Electronic indexing effects on newspaper reading. *Communication Research, 4*, 335–351.

Fico, F., Ku, L., & Soffin, S. (1994). Fairness and balance of newspaper coverage of US in the Gulf War. *Newspaper Research Journal, 15*(1), 30–43.

Fidler, R. (1994). Newspapers in the electronic age. In F. Williams & J. V. Pavlik (Eds.), *The people's right to know: Media, democracy, and the information highway* (pp. 25–45). Northvale, NJ: Lawrence Erlbaum Associates.

Fidler, R. (1997). *Mediamorphosis: Understanding new media.* Newbury Park, CA: Pine Forge Press.

Financial Times. (1995, December 12). *Paper dinosaurs refuse to fold,* 48.

Findahl, O., & Hoijer, B. (1981). Media content and human comprehension. In K. E. Rosengren (Ed.), *Advances in content analysis* (pp. 111–132). Beverly Hills, CA: Sage.

Finnegan, R. H. (1988), *Literacy and orality: Studies in the technology of communication.* Oxford, England: Blackwell.

Flanagin, A. J. (2000). Social pressures on organizational Website adoption. *Human Communication Research, 26*(4), 618–646.

Flanagin, A. J., & Metzger, M. J. (2000). Perceptions of Internet information credibility. *Journalism & Mass Communication Quarterly, 77*(3), 515–540.

Foo, Y. P., Tham, N. I., & Hao, X. (1999). Trends in online newspapers: A look at the U.S. Web. *Newspaper Research Journal, 20*, 52–63.

Forsham v. Harris, 44 U.S.C. sec.330 (1980).

Fredin, E. S. (1997). Rethinking the news story for the Internet: Hyperstory prototypes and a model of the user. *Journalism Monographs, 163.*

Fredin, E. S., & David, P. (1998). Browsing and the hypermedia interaction cycle: A model of self-efficacy and goal dynamics. *Journalism & Mass Communication Quarterly, 75*(1), 35–54.

Freeman, J., Lessiter, J., & Ijsselsteijn, W. (2001). Immersive television. *The Psychologist, 14*(4), 190–194.

Friedland, L. A., & Webb, S. (1996). Incorporating online publishing into the curriculum. *Journalism & Mass Communication Educator, 51*, 54–65.

Fulton, K. (1996, March/April). Tour of our uncertain future [Online]. *The Columbia Journalism Review,* 19–26. Available at: http://www.journalism.now

Galaskicwicz, J.,& Wasserman, S. (1989). Mimetic processes within an interoganizational field: An empirical text. *Administrative Science Quarterly, 34*, 454–479.

Gandy, O. (1993). *The panoptic sort: A political economy of personal information.* Boulder, CO: Westview Press.

Garneau, G. (1994, April 30). Newspapers at the crossroads. *Editor & Publisher,* 11–12.

Garramone, G., Harris, A., & Andersen, R. (1986). Uses of political bulletin boards. *Journal of Broadcasting & Electronic Media, 30*, 325–339.

Garrison, B. (1992). *Professional news reporting.* Hillsdale, NJ: Lawrence Erlbaum Associates.

Garrison, B. (1995). Online services as reporting tools; Daily newspaper use of commercial databases in 1994. *Newspaper Research Journal, 16*(4), 74–86.

Garrison, B. (1996). *Successful strategies for computer-assisted reporting.* Mahwah, NJ: Lawrence Erlbaum Associates.

Garrison, B. (1997a, August). *Online Newsgathering Trends 1994–96.* Paper presented at the meeting of the Association of Educations in Journalism and Mass Communication, Chicago.

Garrison, B. (1998a). *Caught in the Web: Newspaper use of the Internet and other online resources.* Baltimore, MD: Association of Education in Journalism and Mass Communication—Newspaper Division.

Garrison, B. (1998c). *Computer-assisted reporting* (2nd ed.). Mahwah, NJ: Lawrence Erlbaum Associates.

Garrison, B. (1998d). Judging Web site content not always simple. *College Media Review, 36*(1), 29, 31.

Garrison, B. (1999a, August) *Journalists' perceptions of online information gathering problems.* Paper presented to the Newspaper Division, Association for Education in Journalism and Mass Communication, New Orleans.

Garrison, B. (1999b, March). *Online information use in newsrooms.* Paper presented to the Creativity and Consumption Conference, University of Luton, England.

Garrison, B. (1999c, August). *The role of computers in newsgathering.* Paper presented to the Mass Communication and Society Division, Association for Education in Journalism and Mass Communication, New Orleans.

Garrison, B. (2000). Diffusion of a new technology: On-line research in newspaper newsrooms. *Convergence: The Journal of Research into New Media Technologies, 6*(1), 84–105.

Geier, T. (1995, November 20). Tracking the news in cyberspace. *U.S. News & World Report, 119*(20), 106.

George, C. (1997). The Internet and the future of print journalism. Management Information Systems Class Project, George Mason University, Washington, DC. Available at: http://mason.gmu.edu/~corr/papers/news2.htm

Ghose, S., & Dou, W. (1999). Interactive functions and their impact on the appeal of Internet presence sites. *Journal of Advertising Research, 38*, 29–43.

Gilder, G. (1990). *Life after television.* Knoxville, TN: Whittle Direct Books.

Gilder, G. F. (1994). Fidler's electronic news panel is a better bet for the future than homeshopping. *ASNE Bulletin, 10*, 4–8.

Gilhooly, M. (1998). *The law of defamation in Australia and New Zealand.* Liechardt, New South Wales: Federation Press.

Giussani, B. (1997, April 2). A new media tells different stories. *First Monday* [Peer reviewed journal on the Internet]. Available at: firstmonday.com

Glasser, W. (1986). *Control theory in the classroom.* New York: Harper & Row.

Glossbrenner, J. A., & Glossbrenner, E. (1998). *Search engines for the World Wide Web.* Berkeley, CA: Peachpit Press.

Glossbrenner, J. A., & Glossbrenner, E. (1999). *Search engines for the World Wide Web* (2nd ed.). Berkeley, CA: Peachpit Press.

Godfrey, L. v. Demon Internet Ltd. (1999). Royal Courts of Justice, Strand, London, Case No. 1998-G-No 30, March 26.

Godley, S. (2001, July 26). Leaping from free to fee. *The Daily Telegraph*, 2.

Gold, S. (2001, March 22). End of the anonymous net. *The Guardian Online*, 7.

Goldsmith, J. L. (1998). The Internet and the abiding significance of territorial sovereignty. *Indiana Journal of Global Legal Studies, 5*(2). Available at: www.law.indiana.edu/glsj.vol5/no2/6golds.html

Gordon, A. C. (1995). Journalism and the Internet. *Media Studies Journal, 9*, 173.

Gozenbach, J., & Stephenson, L. (1994). Children with AIDS attending public school: An analysis of the spiral of silence. *Political Communication, 11*, 3–18.

Grant, D. (2002). Defamation and the Internet: Principles for a unified Australian (and world) online defamation law. *Journalism Studies, 3*(1), 115–132.

Greenberg, B. S. (1966). Media use and believability: Some multiple correlates. *Journalism Quarterly, 43*, 665–671.

Greenberg, B. S., & Lin C. (1987). *Patterns of teletext use in the UK.* London: John Libbey.

Greenberg, B. S., & Lin C. (1988). *Patterns of teletext use in the UK.* London: John Libbey.

Greenfield Online (1999). *Surfing seniors.* Greenfield Online, Inc. [Internet]. Available at: http://beta.greenfield.com

Grenier, G. (1998). Creating wiley interscience: Moving From ink molecules to computer bits. *The Journal Of Electronic Publishing, 3*. Available at: http://www.press.umich.edu/jep/03-04/grenier.html

Griffin, J. L., & Stevenson, R. L. (1992). Influence of text and graphics in increasing understanding of foreign news content. *Newspaper Research Journal, 13*, 84–99.

Griffin, J. L., & Stevenson, R. L. (1994). The effectiveness of locator maps in increasing reader understanding of the geography of foreign news. *Journalism Quarterly, 71*, 937–946.

Grodsky, J. A. (1988). The Freedom of Information Act in an electronic age. In *Informing the Nation: Federal Information Dissemination in an Electronic Age.* U.S. Congress, Office of Technology assessment, Washington, DC: U.S. Government Printing Office.

Grossman, L. K. (1996). *The electronic republic: Reshaping democracy in the information age.* New York: Penguin.

Grundner, T. (1991, September/October). Free-nets: Networking meets middle America. *Link Letter.*

Gubman, J., & Greer, J. (1997, August). An analysis of online sites produced by U.S. newspapers: Are the critics right. Paper presented at the Newspaper Division, Association for Education in Journalism & Mass Communication, Chicago, IL.

Guenther, N. W. (1998). Good samaritan to the rescue: America online free from publisher and distributor liability for anonymously posted defamation. *Communications and the Law, 20*(2), 35–95.

Gunter, B. (2000). *Media research methods.* London: Sage Publications.

Gunther, A. (1988). Attitude extremity and trust in media. *Journalism Quarterly, 65,* 279–287.

Gunther, M. (1995, November). News you can choose. *American Journalism Review,* 34–38.

Gurak, L. (1994). *The rhetorical dynamics of a community protest in cyberspace: The case of Lotus marketplace.* Unpublished doctoral dissertation, Rensselaer Polytechnic Institute, Troy, NY.

Gyles, B. (1997, February). Bowing to audience requests: Jostling media present multiplying methods for counting users. *Presstime,* 9–10.

Ha, L., & James, E. L. (1998) Interactivity reexamined: A baseline analysis of early business Web sites. *Journal of Broadcasting & Electronic Media, 42*(4), 457–474.

Halloran, J. D. (1965). *The effects of mass communication.* Leicester: Leicester University Press.

Hanson, C. (1997, May/June). The dark side of online scoops. *Columbia Journalism Review.* Available at: http://www.cjr.org/year/97/3/scoops.asp

Harnad, S. (1991). Post-Gutenberg galaxy: The fourth revolution in the means of production of knowledge. *Public-Access Computer Systems Review, 29*(1), 39–53.

Hastie, R. (1984). Causes and effects of causal attribution. *Journal of Personality and Social Psychology, 46,* 44–56.

Havelock, E. A. (1986). *The muse learns to write: Reflections of orality and literacy from antiquity to the present.* New Haven, CT: Yale University Press.

Hayes, D. (2002, April 29). We're going all digital. *The Guardian New Media,* 38–39.

Heeter, C. (1989). Implications of new interactive technologies for conceptualizing communication. In J. L. Salvaggio & J. Bryant (Eds.), *Media use in the information age: Emerging patterns of adoption and consumer use* (pp. 217–235). Hillsdale, NJ: Lawrence Erlbaum Associates.

Heikinnen, K., & Reese, S. D. (1986). Newspaper readers and a new information medium. *Communication Research, 13,* 19–36.

Henderson, B., & Fernback, J. (1998). The campus press: A practical approach to on-line newspapers. In D. L. Borden & K. Harvey (Eds.), *The electronic grapevine: Rumor, reputation and reporting in the new online environment* (pp. 113–141). Mahwah, NJ: Lawrence Erlbaum Associates.

Hetland, P. (1999, November). The Internet in Norway: Dissemination and use. *Nordicom Review, 20,* 33–44.

Hiebert, R. E., & Gibbons, S. J. (2000). *Exploring mass media for a changing world.* Mahwah, NJ: Lawrence Erlbaum Associates.

Hilgemere, M. (1996). *Internet growth* [Online]. Available at: http://www.is-bremen.de/~mhi/inetgrow.html

Hiltz, S. R., & Turoff, M. (1978). *The network nation.* Reading, MA: Addison-Wesley.

Hock, R. (1999). *The extreme searcher's Guide to Web search strategies.* Medford, NJ: CyberAge Books.

Hoffman, D., & Novak, P. (1996). Marketing in hypermedia computer-mediated environments: Conceptual foundations. *Journal of Marketing, 60,* 50–68.

Hoffman, D. L., & Novak, T. P. (1995, June). Business scenarios for the Web: Opportunities and challenges. *Journal of Computer-Mediated Communication* [Online], *1*(3). Available: http://www.usc.edu/dept/annenberg/vol1/issue3/vol1no3.html

Hoogeveen, M. (1997). Towards a theory of the effectiveness of multimedia systems. *International Journal of Human and Computer Interaction, 9,* 151–168.

Hovland, C. I., Lumsdaine, A. A., & Sheffield, F. D. (1949). *Experiments in mass communication.* Princeton: Princeton University Press.

Huizer, E. (1997). *Internet domain survey January, 1997.* Available at: http://www.sex.nl/persons/huizer/Internetgrowth.html

Hutchin's Commission on Freedom of the Press (1947). *A free and responsible press.* Chicago: University of Chicago Press.

Hutton, N. (1997, April). *Electronic newspapers and magazines.* Seminar paper presented at Computer Aided Research and Reporting Course Lecture, Rhodes University, Grahamstown, South Africa.

The Internet Advertising Bureau. (2000). *Internet advertising revenues* [Online]. New York: Author. Available at: www.iab.net..

The Internet Advertising Bureau. (1985). *Attitudes to broadcasting.* London: Author.

Independent Television Commission. (1998). *Television: The public's view—1997.* London: Author.

Independent Television Commission. (1998). *Television: The public's view—1998.* London: Author..

Independent Television Commission. (1998). *Television: The public's view—1999.* London: Author.

Iran-Nejad, A. (1987). Cognitive and affective causes of interest and liking. *Journal of Educational Psychology, 79,* 120–130.

Irish, G. (1997, February). *Interactive newspapers.* Paper presented at the Editor & Publisher Interactive Newspapers '97 Conference in Houston, TX.

Izard, R. S., Culbertson, H. M., & Lambert, D. A. (1994). *Fundamentals of news reporting* (6th ed.). Dubuque, IA: Kendall/Hunt.

Jacobson, T., & Ullman, J. (1989). Commercial databases and reporting: Opinions of newspaper journalists and librarians. *Newspaper Research Journal, 10,* 16.

James, M. L., Wotring, C. E., & Forrest, E. J. (1995). An exploratory study of the perceived benefits of electronic bulletin board use and their impact on other communication activities. *Journal of Broadcasting & Electronic Media, 39,* 30–50.

Jankowski, N.W., & Hanssen, L. (1996). Introduction: Multimedia come of age. In N. W. Jankowski & L. Hanssen (Eds.), *The contours of multimedia: Recent technological, theoretical and empirical development* (pp. 1–21). Luton, England: University of Luton Press.

Jeffres, L., & Atkin, D. (1996). Predicting use of technologies for communication and consumer needs. *Journal of Broadcasting & Electronic Media, 40,* 318–330.

Jenner v. Sun Oil Co. Ltd. (1952). 2 DLR 526 at 526.

Johansen, R., Valle, J., & Spangler, K. (1979). *Electronic meetings: Technical alternatives and social choices.* Reading, MA: Addison-Wesley.

Johnson, T. J., & Kaye, B. K. (1998). Cruising is believing? Comparing Internet and traditional sources on media credibility measures. *Journalism Mass Communication Quarterly, 79,* 325–340.

Jones, B. (1991). Cultural effects of integrated media dissolving the frame: Artist, author and authority. *Leonardo, 24*(2),153–158.

Jones, R. A. (1994). The ethics of research in cyberspace. *Internet Research, 4,* 30–35.

Juliussen, E., & Petska-Juliussen, K. (1999). *The Internet industry almanac.* Glenbrook, NV: Computer Industry Almanac.

Jupiter Communications. (1999). Digital news: Revenue strategies, consumer usage, case studies. Available at : http://www.jup.com/research/

Jurdi, N. A. (1995). Information superhighway and the process of communication. *Arab Journal of Communication, 13,* 392–405.

Kamerer, D., & Bressers, B. (1998, August). *Online newspapers: A trend study of news content and technical features.* Paper presented at the Association for Education in Journalism & Mass Communication, Baltimore, MD.

Katz, E., Blumler, J. G., & Gurevitch, M. (1974). Utilization of mass communication by the individual. In J. G. Blumler & E. Katz (Eds.), *The uses of mass communications: Current perspectives on gratifications research* (pp. 19–32). Beverly Hills, CA: Sage.

Katz, E., Gurevitch, M., & Haas, H. (1973). On the use of the mass media for important things. *American Sociological Review, 38,* 164–181.

Katz, E., & Lazarsfeld, P. F. (1955). *Personal influence.* Glencoe, IL: Free Press.

Katz, J. (1994). Online or not, newspapers suck. *Wired, 9,* 50–58.

Katz, J. (1999). The future is the Net. *Media Studies Journal, 13*(2), 14–15.

Kaye, B. K., & Medoff, N. J. (1999). *The World Wide Web: A mass communication perspective.* Mountain View, CA: Mayfield Publishing.

Keeton, W. P., Dobbs, D. B., Keeton, R. E., & Owen, D. G. (1984). *Prosser and KEeton on tort* (5th ed.). St. Paul, MN: West Publishing Co.

Kehoe, C., Pitkow, J., & Moron, K. (1997). *Graphic visualization and usability center's 8th WWW user survey.* Available at: http://www.gvu.gatech.edu/user_surveys/survey-1997-10/.#exec

Kennedy, D. (2001a, November 14). Internet at the center of Loutchansky appeal. *The Times e-services.* Available at: http://www.thetimes.co.uk/article/0,,706-2001395202,00.html

Kennedy, D. (2001b, December 6). Victory for Times after libel judge's blunder. *The Times,* 6.

Kerr, J., & Niebauer, W. E., Jr. (1986). *A base-line study on the use of outside databases, full text retrieval systems by newspaper editorial page writers.* Paper presented at the annual meeting of the Association for Education in Journalism and Mass Communication, Norman, OK.

Khoo, D., & Gopal, R. (1996). Implications of the Internet on print and electronic media. *Journal of Development Communication, 1,* 21–33.

Kiernan, V., & Levy, M. R. (1999). Competition among broadcast-related web sites. *Journal of Broadcasting & Electronic Media, 43*(2), 271–279.

Kiesler, A. (Ed.). (1997). *Culture of the Internet.* Mahwah, NJ: Lawrence Erlbaum Associates.

Kiesler, S., Siegel, J., & McGuire, T. W. (1984). Social psychological aspects of computer-mediated communication. *American Psychologist, 39,* 1123–1134.

Kimberly, J. R., & Evanisko, M. J. (1981). Organizational innovation: The influence of individual, organizational, and contextual factors on hospital adoption of technological and administrative innovations. *Academy of Management Journal, 24,* 689–713.

Kincaid, D. L. (1979). *The convergence model of communication.* (East-West Institute Paper No. 18.) Honolulu: University of Hawaii.

King, W. R., & Grover, B. (1991). The strategic use of information resources: An exploratory study. *IEEE Transactions on Engineering Management, 38,* 293–305.

Klapper, J. (1960). *The effects of mass communication.* New York: Free Press.

Koch, T. (1996). *The medium is the message: Online all the time for everyone.* Westport, CT: Prager.

Koelman. K., & Hugenholtz, B. (1999, November). *Workshop on service provider liability,* .pdf 221 KB.

Kohl, U. (2000). Defamation on the Internet: A duty free zone after all? Macquarie Bank Limited & Anor v Berg. *Sydney Law Review, 22*(4). Available at: pandora.nla.gov.au/parchive/2000/Z2000-Dec-20/www.law.usyd. edu.au/_slr/v22/nl/Internet.pdf

Kovacs, D. K. (1995). *The Internet trainer's guide.* New York: Van Nostrand Reinhold.

Kraut, R., Patterson, M., Lundmark, V., Kiesler, S., Mukopadhyay, T., & Scxherlis, W. (1998). Internet paradox: A social technology that reduces social involvement and psychological well-being? *American Psychologist, 53*(9), 1017–1031.

Krol, E. (1993). *The whole Internet user's guide and catalog.* Sebastopol, CA: O'Reilly & Associates.

Krugman, D. (1985). Evaluating the audiences of the new media. *Journal of Advertising, 14*(4), 14–19.

Kwan, P. (1996). *Telecommunications and the future of newspapers.* London: School of Printing & Publishing, the London Institute. Available at: http://twinpentium.lcp.linst.ac.uk/default.htm

Lacy, S. (1987). The effects of intracity competition on daily newspaper content. *Journalism Quarterly, 64,* 281–290.

Lacy, S. (1992). The financial commitment approach to news media competition. *Journal of Media Economics, 5*(2), 5–22.

Lancaster, F. W. (1995). The evolution of electronic publishing. *Library Trends, 4,* 519–527.

Landau, G. (1994, June). *Cleaning dirty data.* Paper presented at Investigative Reporters and Editors, St. Louis, ,MO.

Lang, A. (2000). The limited capacity model of mediated message processing. *Journal of Communication, 50,* 46–70.

Lang, K., & Lang, G. E. (1959). The mass media and voting. In E. J. Burdick & A. J. Brodbeck (Eds.), *American voting behavior.* New York: Free Press.

Lapham, C. (1995, July 1). The evolution of the newspaper of the future. *Journal of Computer-Mediated Communication, 7,* 7.

Lasica, J. D. (1996, November). Net gain. *American Journalism Review, 18,* 20–33.

Lasica, J. D. (1997, June). Time to freshen up online newspapers. *American Journalism Review Newslink.* Available at: http://www.newslink.org/ajrlasica697.html

Lasica, J. D. (1997c). When push comes to news. *American Journalism Review, 21,* 18–27. Available at: www.ajr.com

Lasica, J. D. (1998). Get it fast, but get it right. *American Journalism Review, Newslink.* Available at: http://www.newslink.org/ajrlasica697.html

Lasswell, H. D. (1927). *Propaganda technique in the world war.* New York: Knopf.

Lawrence, D. J. (1993). Why future is promising for newspaper industry. *Newspaper Research Journal, 14*(2), 11–17.

Lawson, R. (1996, November). Exploring the anorak myth. *Digital Publishing Strategies,* 5.

Lazarsfeld, P. F., Berelson, B., & Gaudet, H. (1944). *The people' choice.* New York: Duell, Sloan, & Pearce.

Lazarus, D. (1997, January 8). Microsoft goes head-to-head with dailies. *Wired News.* Available at: http://www.wired.com/news/business/story/1372html

Leahy, P. (1991). Electronic Freedom of Information Act of 1991, 102nd Congress, Session 1.

Lea, M., & Spears, R. (1991). Computer-mediated communication, de-individuation, and group decision making. In S. Greenberg (Ed.), *Computer-supported cooperative work and groupware, people and computers* (pp. 155–173). London: Academic Press.

LeBoeuf, R. A., & Matre, M. (1977). How different readers perceive magazine stories and characters. *Journalism Quarterly, 54,* 50–57.

Ledbetter, J. (2000, January/February). Wanted: A way of counting that you can count on. *Columbia Journalism Review* [Internet]. Available at: http://www.cjr.org/year/00-1/ledbetter.asp

Leigh, J. H. (1991). Information processing differences among broadcast media: Review and suggestions for research. *Journal of Advertising, 20,* 71–75.

Leung, L., & Wei, R. (2000). More than just talk on the move: Uses and gratifications of the cellular phone. *Journalism & Mass Communication Quarterly, 77*(2), 308–320.

Lewenstein, F. V. (1995). Do public electronic bulletin boards help create scientific knowledge? The cold fusion case. *Science, Technology & Human Values, 20,* 123–149.

Li, X. (1998). Web page design and graphic use of three U.S. newspapers. *Journalism & Mass Communication Quarterly, 75*(2), 353–365.

Lichtenstein, A., & Rosenfeld, L. B. (1983). Uses and misuses of gratifications research: An explication of media functions. *Communication Research, 10,* 97–109.

Lichtenstein, A., & Rosenfeld, L. B. (1984). Normative expectations and individual decision concerning media gratifications choices. *Communication Research, 11,* 393–413.

Liebman, H. (1993, September 27). About time for on-line. *Media Week, 32,* 36–37.

Lin, C. A. (1994a). Audience fragmentation in a competitive video marketplace. *Journal of Advertising Research, 34*(6), 1–17.

Lin, C. A. (1994b). Exploring potential factors for home videotext adoption. In J. Hanson (Ed.), *Advances in telematics* (Vol. 2, pp. 111–121). New York: Ablex.

Lin, C. A. (1998). Exploring the personal computer adoption dynamics. *Journal of Broadcasting & Electronic Media, 41*(1), 95–112.

Lin, C. A., & Jeffries, L. W. (1998). Factors influencing the adoption of multimedia cable technology. *Journalism & Mass Communication Quarterly, 75,* 341–352.

Lindoo, E. C. (1998). *The future of newspapers: A study of the World Wide Web and its relationship to electronic publishing of newspapers.* Unpublished doctoral dissertation, School of Computer and Information at Nova Southeastern University, Fort Lauderdale, FL.

Lindsay, D. (2000). *Liability for the publication of defamatory material via the Internet* [Research paper No.10]. Melbourne Center for Media, Communications and Information Technology Law, University of Melbourne.

Litman, B. L., & Bridges, J. (1986). An economic analysis of daily newspaper performance. *Newspaper Research Journal, 7,* 9–26.

Liu J. (1996). *The impact of new media on journalism: Journalism in cyberspace* [Online]. Available at: http://www.swin.edu.au/sbs/subjects/mlf/am209/victor/!nine.html

Lloyd, C. (1996, January 7). Mission control keeps data flowing. *The Sunday Times,* Innovation Section, 2.

Long v. Internal Revenue Service, 596 F. 2d 362 (9th Cir., 1979).

Long, E. V. (1994, January). To our readers. *Time.*

Luge, T. (1999). *Usage patterns and information needs of journalists on the Internet: An empirical study at USUA—the usually useful Internet guide for journalists.* Master's thesis, Institute for Communication Sciences, University of Munich.

MacArthur, B. (1998, March 6). Newspapers not yet a dying breed. *The Times,* Media Section, 3.

Macquarie Bank Limited & Anor v. *Berg* (1999). New South Wales Supreme Court, NSWSC 526. Available at: www.austlii.edu.au/au/cases/nsw/supreme_ct/1999/526.rtf

Maddox, K. (1998). Survey shows increase in online usage, shopping. *Advertising Age, 69*(43), S6, S34.

Maddox, L. M., Darshn, M., & Dubek, H. G. (1997). The role and effect of Web addresses in advertising. *Journal of Advertising Research, 37,* 47–59.

Maier, S. R. (1999, May). *Digital diffusion in the newsroom: The slow embrace of computer-assisted reporting.* Paper presented to the Communication and Technology Division, International Communication Association, San Francisco, CA.

Maier, S. R. (2000). Digital diffusion in newsrooms: The uneven advance of computer-assisted reporting. *Newspaper Research Journal, 21,* 95–110.

Mancini, P. (1994). The ligitimacy gap: A problem of mass media research in Europe and the United States. In M. Levy & M. Gurevitch (Eds.), *Defining media studies: Reflections on the future of the field.* Beverly Hills: Sage.

Mannes, G. (1995, November). The new news "paper": Electronic editions of newspapers. *Popular Mechanics, 172*(11), 66.

March, J. G., & Simon, H. A. (1958). *Organizations.* New York: Wiley.

Marlatt, A. (1999). Advice to newspapers: Stop the shoveling. *Internet World,* online edition. Available at: http://www.iw.com/print/current/content/19990715shoveling.html

Martin, S. E. (1998). How news gets from paper to its online counterpart. *Newspaper Research Journal, 19,* 64–73.

Martinson, J. (2000, May 3). U.S. courts free Internet firms from libel laws. *The Guardian,* 9.

Massey, B. L. (2000). Market-based predictors of interactivity at Southeast Asian online newspapers. *Internet Research: Electronic Networking Applications and Policy, 10*(3), 227–237.

Massey, B.L., & Levy, M. R. (1998). Interactivity, online journalism, and English-language Web newspapers in Asia. *Journalism & Mass Communication Quarterly 67,* 138–151.

Massey, B. L., & Levy, M. R. (1999). Interactive online journalism at English-language Web newspapers in Asia: A dependency theory analysis. *Gazette, 61*(6), 523–538.

Massey, S. W. (1996). *Cyberjournalism: A look at the future of newspapers and print education.* Newspaper Division, Association of Education in Journalism and Mass Communication.

McAdams, M. (1995b). *The sad story of videotext* [Online]. Available at: http://www.well.com/user/mmcadams/videotext.html

McChesney, R. (1999). *Rich media, poor democracy: Communication politics in dubious times.* Urbana, IL: University of Illinois Press.

McCombs, M. E., & Shaw, D. C. (1972). The agenda setting function of the press. *Public Opinion Quarterly, 18,* 239–244.

McCoy, M. E. (2001). Dark alliance: News repair and institutional authority in the age of the Internet. *Journal of Communication, 51*(1), 164–193.

McDermott, K., & Fay, J. (1997). *Multimedia planning information for Europe.* Mag-Pie: Multimedia Action Groups—Planning Information For Europe.

McGuire, M., Stilborne, L., McAdams, M., & Hyatt, L. (1997). *The Internet handbook for writers, researchers and journalists.* Toronto, Canada: Trifolium Books.

McLuhan, M., & Powers, B. R. (1989). *The global village: Transformations in world life and media in the 21st Century.* New York: Oxford University Press.

McMillan, S. (1998). Who pays for content? Funding in interactive media. *Journal of Computer-Mediated Communication, 4*(1), 16–23.

McMillan, S. (2000). Moving target: The challenge of applying content analysis to the World Wide Web. *Journalism & Mass Communication Quarterly, 77*(1), 80–98.

McMillan, S. J. (2001). Moving target: The challenge of applying content analysis to the World Wide Web. *Journalism & Mass Communication Quarterly, 77*(1), 80–98.

McNamara, J. B. (1998). Legal issues on the Internet: An analysis and comparison of law and policy relating to the use and regulation of the Internet in Great Britain and Australia. *Dickinson Journal of International Law, 17*(159). Available at: www.chinalawinfo.com/fljy/flkc/first_amendment/22htm

McQuail, D. (1997). *Audience analysis.* Thousand Oaks, CA: Sage.

Medphone Corp v. *Denigris,* No. 92-CV-3785 (D. N. J. filed Sept.11, 1992).

Medsger, B. (1996). Winds of change: Challenges confronting journalism education. Available at: http://www.freedomforum.org/freedomforum/resources/journalism/

Mencher, M. (1994). *News reporting and writing* (8th ed.). Madison, WI: Brown & Benchmark Publishers.

Mencher, M. (1997). *News reporting and writing* (7th ed.). Madison, WI: Brown & Benchmark Publishers.

Mensing, D. (1998, August). *The economics of online newspapers.* A paper presented to the annual meeting of the Association of Education in Journalism and Mass Communication Newspaper Division, Baltimore, MD.

Mensing, D., Greer, J., Gubman, J., & Louis, S. (1998, August). *Measuring recall of linear and non-linear online news stories.* Paper presented at the meeting of the Association for Education in Journalism & Mass Communication, Baltimore, MD.

Meyer, E. (1998). *An unexpectedly wider Web for the world's newspapers* [Online]. Available at: www.njr.com

Meyer, E. (1999). The 10 myths of online publishing. *American Journalism Review, 21*(2).

Meyer, E. K. (1998). An unexpected wider Web for the world's newspapers. *American Journalism Review Newslink.* Available at: http://www.ajr.newslink.org/emcol10.html.org/July

Middlcbcrg, D., & Ross, S. (1997, July). *The media in cyberspace* [Online]. Available at: http://www.mediasurce.com/study/cont.htm

Middleberg, D., & Ross, S. (2000, June). *Media in cyberspace* [Online]. Available at: http://www.middleberg.com/sub_cyberspacestudy.html

Miller, L. C. (1998). *Power journalism: Computer-assisted reporting.* Fort Worth, TX: Harcourt Brace.

Miller, T. (1983, September). Information please and fast: Reporting's revolution: Data bases. *Washington Journalism Review,* 51–53.

Miller, T. (1984, April 28). The database as a reportorial resource. *Editor and Publisher,* 70–71, 104.

Mings, S. (1997a, July). The online newspaper pilot study. *CMC Magazine* [Online serial]. Available at http://www.december.com/cmc/mag/1997/ mingpilo.html

Mings, S. (1998). *Uses and gratifications of online newspapers: An audience-centered study.* Unpublished doctoral dissertation, Rensselaer Polytechnic Institute, Rensselaer, NY.

Moncrieff, M. (2002, April 8). No names ... unless the court decides otherwise. *The Guardian* [Media Guardian Section], 6–7.

Moon, J. L., Ferguson, M. A., & Tedder, M. C. (1999, August). The effects of three different computer texts on readers' recall. Paper presented at the meeting of the Association for Education in Journalism & Mass Communication, New Orleans, LA.

Morris, M., & Ogan, C. (1996). The Internet as mass medium. *Journal of Computer-Mediated Communication* [Online], *1*(4). Available at: http://www. cwis.usc.edu/dept/annenberg.vol1/issue4/vol1no.4.html

Mueller, J., &. Kamerer, D. (1995). Reader preference for electronic newspapers. *Newspaper Research Journal, 16,* 2–12.

Murray, D. E. (1991). The composing process for computer conversation. *Written Communication, 8*(1), 35–55.

NAA. (1997). Newspapers circulation vs. readership. *Newspapers Association of America.* Available at: http://www.naa.org/presstime/9901/images.gif

Nass, C., & Moon, Y. (2000). Machines and mindlessness: Social responses to computers. *Journal of Social Issues, 56*(1), 81–103.

Nass, C., & Steuer, J. (1993). Voices, boxers, and sources of messages: Computers and social actors. *Human Communication Research, 19,* 504–527.

Nass, C., Steuer, J., Henriksen, L., & Dryer, D. C. (1994). Machines, social attributions and ethics: Performance assessment of computers subsequent to "self" or "other" evaluation. *International Journal of Human Computer Studies, 40,* 543–559.

National Opinion Poll. (1997). *Internet surveys: One in twenty-five British households now linked to the Internet* [Online]. Available at: http://www.nopres. co.uk/surveys/Internetsurvey.htm

Negroponte, N. (1995). *Being digital.* London: Hodder & Stoughton.

Neuberger, C., Tonnemacher, J., Biebl, M., & Duck, A. (1998). Online—The future of newspapers? Germany's dailies on the World Wide Web. *Journal of Computer Mediated Communication, 4* [Online].

Neuendorf, K. A., Atkin, D., & Jeffries, L. W. (1998). Understanding adopters of audio information innovations. *Journal of Broadcasting & Electronic Media, 42,* 80–94

Neuman, J. (1995). *Lights, camera, war.* New York: St. Martin's Press.

Neuman, R. W., Just, M. R., & Crigler, A. N. (1992). *Common knowledge: News and the construction of political meaning.* Chicago, IL: University of Chicago Press.

Newhagen, J. E., Cordes, J. W., & Levy, M. R. (1995). Nightly@nbc.com: Audience scope and the perception of interactivity in viewer mail on the Internet. *Journal of Communication, 45*(3), 164–175.

Newhagen, J. E., & Levy, M. R. (1998). The future of journalism in a distributed communication architecture. In D. L. Borden & K. Harvey (Eds.), *The electronic grapevine: Rumor, reputation, and reporting in the new online environment* (pp. 9–21). Mahwah, NJ: Lawrence Erlbaum Associates.

Newhagen, J. E., & Nass, C. (1989). Differential criteria for evaluating credibility of newspapers and TV news. *Journalism Quarterly, 66*(2), 277–284.

Newhagen, J., & Rafaeli, S. (1996). Why communication researchers should study the Internet. *Journal of Communication, 46*(1), 4–14.

New York Times v. Sullivan (1964). 376 US 254 at 2790280, 283.

Nicholas, D. (1996). An assessment of the online searching behavior of practitioner and users. *Journal of Documentation, 52*(3), 227–251.

Nicholas, D., Erbach, G., Pang, Y. W., & Paalman, K. (1988). *End-users of online information systems.* London: Mansell.

Nicholas, D., & Fenton, D. (1997, January/February). The Internet and the changing information environment. *Managing Information,* 30–33.

Nicholas, D., & Frossling, D. (1996). The information handler in the digital age. *Managing Information, 3*(7/8), 31–34.

Nicholas, D., Frossling, I., Martin, H., & Buesing, P. (1997). (Really) getting to grips with the Internet: What it has to offer in the way of newspapers. *Vine, 52*(3), 98–114.

Nicholas, D., Huntingdon, P., Lievesley, N., & Withey, R. (1999). Cracking the code: Web log analysis. *Online & CD-ROM Review, 23*(5), 263–269.

Nicholas, D., & Martin, H,. (1993). Should journalists search themselves? (And what happens when they do?) *Online Proceedings 93,* 227–234.

Nicholas, D., & Martin, H. (1997). Assessing information needs: A case study of journalists. *Aslib Proceedings, 49*(2), 43–52.

Nicholas, D., Williams, P., Cole, P., & Martin, H. (1998). Journalists—not true to type? *Library Association Record, 100*(2), 84–85.

Nicholas, D., Williams, P., Cole, P., & Martin, H. (1998). *The media and the Internet.* London: Aslib.

Nicholas, D., Williams, P., Cole, P., & Martin, H. (2000). The impact of the Internet on information seeking in the media. *Aslib Proceedings, 52*(3), 98–114.

Niebauer, W. E., Jr., Abbott, E. A., Corbin, L., & Neibergall, J. (1999). *Computer adoption by Iowa newspapers—News/information flow management, production and business uses.* Unpublished paper, Iowa State University, Ames.

Niebauer, Jr., W. E., Abbott, E. A., Corbin, L., & Neibergall, J. (2000). Computer adoption levels of Iowa dailies and weeklies. *Newspaper Research Journal, 21,* 84–94.

Niekamp, R. (1996, August). *TV station sites on the World Wide Web.* Paper presented at the meeting of the Association for Education in Journalism & Mass Communication, Anaheim, CA.

Niekamp, R. (1997, August). *Television station Web sites: Interactivity in news stories.* Paper presented at the meeting of the Association for Education in Journalism & Mass Communication, Chicago, IL.

Nielsen Media Research (1996). *Internet demographics survey* [Online]. Available at: http://www.nielsenmedia.com/demo.htm. Nielsen media research.

Nielsen, J. (1998). *The end of legacy media* [Online]. Available at: http://www.useit.com/alertbox/980823.htm.

Noack, D. (1999). eBuy: Users of newspaper web sites open their cyberwallets. *Editor & Publisher, 132*(28), 18–21.

Noelle-Neuman, E. (1993). *The spiral of silence: Our social skin.* Chicago: Chicago University Press.

Noelle-Neuman, E. (1993). *The spiral of silence* (2nd ed.). Chicago: University of Chicago Press.

NPD Group. (1997, April 8). *NPD Survey—Market Survey.* Advertising Research Foundation Conference, New York.

NUA. (2000). *How many online-Internet surveys* [Online]. Available at: http://www.nua.ie/surveys/how_many_online/index.html

Office of Research (1999, August 16). *Study by Nielsen Media Research and CommerceNet.* Research memorandum. Washington, DC: International Broadcasting Bureau, U.S. Information Agency.

Orr, G. (1997). *The Internet and the future of print journalism : A project for management information systems class, Spring '97.* Project as part of the MBA program at George Mason University, Virginia.

Osborne, D. J., & Holton, D. (1988). Reading from screen versus paper: There is no difference. *International Journal of Man–Machine Studies, 28,* 1–9.

Outing, S. (1996, February). Hold on(line) tight. *Editor & Publisher,* 41–61.

Outing, S. (1998, February). Too many newspaper web sites get poor grades. *E & P Interactive.* Available at: http://www.mediainfo.com/@@cd08tbuahsdewaa/plwebcqi/fastweb?getdoc+archives+interactive+417+96++electronic%20newspapers.

Pailliart, I. (1989). France: Experimenting with pay TV and viewdata. In L. Becker & K. Schoenbach (Eds.), *Audience responses to media diversification: Coping with plenty* (pp. 159–166). Hillsdale, NJ: Lawrence Erlbaum Associates.

Paivio, A. (1986). *Mental representations: A dual-coding approach.* New York: Oxford University Press.

Pang, A. S. (1998). Hypertext, the next generation: A review and research agenda. *First Monday, 3* [Peer reviewed journal on the Internet]. Available at: http://firstmonday.dk/subjects/technical.html

Papacharissi, Z., & Rubin, A. M. (2000). Predictors of Internet use. *Journal of Broadcasting & Electronic Media, 44*(2), 175–196.

Parsons, P., & Johnson, R. B. (1996). Profnet: A computer-assisted bridge to academia. *Newspaper Research Journal, 17*(3/4), 29–38.

Paul, N. (1995, February). *Content: A re-visioning.* Paper presented to the conference on Interactive Newspapers '95. Available at: http://www.poynter.org/research/nm/nm_revision.html

Paul, N., & Williams, M. (1999). *Great scouts! Cyberguides for subject searching on the Web.* Medford, NJ: CyberAge Books.

Pavlik, J. (1999). New media and news: Implications for the future of journalism. *New Media & Society, 1*(1), 54–59.

Pavlik, J. V. (1994). Citizen access, involvement, and freedom of expression in an electronic environment. In F. Williams & J. V. Pavlik (Eds.), *The people's right to know: Media, democracy, and the information highway* (pp. 139–169). Hillsdale, NJ: Lawrence Erlbaum Associates, pp. 139–169.

Pavlik, J. V. (1996). *New media and the information superhighway.* Boston: Allyn & Bacon.

Pavlik, J. V. (2001). *Journalism and new media.* New York: Columbia University Press.

Pavlou, P. A., & Stewart, D. W. (2000). Measuring the effects and effectiveness of interactive advertising; A research agenda. *Journal of Interactive Advertising, 1*(1). Available at: http://jiad.org/vol1/no1/pavlou/index.html

Peng, F. Y., Tham, N. I., & Xiaoming, H. (1999). Trends in online newspapers: A look at the U.S. Web. *Newspaper Research Journal, 20,* 52–63.

Perritt, H. H. Jr. (1997). Jurisdiction in cyberspace: The role of intermediaries. In B Kahin & C. Nesson (Eds.), *Borders in cyberspace* (pp. 164–205). Boston, MA: MIT Press.

Perse, E. M., & Courtright, J. A. (1993). Normative images of communication media: Mass and interpersonal channels in the new media environment. *Human Communication Research, 19*, 485–503.

Perse, E. M., & Dunn, D. G. (1998). The utility of home computers and media use: implications of multimedia and connectivity. *Journal of Broadcasting & Electronic Media, 42*(4), 435–456.

Pew Research Center (1996, September). The 1996 Pew Research Center survey of Technology [Online]. Available at: http://www.people-press.org/index.htm

Pew Research Center (2000, January). *The Internet news audience goes ordinary* [Online]. Available at: http://www.people-press.org/tech98sum.htm

Pfaffenberger, B. (1996). *Web search strategies.* New York: MIS Press.

Phillips, C. (1998). Market overview. *Editor & Publisher,* Interactive Newspapers Conference '98, New York.

Phipps, J. C. (1999, July). Local is everything on newspaper Web sites. *Editor & Publisher Mediainfo.com, 23,* 26.

Phipps, J. L. (1998, November). Hackers: Can you stop them? *Mediainfo.com,* 4–8.

Phipps, J. L. (1999a, July). Local is everything on newspaper Web sites. *Editor & Publisher Mediainfo.com,* 23, 26.

Phipps, J. L. (1999b). Superfast Internet access will change reporting and broadcasting. *Editor & Publisher Mediainfo.com,* July, 28–34.

Pitkow, J., & Kehoe, C. (1996). *GVU* [Graphic Visualization and Usability] Center's 6th WWW user survey [Online]. Available at: http://www.cc/gatech.edu/gvu/user_survey/survey-10.1996/

Porter, L. V., Sallot, L. M., Cameron, G. T., & Shamp, S. (2001). New technologies and public relations: Exploring practitioners' use of online resources to earn a seat at the management table. *Journalism & Mass Communication Quarterly, 78*(1), 179–190.

Poster, M. (1995). *The second media age.* Cambridge, MA: Polity Press.

Potter, W. J., Cooper, R., & Dupagne, M. (1993). The three paradigms of mass media research in mainstream communication journals. *Communication Theory, 3*(4), 317–335.

Powell, A. C. III (2000). *Portable, high-tech reporting system: Journalism, anyone?* [Online]. Available at: http://www.freedomforum.org/technology/1999/7/29urbanjunglepack.asp

Powers, W. (1997, May 12). Raising Caen. *The New Republic,* 9–10.

Preece, J. (2000). *Online communities: Designing usability, supporting sociability.* Chichester, England: Wiley.

Priest, S., & Talbot, J. (1994). Mass media and the ultimate technological fix: Newspaper coverage of biotechnology. *Southwestern Mass Communication Journal, 10*(1), 76–85.

Protess, L. D., & McCombs, M. E. (Eds.). (1991). *Agenda setting: Readership on media, public opinion, and policy making.* Hillsdale, NJ: Lawrence Erlbaum Associates.

Public Citizen v. Occupational Safety and Health Administration, OSHA Civil Action No. 86-0705 (D.C. District Court 1986).

Rackiewicz, C. (1996). *Internet growth: Work displaces home as the driving force according to new INTECO research* [Online]. Available at: http://www.inteco.com/p~961205.html

Rademann, T. (1997). *Socio-cultural studies online: Employing Internet news services in higher education.* Prague, Czech Republic: Czech Technical University.

Rafaeli, S. (1986). The electronic bulletin board: A computer-driven mass medium. *Computers and the Social Sciences, 2,* 123–136.

Rafaeli, S. (1988). Interactivity: From new media to communication. In R. Hawkins (Ed.), *Advancing communication science: Merging mass and interpersonal process* (pp. 10–134). Newbury Park, CA: Sage.

Ramsey, S. A. (1993). Issues management and the use of technologies in public relations. *Public Relations Review, 19*(3), 261–275.

Randall, N. (1997, October 7). Who goes there? Seven inexpensive Web analysis tools can help you determine who's visiting your site. *PC Magazine, 8.*

Randle, Q. B. (1996, August). *The fair use of video clips in electronic publication on the World Wide Web.* Paper presented to the Annual Meeting of the Association of Education in Journalism and Mass Communication, Communication Technology& Policy Division, Baltimore, MD.

Reagan, J. (1987). Classifying adopters and nonadopters for technologies using political activity, media use and demographic variables. *Telematics and Informatics, 4,* 3–16.

Reagan, J. (1989). New technologies and news use: Adopters v. nonadopters. *Journalism Quarterly, 68,* 871–875, 887.

Reddick, R., & King, E. (1997). *The online journalist: Using the Internet and other electronic resources.* Fort Worth, TX: Harcourt Brace College Publishers.

Reeves, B., & Nass, C. (1996). *The media equation: How people treat computers, television and new media like real people and places.* Stanford, CA: CSCI Publications & Cambridge University Press.

Regan, J. (1989). New technologies and news use: Adopters v. non adopters. *Journalism Quarterly, 68,* 871–879, 887.

Regan, J. (1999, July 15). *Tools of the trade.* [OJR contributor, mobile reporting with the Palm VII].

Rheingold, H. (1943). *The virtual community: Homesteading on the electronic frontier.* Reading, MA: Addison-Wesley.

Riley, P., Keough, C. M., Christiansen, T., Meilich, O., & Pierson, J. (1998). Community or colony: The case of online newspapers and the Web. *Journal of Computer Mediated Communication, 4* [Online serial]. Available at: http://www.jcmc.huji.ac.il/vol4/issue1/keough.htm

Rimmer, T., & Weaver, D. (1987). Different questions, different answers? Media use and credibility. *Journalism Quarterly, 64,* 28–36.

Rindos v. Hardwick (1994). Supreme Court of Western Australia, No. 1994 of 1993. Available at: www.jmls.edu/cyber/cases/rindos.html

Roberts, H. (1996). *Can the Internet be regulated?* Parliamentary research paper 35, Canberra Parliament House Library. Available at: www.aph.gov.au/library/pubs/rp/1995-96/96rp35.htm

Robinson, J. P., & Levy, M. R. (1986). *The main source.* Beverly Hills, CA: Sage.

Robinson, M. J., & Kohut, A. (1988). Believability and the press. *Public Opinion Quarterly, 52,* 174–189.

Rogers, E. M. (1986). *Communication technology.* New York: Free Press.

Rogers, E. M. (1990). *Communication technology: The new media in society.* New York: The Free Press.

Rogers, E. M. (1995). *Diffusion of innovations* (4th ed.). New York: Free Press

Rogers, E. M., & Shoemaker, F. (1971). *Diffusion of innovations.* (2nd ed.). New York: Free Press.

Roper Organization (1983). *Trends in attitudes towards television and other media: A twenty-year review.* New York: Television Information Office.

Rosen, J. (1992, Winter). Forming and informing the public. *Kettering Review, 22,* 60–70.

Rosen, J. (2000). *The e-commerce question and answer book: A survival guide for business managers.* New York: AMACOM.

Ross, S. S., & Middleberg, D. (1997, November 12). *Media in cyberspace study III: A research study* [Online]. Available at: http://www.mediasource.com/ cyberstudy/ intro.htm

Ross, S. S., & Middleberg, D. (1998, November 11). *Media in cyberspace study: 1997 Fourth Annual National Survey* [Online]. Available at: http://mediasource.com/ intro.htm

Rubin, A. M. (1981). An examination of television viewing motivations. *Communication Research, 8,* 141–165.

Rubin, A. M. (1983). Television uses and gratifications: The interactions of viewing patterns and motivations. *Journal of Broadcasting, 27,* 37–51.

Ruggiero, E. (1998, August). *Perceptions of traditional American journalists toward the Internet as a news source: A critical approach.* Paper presented to the Mass Communication & Society Division of the 1998 Association of Education in Journalism and Mass Communication Convention, Baltimore, MD.

Rusbridger, A. (1999, January 11). Get the net: Whatever the opposite of an anorak is, I'm it. But in my simple, untutored way, I love the Internet. *The Guardian,* 15.

Ryan, J. (1995). A uses and gratifications study of the Internet social interaction site Lambdamoo: Talking with "dinos." Master's thesis, Ball State University, Indiana.

Salem, S. (1996). *Electronic publishing development—With special emphasis on the Arab countries.* Paper presented at the International seminar, "The Global Information Society and Development—The Role of Electronic Publishing," Frankfurt, Germany.

Samuelson, P. 1995, Copyright and digital libraries. *Communications of the ACM, 8*(3), 15–22.

Sands, K. (1999). *How to get customized news: Net guide.* Available at: http:// www.netguide.com

Sargent, L. W. (1965). Communicator image and news reception. *Journalism Quarterly, 42,* 35–42.

Savage, M. (2000, May). *Beware the Net traps. Research.* London: Market Research Society.

Schiel, M. (1996, July). The publisher's perspective. In *The legal implications of publishing on the Internet seminar* (pp. 14–16; Research paper No.1). Melbourne: Center for Media, Communications and Information Technology Law, University of Melbourne.

Schierhorn, C., Wearden, S. T., Schierhorn, A. B., Taber, P. S., & Andrews, S. C. (1998, August). *Digital formats for the future: The Web vs. paper vs. a vertical-screen, page-based design.* Paper presented to Newspaper Division of the Association for Education in Journalism and Mass Communication, Baltimore, MD.

Schiller, H. I. (1989). *Culture, Inc.: The corporate takeover of public expression.* New York: Oxford University Press.

Schlossberg, E. (1999). A question of trust. *Brill's content, 292,* 68–70.

Schudson, M. (1996). *New technology, old values … and a new definition of news.* Washington, DC: Radio and Television News Directors Foundation.

Schuler, D. (1996). *New community networks, wire for change.* Reading, MA: Addison-Wesley.

Schultz, T., & Voakes, P. (1999). Prophets of gloom: Why do journalists have so little faith in the future of newspapers? *Newspaper Research Journal, 20,* 23–40.

Schwarz, E. (1998). An Internet resource for neighborhoods. In R. Tsagaousianou, D. Tambini, & C. Bryan (Eds.), *Cyberdemocracy technology: Cities and civil networks.* London: Routledge.

Scott, W. R. (1995). *Institutions and organizations.* Thousand Oaks, CA: Sage.

Scott, W. R., & Christensen, S. (Eds.). (1994). *Institutional environments and organizations: Structural complexity and individualism.* Thousand Oaks, CA: Sage.

Scott, W. R., & Christensen, S. (Eds.). (1995). *The institutional construction of organizations: International and longitudinal studies.* Thousand Oaks, CA: Sage.

Scott, W. R., & Meyer, J. W. (Eds.). (1994).*Institutional environments and organization: Structural complexity and individualism.* Thousand Oaks, CA: Sage.

Scupola, A. (1999). The impact of electronic commerce on the publishing industry: Towards a business value complementarity framework of electronic publishing. *Journal of Information Science, 25,* 133–145.

Self, C. C. (1988). Perceived task of news report as a predictor of media choice. *Journalism Quarterly, 65,* 119–125.

Semonche, B. P. (1993). Computer-assisted journalism: An overview. In B. P. Semonche (Ed.), *News media libraries: A management book.* Westport, CT: Greenwood Press.

Severin, W. J. (1967). Pictures as retrieval cues in multi-channel communications. *Journalism Quarterly, 44,* 17–22, 52.

Severin, W. J., & Tankard, J. W. (1992). *Communication theories: Origins, methods, and uses in the mass media* (3rd ed.). New York: Longman.

Severin, W. J., & Tankard, J. W. (1997). *Communication theories: Origins, methods, and uses in the mass media* (4th ed.). New York: Longman.

Shade, L. R. (1994). Computer networking in Canada: From CA* Net to CANARIE. *Canadian Journal of Communication, 19,* 68–82.

Shank, G. (1993). Abductive multiloguing: The semiotic dynamics of navigating the net. *The Arachnet Electronic Journal on Virtual Culture* [Online], *1*(1). Available at: ftp://byrd.mu.wvnet.edu/pub/ejvc/SHANK.V1N1

Shaw, E. F. (1973). Media credibility: Taking the measure of a measure. *Journalism Quarterly, 50,* 306–311.

Shay, O. (1995). *Electronic typography publishing.* Computer Scince 547 Project, Calgary University, Canada. Available at: http://ksi.cpsc.ucalgary.ca/courses/547-95/shay/index-13.html

Shepard, A. C. (1997, March). Webward ho! *American Journalism Review,* 32–36, 38.

Shoemaker, P. (1994). Communication in crisis: Theory, curricula, and power. In M. R. Levy, & M. Gurevitch (Eds.), *Defining media studies: Reflections on the future of the field* (pp. 388–395). Oxford: Oxford University Press.

Siegel, D. (1999). *Futurise your enterprise: Business strategy in the age of the e-customer.* New York: Wiley.

Sikes, A.C. (1997). Foreward. In R. Fidler (Ed.), *Mediamorphosis: Understanding new media* (pp. XV–XVIII). California: Pine Forge Press.

Singer, J. B. (1996, August). *Changes and consistencies: Newspaper journalists contemplate an online future.* Paper presented to the Association for Education in Journalism & Mass Communication conference, San Francisco, CA.

Singer, J. B. (1998). Online journalists: Foundations for research into their changing roles. *Journal of Computer Mediated Communication, 4*(1), Available at: http://www.ascusc.org/jcmc/vol4/issue1/singger.html

Singer, J. B. (1999, August). *The metro wide web: How newspapers' gatekeeping role is changing online.* Paper presented to the Newspaper Division, Association for Education in Journalism & Mass Communication, New Orleans, LA.

Singer, J. B. (2001). The metro wide Web: Changes in newspapers; gate keeping role online. *Journalism & Mass Communication Quarterly, 78*(1), 65–80.

Singer, J. B., Tharp, M. P., & Haruta, A. (1999). Online staffers: Superstars or second-class citizens? *Newspaper Research Journal, 20,* 29–47.

Slater, M. D., & Rouner, D. (1996). How message evaluation and source attributes may influence credibility assessment and belief change. *Journalism & Mass Communication Quarterly, 73,* 974–991.

Slywotzky, A. J., & Morrison, D. J. (2000). *How digital is your business?* London: Nicholas Brealey.

Smith, A. (1980). *Goodbye Gutenberg: The newspaper revolution of the 1980s.* New York: Oxford University Press.

Spears, R., & Lea, M. (1992). Social influence and the influence of the "social" in computer-mediated communication. In M. Lea (Ed.), *Contexts of computer-mediated communication* (pp. 30–65). New York: Harvester Wheatsheaf.

Spears, R., Lea, M., & Lee, S. (1990). De-individuation and group polarization in computer-mediated communication. *British Journal of Social Psychology, 29,* 121–134.

Spitzer, M. (1986). Writing style in computer conferences. *IEEE Transactions on Professional Communications, 29*(1), 19–22.

Springston, J. K. (2001). Public relations and new media technology: The impact of the Internet. In R. Heath (Ed.), *Public relations handbook* (pp. 603–614). Newbury Park, CA: Sage.

Starr, S. (2002). Self-regulation makes us all blind. *Sp!ked-IT* [Online]. Available at: http://www.spiked-online.com/printable/00000002D46B.htm

Stephens v. Western Australian Newspapers (1994). High Court of Australia, 182 CLR 211 at 232. Available at: www.austlii.edu.au/au/cases/cth/high_ct/182clr211.html

Strangelove, M. (1994). The Internet as catalyst for a paradigm shift. *Journal of Computer-Mediated Communication, 1,* 7.

Strauss, R., & Schoder D. (1994). *Individualized printed newspaper: Technology pushes and organizational requirements in the printing and publishing industry.* Germany: Institut Für Informatik Und Gesellschaft.

Sullivan, A. (2002, ,February). Out of the ashes, a new way of communicating. *The Sunday Times,* News Review, 8.

Sundar, S. S. (1999). Exploring receivers' criteria for perception of print and on-line news. *Journalism & Mass Communication Quarterly, 76*(2), 373–386.

Sundar, S., & Nass, C. (1996, May). *Source effects in users' perceptions of online news.* Paper presented at the 46th annual conference of the International Communication Association, Chicago, IL.

Sunder, S. S. (2000). Multimedia effects on processing and perception of online news: A study of picture, audio, and video downloads. *Journalism & Mass Communication Quarterly, 77*(3), 480–499.

Tambini, D. (1999). New media and democracy: The civic networking movement. *New Media & Society, 1*(3), 305–329.

Tankard, J. W., & Ban, H. (1998, August). Online newspapers: Living up to their potential? Paper presented at the meeting of the Association for Education in Journalism & Mass Communication, Baltimore, MD.

Tedford, T. L. (1993). *Freedom of speech in the United States* (2nd ed.). New York: McGraw-Hill.

Temple, P. (2000). *The new online investor: The revolution continues.* Chicester, England: Wiley.

Thalhimer, M. (Ed.). (1994). *Media industry news roundup.* Associated Press, The Freedom Forum Media Studies Center.

Theophanous v. The Herald and Weekly Times Ltd. (1994). High Court of Australia, Sydney, Australia, unreported. Available at: www.austlii.edu.au/au//cases/cth/high_ct/unrep297.htm

Thomsen, S. R. (1995). Using online databases in corporate issues management. *Public Relations Review, 21*(9), 103–122.

Thompson, D. R. (1995, March). *The digital daily: How will readers react?* Paper presented to the Newspaper Division, Association for Education in Journalism and Mass Communication, Southeast Colloquium, Gainesville, FL.

Tolbert, P. S., & Zucker, L. G. (1983). Institutional source of change in the formal structure of organizations: the diffusion of civil service reform, 1880–1935. *Administrative Science Quarterly, 28*, 22–39.

Tornazky, L. G., & Klein, K. J. (1982). Innovation characteristics and innovation adoption implementation: A meta-analysis of findings. *IEEE Transactions on Engineering Management, EM-29*, 28–45.

Traynor, I. (1998, May 29). Child porn verdict stuns Net lawyers. *The Guardian,* 2.

Tremayne, M. W. (1997, August). *The Internet: Is the medium the message?* Paper presented to the meeting of the Association for Education in Journalism & Mass Communication, Chicago, IL.

Trench, B. (1997). *Interactive newspapers: From access to participation.* Paper presented to the Society of Newspaper Design, Scandinavia, Denmark.

Trevino, L., Lengel, R. H., Bodensteiner, W., Gerloff, E., & Muir, N. K. (1990). The richness imperative and cognitive style: The role of individual differences in media choice behavior. *Management Communication Quarterly, 4*, 176–197.

UCLA [University of California at Los Angeles] Center for Communication Policy (2000). The UCLA Internet report: "Surveying the digital future." Available at: www.ccp.ucla.edu/ucla-Internet.pdf

Ungaro, J. (1991). Newspapers I: First the bad news. *Media Studies Journal, 5*, 101–114.

U.S. Senate (1974). *The Freedom of Information Act source book.* Committee on the Judiciary, Subcommittee on Administrative Practice and Procedure, 93rd Congress, 2nd Session, Washington DC.

Van Oostendorp, H., & van Nimwegen, C. (1998). Locating information in an online newspaper. *Journal of Computer Mediated Communication, 4*(1). Available at: http://www.ascusc.org/jcmc/vol4/issue1/oostendorp.html

Vargo, K., Schierhorn, C., Wearden, S. T., Schierhorn, A. B., Endres, F., & Tabar P. (1998, August). Readers' response to digital news stories presented in layers and links. Association for Education in Journalism and Mass Communication, Newspaper Division, Baltimore, MD.

Vattyam, S., & Lubbers, C. A. (1999, August). *A content analysis of the Web pages of large U.S. corporations: What is the role of public relations and marketing?* Paper presented to the Annual Meeting of Association of Education in Journalism and Mass Communication, New Orleans.

Vickers, P., & Martyn, J. (1994). *The impact of electronic publishing on library services and resources in the UK.* The British Library Board.

Viswanath, K., & Finnegan, J. R. (1995). The knowledge-gap hypothesis: Twenty-five years later. In B. R. Burleson (Ed.), *Communication yearbook* (pp. 245–261). Thousand Oaks, CA: Sage.

Vitalari, N. P., Venkatesh, A., & Gronhaug, K. (1985). Computing in the home: Shifts in the time allocation patterns of households. *Communications of the ACM, 28,* 512–522.

Volkmer, I. (1997). Universalism and particularism: The problem of cultural sovereignty and global information flow. In B. Kahin & C. Nesson (Eds.), *Borders in cyberspace* (pp. 48–84). Cambridge, MA: MIT Press.

Wall, D. S. (1999, March). *On the politics of policing the Internet: Striking the right balance.* Paper presented at the 14th Annual BILETA Conference. Available at: www.bileta.ac.uk/99papers/wall.htm

Walther, J. B., & Burgoon, J. K. (1992). Relational communication in computer-mediated interaction. *Human Communication Research, 19*(1), 50–88.

Wanta, W., & Hu, Y.-W. (1994). The effects of credibility, reliance, and exposure on media agenda-setting: A path analysis model. *Journalism Quarterly, 71,* 90–98.

Ward, J., & Hansen, K. A. (1997). *Search strategies in mass communication* (3rd ed.). New York: Longman.

Warnick, B. (1997, November). *From print to computer-mediated communication: Modality shift and its implications for communication in the 21st century.* Paper presented at the annual conference of the National Communication Association, Chicago.

Weaver, D. H., Hopkins, W. W., Billings, W. H., & Cole, R. R. (1974). Quotes vs. paraphrases in writing: Does it make a difference to readers? *Journalism Quarterly, 51,* 400–404.

Weaver, R. L. (2000). Defamation Law in turmoil: The challenges presented by the Internet. *Journal of Information Law and Technology, 3.* Available at: elj.warwick.ac.uk/jilt/00-3/weaver.html

Webber, S. (1998). Search engines and news services: Developments on the Internet. *Business Information Review, 15*(4), 229–237.

Wells, M. (2000a, April 15). Alarm as libel threats curb Web's freedom of speech. *The Guardian,* 3.

Wells, M. (2000b, April 3). Freedom fear on Website closure. *The Guardian,* 3.

Wells, M. (2002, January 21). Courting contempt online. *The Guardian,* Media Law, 10.

Wells, R., & King, E. (1994). Prestige newspaper coverage of foreign affairs in the 1990 congressional campaigns. *Journalism Quarterly, 71,* 652–664.

Whillock, R. K. (1997). Cyberpolitics: The online strategies of '96. *American Behavioral Scientist, 40*(8), 1208–1225.

Williams, P., & Nicholas, D. (1999). Not an age thing! "Greynetters" in the newsroom defy the stereotype. *New Library World, 99*(142), 143–148.

Williams, F., Phillips, A. F., & Lum, P. (1985). Gratifications associated with new communication technologies. In K. E. Rosengren, L. A. Wenner, & P. Palmgreen (Eds.), *Media gratifications research: Current perspectives* (pp. 241–252). Beverly Hills, CA: Sage.

Williams, F., & Rice, R. E. (1983). Communication research and the new media technologies. In R. N. Bostrom (Ed.), *Communication Yearbook 7* (pp. 200–224). Beverly Hills, CA: Sage.

Williams, F., Rice, R. E., & Rogers, E. M. (1988). *Research methods and the new media*. New York: Free Press.

Williams, P., & Nicholas, D. (1998a). The Internet, a regional newspaper and the provision of "value added" information. *Aslib Proceedings, 50*(9), 255–263.

Williams, P., & Nicholas, D. (1998b). Not an age thing! "Greynetters" in the newsroom defy the stereotype. *New Library World, 99*(1142), 143–148.

Williams, P., & Nicholas, D. (1999). The migration of news to the web. *Aslib Proceedings, 51*(4), 122–134.

Williams, P., & Nicholas, D. (2001). *The Internet and the changing information environment*. London: Aslib.

Williams, W. S. (1998). The blurring of the line between advertising and journalism in the on-line environment. In D. L. Borden & K. Harvey (Eds.), *The electronic grapevine: Rumor, reputation and reporting in the new online environment* (pp. 31–41). Mahwah, NJ: Lawrence Erlbaum Associates.

WIPO [World Intellectual Property Organization] Copyright Treaty (1996), Article 8, p. 4, .pdf318KB.

Wiss, U. (1996). *Readers of a local newspaper on the WWW: Who are they and how do you find out?* Sweden: Center For Distance-Spanning Technology, University Of Lule.

Woodward, W. (2000, March 31). Net firm pays out for alleged libel. *The Guardian*, 3.

World Bank (1999). *World development indicators, 1999*. Washington, DC: Author.

Yeager v. Drug Enforcement Agency, Decision and Order of the Department of Energy, 678 F. 2d. 315 (Office of Hearings and Appeals, 1982).

Zachary, G. P. (1992, February 21). many journalists see a growing reluctance to criticize advertisers: They say some newspapers, suffering tough times, are softening coverage. *The Wall Street Journal*, A1.

Author Index

Lindoo, E. C., 26, 36
Lindsay, D., 132
Litman, B. L., 76
Liu, J., 28
Lloyd, C., 67
Long, E. V., 22
Louis, S., 85
Lubbers, C. A., 90
Luge, T., 95, 96
Lum, P., 151
Lumsdaine, A. A., 5
Lundmark, V., 151

M

MacArthur, B., 71
Maddox, K., 144
Maddox, L. M., 37
Maier, S. R., 9, 90
Mancini, 8
Mannes, G., 59
March, J. G., 176
Marchetti, P. G., 147
Marlatt, A., 96
Martin, H., 3, 24, 69, 71, 93, 99,
    101, 112
Martin, S. E., 65
Martinson, J., 128
Martyn, J., 18
Massey, B. L., 78, 79, 81, 83, 84, 95
Massey, S. W., 88
Maston, T., 90
Matre, M., 156
McAdams, M., 21, 35, 71, 91, 100
McClung, S., 78, 79
McCombs, M. E., 6, 173
McConnell, M., 161
McCoy, M. E., 167, 173
McDermott, K., 25, 36, 45
McGuire, M., 91, 100
McGuire, T. W., 74
McLuhan, M., 74
McMillan, S., 51, 75
McNamara, J. B., 132
McQuail, D., 5, 10
Medof, N. J., 8, 98
Medsger, B., 35
Meilich, O., 39
Mencher, M., 98, 155
Mensing, D., 52, 85
Metzger, M. J., 159
Meyer, E. K., 30, 39, 85, 94, 145

Meyer, J. W., 38
Middleberg, D., 38, 87, 89, 91, 93,
    94, 98, 99, 104
Miller, L. C., 89
Miller, T., 92
Mings, S., 44, 85
Moen, D. R., 155
Mohr, L. B., 37
Moncrieff, M., 138
Moon, J. L., 85
Moon, Y., 160
Moron, K., 60
Morris, M., 7, 13, 16, 61, 86, 146
Morrison, D. J., 166
Mueller, J., 21, 61, 85, 154, 156
Muir, N. K., 74
Mukopadhyay, T., 151
Murray, D. E., 74

N

Nass, C., 17, 159, 160, 161, 170
Negroponte, N., 2
Neibergall, J., 9, 90
Neuberger, C., 31, 91, 110
Neuendorf, K. A., 89, 90, 150
Neuman, J., 62
Neuman, R. W., 161
Newhagen, J., 170
Newhagen, J. E., 159, 170
Nicholas, D., 3, 20, 24, 51, 59, 66,
    69, 70, 71, 91, 92, 93, 99,
    101, 110, 111, 112
Niebauer, W. E., Jr., 9, 90, 92
Niekamp, R., 79, 80
Nielsen, J., 32, 42, 60
Noack, D., 4
Noelle-Neuman, E., 73
Novak, P., 7, 16

O

Ogan, C., 7, 13, 16, 61
Orr, G., 23, 31, 35, 42, 67
Osborne, D. J., 155
Outing, S., 39, 95
Owen, 126

P

Paalman, K., 92
Pailliart, I., 20

Subject Index

Note: Page numbers followed by a *t* indicate a table.